4/09

Frommer's®

25
GREAT
drives in
CALIFORNIA

WITHDRAWN

Written by Robert Holmes

First published 1997
Revised second edition 1999
Reprinted 2000
Revised third edition 2001
Revised fourth edition 2003
Revised fifth edition 2005
Revised sixth edition 2007
Revised seventh edition 2009

Edited, designed and produced by AA Publishing.

Published by AA Publishing

Published in the United States by
John Wiley & Sons, Inc.
111 River Street, Hoboken, NJ 07030

Find us online at Frommers.com

Frommer's is a registered trademark of Arthur
Frommer. Used under license.

ISBN 978-0-470-42335-6

Cataloging-in-Publication Data is available from the
Library of Congress.

Color separation: Daylight Colour Art, Singapore

Printed and bound by G. Canale & C. S.P.A., Torino, Italy

Right: *satisfied customer, Fisherman's Wharf*

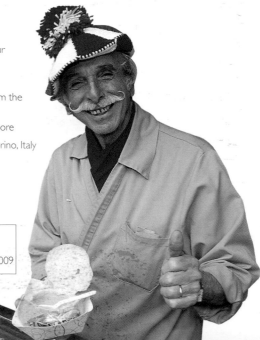

A03666
Atlas mapping in this title produced from
mapping © MAIRDUMONT / Falk Verlag 2009

CONTENTS

ABOUT THIS BOOK

This book is not only a practical touring guide for the independent traveler, but is also invaluable for those who would like to know more about California. It is divided into 8 regions, each with city and driving tours. The driving tours start and finish in those cities considered to be the most interesting centers for exploration. There are special features on theme parks, the Wine Country, the Gold Country and California's missions. Each tour has details of the most interesting places to visit. Boxes catering to special interests follow some of the main entries – for those whose interest is in history or walking or those who have children. There are also boxes which highlight scenic stretches of road and give details of special events, crafts and customs. The simple route directions are accompanied by an easy-to-use map at the beginning of each tour, along with a chart showing how far it is from one town to the next in miles and kilometers. (All distances quoted are approximate.) Before setting off it is advisable to check with the information center listed at the start of the tour for recommendations on where to break your journey, and for additional information on what to see and do, and when best to visit.

★ This symbol on the maps represents other attractions seen along the routes, often mentioned in the panels.

<table>
<tr><td>

Tour Information
See pages 172–6 for addresses, telephone numbers and opening times of the attractions, including telephone numbers of tourist offices.

Accommodations and restaurants
See pages 165–9 for a list of recommended hotels and restaurants for each tour.

Motoring
For information on aspects of motoring in California see page 161.

</td><td>

INFORMATION FOR NON-U.S. RESIDENTS
Banks

Banks in California have traditionally opened from 9–3, Mon–Fri (except national holidays), but recent competition has resulted in longer hours (9–6), and Saturday opening (9–2). Most banks do not offer foreign exchange facilities, but it is possible to exchange money at the airport or some hotels.

It is better to take U.S. dollar travelers' checks, which are accepted as currency in most shops, hotels and restaurants, and can be replaced if lost or stolen.

</td><td>

Credit Cards

Major credit cards are accepted almost everywhere and their use is often the best way to take advantage of the most favorable exchange rates.

Currency

The U.S. dollar bill is available in denominations of 1, 5, 10, 20, 50 and 100. There is a 2-dollar bill, but it's rarely seen. Coins come in denominations of 1 cent (penny), 5 cents (nickel), 10 cents (dime), 25 cents (quarter) and one dollar.

A host of golden pumpkins at the Half Moon Bay Pumpkin Festival

</td></tr>
</table>

Customs Regulations

Personal allowances include up to one liter of alcoholic beverages (for visitors age 21 or over), 200 cigarettes, 1.4kg tobacco, or 50 cigars plus $100 worth of gifts. In practice, most of these items are far cheaper within the U.S. than at airport duty free shops, so there is little point in importing them. There is no restriction on the amount of currency imported or exported, but anything over $10,000 must be declared. U.S. customs are particularly concerned about drugs, animals, meat (both fresh and processed), plants and fresh fruit. Penalties are severe.

Emergency Telephone Numbers

For police, fire and ambulance dial 911 from any telephone.

Entry Regulations

Visas are required for all visitors to the U.S., except for Canadian citizens or nationals of Britain, France, Germany, Italy, the Netherlands, Sweden, Switzerland or Japan visiting the U.S. for business or tourist purposes, for a stay not exceeding 90 days, and provided that a return or onward ticket is held. In these instances a passport only is required. Visa waiver travelers from all Visa Waiver Program countries must present either a machine-readable passport or a valid US visa upon entering the US. Visitors with a valid US visa will not be required to have machine-readable passports. However, visa requirements can change, so seek advice before traveling.

Health

The standard of health care is extremely high – but so are costs. It is essential to have a good health insurance policy. Doctors and hospitals may refuse treatment unless proof of insurance can be given. Most major hospitals have 24-hour emergency rooms. Information on doctors can be obtained from hotels.

California does not have any specific health problems but it is a rabies risk area. If bitten, seek a doctor immediately. Tap water is drinkable, but if hiking in the back country do not drink from streams, which often carry the parasite Giardia.

AIDS is a continuing concern, particularly in the San Francisco area. AIDS Hotline number is 415/863-2437 or 1-800/367-2437.

Post Offices

Post office opening hours can vary, so it is best to double-check. Stamps may be purchased from vending machines in a range of places, such as hotels, motels, drugstores and transportation terminals, but they cost more at these outlets than they do if you buy them at the post offices.

Sombreros for sale in Los Angeles

Telephones

All public telephones accept 5, 10 and 25 cent coins. The minimum charge varies but is usually 35 cents. Hotels usually charge a high premium for calls from rooms. Always check rates before making a call, to avoid any unpleasant surprises.

Dial 0 for a local operator or 00 for a long-distance operator. For direct-dialing international calls, dial 011, the country code and then the number. International codes are:
Australia 61, Canada 1, New Zealand 64, U.K. 44.

Time

California is on Pacific Standard Time, eight hours behind GMT.

GREATER LOS ANGELES & THE INLAND EMPIRE

In all America, nowhere is the car more important than in this giant metropolis. The size of Los Angeles is difficult to comprehend until you try driving from one neighborhood to another. It is impossible to tell where LA begins or ends. Los Angeles County has a population of more than 11 million and covers an area of 4,083 square miles (10,575sq km) with 88 incorporated cities, but the continuous urban sprawl goes way beyond this. Development stretches from Ventura County in the north to Orange County in the south, and from the Pacific coast to Riverside County and the Inland Empire in the east.

This five-county area is bigger than any state excluding California, New York or Texas. Altogether there are more than 16 million people in an area of 34,149 square miles (88,446sq km). As you would expect, an area of this size has it all – except clean air. Only on rare days, when the Santa Ana winds flush away the smog, can you see the spectacular backdrop of the Inland Empire's San Bernardino Mountains. The region has beaches, mountains and desert, and some of the world's best entertainment. On the same day it is possible to swim in the Pacific and ski in the mountains, returning in the evening for dinner in one of America's great restaurants.

Los Angeles was founded by a group of settlers in 1781, on the banks of the Los Angeles River, but it was not until the sunshine lured film-makers in the early 1900s that the city achieved its present prominence and Hollywood became the movie capital of the world. On any day, somewhere on the city streets, there will be a film crew out shooting – although today it is often for television, rather than the cinema. This emphasis on show business has helped Los Angeles become the barometer of popular culture in the nation, and the city likes to think it is on the cutting edge of fashion. There is nothing modest here. Everything is larger than life and the more flamboyant the attitude, the greater the respect – or so it often seems.

This is a city of acceptance. Anything goes, and you will be greeted equally whether you are in jeans and a T-shirt or a tuxedo, although jeans and a tuxedo may give you an edge! It is a cosmopolitan city in the greatest sense.

A large Asian population has grown up over the last few years and whole neighborhoods have distinct ethnic characteristics. Koreans, Vietnamese, Chinese and Filipinos represent a high percentage of the population and this is reflected most noticeably in the proliferation of ethnic restaurants. This is a true Pacific Rim community. Unfortunately, not all of Los Angeles is equally safe, and although the dangers are often exaggerated by the press, some of the neighborhoods, particularly South Central and the Downtown area at night, are best avoided or visited with care.

Tour 1

Drive the freeways of this great city to visit the most interesting sites, from the glamor of Hollywood to the splendor of the *Queen Mary* at Long Beach. The freeways are as much part of Los Angeles as the sites. Without them the place would come to a standstill; at rush hour it often does come to a standstill, even with them! Locals spend a good percentage of their lives on these urban arteries so to get a feel for the real Los Angeles, join them on their home ground and include several of the most interesting attractions for good measure. Visit the city's best beaches along the Pacific, from Hermosa to Santa Monica, and on the way stop at some of its great museums, art galleries and stores.

Tour 2

To experience the real LA, walk along the boardwalk at Venice Beach. The street life, from roller-bladers and bodybuilders to jugglers and acrobats, provides a continuous theater. This is the one beach that should be on everyone's itinerary. It is a microcosm of everything visitors to Los Angeles would expect. Bikini-clad beauties, muscle-bound hunks and every weird and wonderful form of humanity

Left: Mann's Chinese Theatre, where the stars leave their marks

A portrait of America's past at the Gene Autry Western Heritage Museum, Griffith Park

in between. On top of all this there is sand, sun and the sea – although these seem to take second place to the more exotic activities on land. At the southern end of the beach is an area of graceful canals modeled on Venice, Italy, where you can enjoy a quiet stroll, watch the world go by, or feed the ducks.

Tour 3

The Inland Empire is a dormitory extension of the sprawling mass of Los Angeles. Every morning traffic fills the freeways as commuters head into the business districts, but they are leaving behind some of the most unexpected landscape in Greater Los Angeles. Drive along Route 66 through the orange groves and Victorian mansions of Redlands to the alpine lakes of Big Bear and Arrowhead. During the winter this is an important winter sports area, attracting thousands of Los Angeles ski fanatics on weekends and, in the summer, the lakes provide all kinds of water activities, from fishing to waterskiing. One of the more attractive aspects of the area comes from its high elevation. Even when smog is descending on downtown Los Angeles, clean, fresh air can be found only a few miles' drive away in these delightful mountains.

TOUR
1

Los Angeles

Los Angeles is overwhelming. This tour can take a long day, as a broad introduction to the city's attractions, or several days, visiting sites *en route*. Covering LA County's valleys and beaches, it involves a considerable amount of freeway driving: an important part of LA lifestyle.

1/3 DAYS • 127½ MILES • 207KM

i *Hollywood Visitors Information Center, 6801 Hollywood Boulevard*

▶ *Start at Hollywood Boulevard.*

❶ Hollywood Boulevard

Hollywood has been revitalized with the completion of Hollywood & Highland, a massive new entertainment, shopping and dining complex that incorporates the Kodak Theater, permanent home to the Academy Awards.

Adjoining the development is Mann's Chinese Theatre, outside which the hand- and Hollywood – the name that has drawn many a starry-eyed hopeful

footprints of several generations of Hollywood stars have been preserved in cement since it opened in 1927. Over 200 stars have been immortalized here, from Mary Pickford and Douglas Fairbanks to Johnny Depp and Morgan Freeman.

The Hollywood Walk of Fame passes in front of the theater where the "stars" of the famous and not-so-famous have been embedded into the pavement.

SCENIC ROUTES

Just north of Hollywood, take Mulholland Drive west off 101 north and climb up into the Hollywood Hills and Santa Monica Mountains for spectacular views over Hollywood and Los Angeles. The drive is scattered with the palatial homes of many film and television stars.

▶ *Continue east on Hollywood Boulevard to Western Avenue and turn north. Western veers right into Los Feliz and continues up into Griffith Park.*

❷ Griffith Park

This 4,000-acre (1,619-hectare) oasis of greenery sits astride the Hollywood Hills. It provides outdoor recreational facilities for the neighborhood, including an 18-hole golf course, more than 53 miles (85km) of jogging, hiking and bridle trails, and pony rides for youngsters. It even has a polo ground and cricket pitch, and is the home of several major attractions.

Off Western Drive, turn right onto West Observatory Drive for Griffith Observatory. Although it is doubtful whether the telescopes could now penetrate more than a few feet of Los Angeles smog, the observatory is still the major landmark of Griffith Park. On a clear day the views of Hollywood and downtown Los Angeles are spectacular. The 1930s architecture has provided a backdrop for many Hollywood films, most notably for James Dean in *Rebel Without a Cause*. The Hall of

Sciences has displays on astronomy and meteorology, and the planetarium is probably the only way to view stars at the observatory these days. Continue down East Observatory Drive to Vermont, and back to Los Feliz and turn east. Then turn north on Crystal Springs Drive to reach the Autry National Center, on the northeastern edge of the park. This impressive museum, dedicated to the Wild West, opened in 1988. Anyone with even the slightest interest in cowboys will be fascinated by the two floors of exhibits of historic artifacts and Western film memorabilia, such as the jacket worn by Robert Redford in *Butch Cassidy and the Sundance Kid* or John Wayne's gun belt. Film clips from old Westerns can be seen throughout the museum.

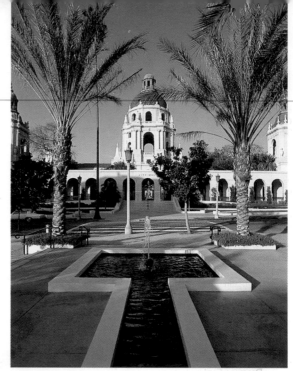

Pasadena's elegant City Hall, a world away from downtown LA

FOR CHILDREN

Travel Town, in Griffith Park, is a transportation museum with just about every form of vehicle possible represented. There are more than 30 steam locomotives and railroad cars, an 1849 circus wagon and a horse-drawn milk cart. Particularly popular is the narrow-gauge railroad that takes children on a circuit of the park.

---

i *Visitor Center, 4730 Crystal Springs Drive (24-hours)*

▶ *Take I-5 south to the Glendale East exit. Continue along South Glendale Avenue.*

❸ Forest Lawn
Cemeteries may not be a normal tourist attraction, but Forest Lawn on South Glendale Avenue is said to have in excess of a million visitors a year. There you will be able to find the final resting places of stars such as Clark Gable and Jean Harlow. This perfectly manicured park is also home to larger-than-life-sized reproductions of some of

the world's great masterpieces, including Michelangelo's *David* and Leonardo da Vinci's *Last Supper* in stained glass. You can also see the world's largest religious painting on canvas, Jan Stryka's *The Crucifixion*. The 300 acres (121 hectares) of lush lawns are a popular, if macabre picnic site.

▶ *Take the Glendale Freeway north to **Hwy 134** East and exit onto Fairoaks Avenue. Head south to Colorado Boulevard.*

❹ Pasadena
This small, wealthy community came to prominence in the 1930s because of its agreeable climate. It is only 20 minutes from downtown Los Angeles by freeway but, sitting at the foot of the San Gabriel Mountains, it feels like a different part of the country. The historic town center known as Old Town has been restored, preserving many of the fine old Victorian facades.

At 411 West Colorado Boulevard is an unusual modern group of buildings housing the Norton Simon Museum of Art, a collection that spans 2,500 years,

including paintings by Rembrandt, Raphael and Rubens, drawings by Goya, sculpture by Rodin and Henry Moore and works by Cézanne, Van Gogh and Degas. The biggest display is of French art, from Poussin and Wateau through to the Impressionists and on to the Cubists, with important works by most of the major artists of each movement. One whole gallery is devoted to 88 works by Degas.

From Colorado Boulevard, take Fairoaks south and turn left onto California Boulevard. At Allen Avenue, turn right and go two blocks to the gates of Huntington Library. It would be difficult to find a more impressive collection of paintings and manuscripts anywhere. Of the 4 million items in the library, many are unique and invaluable. *The Ellesmere Manuscript* from Chaucer's *Canterbury Tales* dates back to 1410. There is a two-volume Gütenberg Bible printed on parchment in 1455, a Shakespeare folio edition and

Audubon's original edition of *Birds of America*. The collection of American art is impressive, but you will also find Gainsborough's *Blue Boy* and Thomas Lawrence's *Pinkie* among the paintings. As if this is not enough, the grounds of the Huntington match the galleries in interest, with several gardens, each devoted to a different theme. The Japanese Garden is the most popular, but there is also a herb garden, a rose garden, a subtropical garden and a Shakespeare garden, where only the plants that existed in the playwright's time are grown. The Huntington deserves far more time than can be allocated on a driving tour, and is well worth a return visit.

BACK TO NATURE

The Descanso Gardens lie at the junction of I-210 and the Glendale Freeway just to the north of Pasadena. Once a private estate, these 165-acre (67-hectare) gardens contain 100,000 camellias from around the world, and from October to May they present a riot of color. From May to December the roses are in bloom and April is the peak month for lilacs and outdoor orchids.

▶ *Return to the Pasadena Freeway and go south to Cesar Chavez Parkway; follow it to Olvera Street.*

5 El Pueblo de Los Angeles State Historic Park

Downtown Los Angeles is generally considered to be a cultural desert. First impressions certainly suggest that the center of the city consists of high-rise offices and little else, but this seemingly sterile area should not be dismissed: it has more to offer than many other parts of the Los Angeles conurbation.

Typical tilework, Olvera Street

RECOMMENDED WALKS

Los Angeles Chinatown, although nowhere near as extensive as the Chinatown in San Francisco, consists of several blocks of intriguing stores filled with wares from exotic foods to oriental antiques. Several good restaurants offer moderately priced meals and serve tank-fresh seafood. The most authentic section is North Spring Street, south of the tourist zone. Walking maps of the area can be obtained from the Chinese Historical Society of Southern California at 970 North Broadway or 982 Gin Ling Way.

At the very heart of Los Angeles there remains a block of buildings dating back to the birth of the city. El Pueblo de Los Angeles State Historic Park preserves the area that was first settled in 1781. The Avila Adobe is the oldest building in the city and was constructed around 1818. Other buildings line either side of Olvera Street, a walkway that is a permanent Mexican marketplace, with craft shops and cafés almost obscuring the historic buildings behind them. It gives a very strong flavor of early Spanish California.

▶ *Go a few blocks west from Olvera Street to reach Grand Avenue and First Street.*

6 Music Center

Three performance spaces combine to form an impressive arts complex that is home to companies such as the Joffrey Ballet and the Los Angeles Philharmonic. The Dorothy Chandler Pavilion provides the concert hall, the Mark Taper Forum is for contemporary theater and the Ahmanson Theater is a 2,000-seat auditorium for traditional drama. The three buildings are linked by landscaped malls with fountains.

▶ *From the Music Center go south on Grand Avenue into what appears to be a canyon of high-rise office buildings.*

7 Museum of Contemporary Art (MOCA)

Nestling at the feet of the office buildings is a striking red sandstone and glass structure designed by Japanese architect Arata Isozaki. This is the Museum of Contemporary Art, which, surprisingly for one of the most trendy cities on earth, did not open until 1986. It houses a small permanent collection from major modern movements, particularly artists who have

Prehistoric exhibits at Exposition Park's Natural History Museum

worked in California, such as Mark Rothko and Clyfford Still, but it is the special exhibits that have generated the attention of the art world. They are often so cutting-edge that they beg description.

▶ *Head two blocks east of the MOCA to Broadway and Third Street.*

8 Grand Central Market

This huge covered market – one of the most colorful and vibrant in California – sells all manner of food, and although there is a strong Central American atmosphere, you can find produce from all over the world.

▶ *Leave the downtown area on Figueroa and travel south to Exposition Boulevard.*

9 Exposition Boulevard

This south Los Angeles neighborhood is dubious at best, but on the corner of Figueroa and Exposition is one of the finest – and most expensive – universities in the state, the

University of Southern California (USC). The film school here is particularly strong and has produced the likes of George Lucas, who is now a

FOR HISTORY BUFFS

Travel south of Exposition Park along the Harbor Freeway and take Wilmington Avenue north off I-105 to East 107th Street to see a bizarre group of 99-foot (30m)-high towers constructed from concrete-coated steel rods and encrusted with shells, tile, pottery and glass. It took Simon Rodia 33 years to complete the towers, which stand as a monumental example of true folk art. They were completed in 1954 and have since been designated a State Historic Park. The Watts Towers Art Center is next door, sponsoring exhibits and cultural events. This area of Los Angeles is not the safest, and care should be taken when traveling from the freeway to the towers.

major benefactor. The campus is quite beautiful and the classical buildings have frequently been used as Hollywood film locations. Tours of the campus are available.

Directly across the road from the university is the Los Angeles Coliseum, site of both the 1932 and the 1984 Olympics (surrounding areas can be dangerous), and next to the Coliseum, at Exposition Park, are two of the best museums in the city. The Natural History Museum is the biggest of its kind in the West. Apart from the usual dioramas of stuffed animals in their habitats, there are very good exhibits of artifacts from Maya, Aztec and Inca civilizations; bird and insect halls; and an exceptional collection of rocks, minerals and gems. The Cenozoic Hall has an intriguing exhibit chronicling the evolution of the horse through fossil remains.

The adjacent California Science Center extends through several buildings, with displays on subjects as diverse as AIDS and earthquakes. This is a hands-on museum and many exhibits are interactive. Visitors can finger-paint on a computer, walk through a space shuttle and take a spin on a General Motors test track. The Aerospace Complex houses a collection of aircraft and spacecraft and also an IMAX theater screening the latest spectacles in 70mm surround vision.

▶ *Take the Harbor Freeway South (I-110) to I-105 East, and then the Long Beach Freeway South (I-710) to Long Beach. Exit at the end of the freeway.*

10 Long Beach

Long Beach is so far from central Los Angeles that it is difficult to think of it as part of the same county. It sits on the Pacific coast, by one of the world's biggest natural harbors, and the major attraction in town is the *Queen Mary*. This majestic ship is now operated as a hotel, but visitors can tour the public areas of the ship.

▶ *Follow Ocean Boulevard east to Naples.*

🄰 Naples
South of downtown Long Beach is Naples, built around a network of canals, complete with gondolas and serenading gondoliers.

▶ *Take Ximeno Avenue north to the Pacific Coast Highway and drive west to Redondo Beach.*

🄱 The Beaches
The Pacific Coast Highway (PCH) hugs the coast, as its name suggests, and passes close to all the beach resorts of southern California. To see the beaches, turn off the PCH and head a couple of blocks west.

Just north of Long Beach, the older seaside resorts of Redondo, Hermosa and Manhattan Beach have little of the glamor of Venice or Santa Monica, but they are usually hopping with young people surfing, playing volleyball, rollerblading or just hanging out. All three resorts have public piers that allow fishing.

▶ *Continue north on the PCH, which changes to Sepulveda Boulevard, past the Los Angeles Airport to Marina del Rey, the largest small craft harbor in the world. (To reach the visitor center turn west on Mindanao Way to 4701 Admiralty.) Continue north on **Hwy 1**, which becomes Lincoln Boulevard, and turn west onto Venice Boulevard. Continue to the end; go north on Pacific Avenue, which becomes Main Boulevard, to Santa Monica.*

🄲 Santa Monica
This trendy coastal resort was originally developed to funnel goods by railroad out of the rapidly expanding Los Angeles area: the Santa Monica piers were, in fact, railroad piers. Eventually, the beautiful expanse of sandy beaches became the main attraction, and established Santa Monica as the premier resort area of the city.

The pier is the most famous landmark in town. It was built in 1909 and is best known for its fully restored, turn-of-the-20th-century carousel featured in *The Sting*. The 1930s ambience of the pier has resulted in its being a popular location for several other movies. It is the best place to view the multitude of activities on the beach. The rest of Santa Monica is filled with chic boutiques, art galleries and some of the finest restaurants in Los Angeles.

▶ *Drive east on Santa Monica Boulevard, turn north onto **I-405** for 2 miles (3km), then turn left onto Getty Center Drive.*

🄳 Getty Center
One of the world's greatest collections of art is housed in a dramatic group of buildings perched high on a 110-acre (44 hectare) campus above the San Diego Freeway. Five pavilions house a remarkable collection that ranges from Renaissance masterpieces to seminal works

Santa Monica's turn-of-the-century Ferris wheel silhouetted at sunset of the 20th century. The exhibits cover manuscripts, sculpture, painting, drawing and the decorative arts. The collection of Impressionist paintings attracts big crowds and includes such masterpieces as Van Gogh's *Irises* and *Still Life with Apples* by Cézanne.

► *Return to I-405, head south, then turn left onto Wilshire Boulevard. Cross Santa Monica Boulevard to Beverly Hills.*

15 Beverly Hills

The very name conjures up images of the rich and famous. Santa Monica Boulevard passes through the heart of the area and, for a glimpse of the high life (what can be seen of it, through gated driveways and over high walls), you can take Beverly Drive north and just meander through some of the immaculate streets. Return to Santa Monica Boulevard and exit south onto

SPECIAL TO...

Everyone wants to see a star and a whole industry has grown up in Hollywood, giving visitors the opportunity to peek at the lifestyle of the stars of the silver screen. Many of today's stars live in the Hollywood Hills, the canyons of Beverly Hills, Bel Air and as far out as Malibu, but tour companies offer trips that point out the homes of the stars from Hollywood's golden years. Hawkers along Sunset Boulevard sell maps to the stars' homes and, while they are not necessarily very accurate, they are a fun way to pass a couple of hours.

Rodeo Drive, arguably the most exclusive shopping street in North America. Drive past the Rolls Royces and Mercedes to see virtually every designer name in the fashion industry displaying their very best wares.

Behind the facade of a modern glass-fronted structure, reflecting the palm trees that line Wilshire Boulevard, is one of the great art collections of North America in the largest museum in the West. The Los Angeles County Museum of Art covers the history of art from pre-Columbian gold ornaments to late 20th-century paintings. It is a museum of international importance, occupying four main buildings around a central courtyard. The Pavilion for Japanese Art houses the Shin'enkan collection of Japanese paintings and *objets d'art*. The Ahmanson Building houses an outstanding collection of Indian and Buddhist art, along with collections from Africa, the South Seas and Egypt and some of the great masterpieces of the Renaissance.

Sitting incongruously next to the clean architecture of the LA County Museum of Art, 6 miles (10km) east of Beverly Hills, on Wilshire, are La Brea Tar Pits, bubbling with black asphalt. During the Pleistocene era, more than 200 different kinds of animal were trapped in this primordial ooze, which perfectly preserved their skeletons. As a result, these are still being discovered by paleontologists in one of the richest fossil deposits that has ever been found.

Adjacent to the tar pits is the George C. Page Museum, where many of the Ice Discoveries have been put on display, including the impressive skeletons of mastodons, mammoths and ancient horses.

► *Take Highland Avenue north off Wilshire to Melrose Avenue, where ultra-trendy boutiques, fashionable restaurants and beautiful people make a walk a fun interlude. Return north on Highland Avenue to Hollywood Boulevard.*

The smooth glass facade of the LA County Museum of Art

Venice
Walk

Venice was developed by tobacco magnate Abbot Kinney in 1904, as part of an attempt to create a cultural renaissance in America. For more than 20 years it was a thriving center of entertainment, built on a series of canals modeled after Venice in Italy. It was Kinney's intention to go even further and have gondolas ferrying people around, but by the end of the 1920s, the area had fallen into decline and most of the canals had been filled in. In recent years, Venice has undergone a remarkable recovery, reclaiming its unique character. Most of the Los Angeles beach resorts are relaxing; Venice is not. This must be the liveliest spot on the coast and any walk here can never fail to be entertaining.

2 HOURS

[i] *Hollywood Visitors Information Center, 6801 Hollywood Boulevard*

▶ *Start at Windward Avenue, turning west off Pacific Avenue.*

❶ Windward Avenue

In Kinney's day, the avenue was lined with grand hotels. For a glimpse of the old days, visit the Italian-style colonnades near Pacific Avenue – one of the few surviving elements of old Venice. Today's commercial enterprises are a little less grand. The inevitable T-shirt stores rub shoulders with tattoo parlors and body-piercing establishments. Parking is not easy in this area, but there are some private lots at the end of Windward that are relatively inexpensive. Just follow the dubious-looking kids who are touting for business. Do not leave your valuables on display and you should not have any problems.

North of Windward are several good sidewalk cafés, where the floorshow is free, as all kinds of entertainers perform on Ocean Front Walk. The quintessential Venice café is The Sidewalk Café at 1401 Ocean Front Walk. The food is really an afterthought, as you sit watching the sun set over the Pacific behind some of the best street entertainers in the country.

▶ *Walk south to 18th Avenue to Muscle Beach, past some of the murals which reflect the level of artistic talent here. The Rebirth of Venus, on the old St. Mark's Hotel at Windward and Ocean Front, is a particularly fine parody of Botticelli's masterpiece.*

❷ Muscle Beach

This is perhaps the most well-known spot in Venice, where narcissistic bodybuilders can be seen almost every day, posing on the outdoor apparatus outside the Muscle Beach Gym. The whole section down to the beach is littered with parallel bars, rings and other instruments of

A surfer prepares to join the throng of Venice fun-seekers

torture, where these sun-bronzed Adonises impress the mortal passersby, swinging and pulling with the greatest of ease.

▶ *Continue south along Ocean Front Walk.*

❸ Ocean Front Walk

A stroll along the Walk guarantees a thoroughly entertaining display of wild Los Angeles. Try to avoid bikini-clad roller-bladers zooming past, and take in the continuous street circus being played out daily. Jugglers, magicians and musicians, fire-eaters and fortune-tellers all try to out-do each other and to direct a few more dollars into the hat. All the way along are more cafés and stores, where you can break your journey if the entertainment starts to pall. It would

The daily promenade continues along Ocean Front Walk

seem that this is the junk food capital of the country, by the number of pizza, hot dog and hamburger vendors lining Ocean Front Walk. Don't come here for the food: the cafés all face west, so this is a perfect afternoon and evening location to stop and nurse a drink for an hour or two and enjoy the California sunset.

▶ *Continue to South Venice Boulevard and turn inland across Pacific Avenue to a small bridge on the south side of the road that crosses the Grand Canal. Steps lead down to a sidewalk that runs along the side of the canal.*

FOR CHILDREN

Venice is really a grown-ups' playground, but young children will be kept amused for hours by the multitude of performers along Ocean Front Walk. Jugglers, conjurers and acrobats seem to be particularly popular with most children and for a few dollars in tips this is the cheapest entertainment in town.

4 The Canals

This quiet, residential neighborhood is a total contrast to the frenetic activity of Ocean Front Walk – yet it is only two blocks away. This is the sole surviving area of Abbot Kinney's canals. Originally there were 16 miles (26km) of waterways; now only this one section, centering on the Grand Canal, remains. Wander along the banks and cross the bridges that link four smaller canals, running at right angles to the Grand Canal. The houses are an interesting mix of modest cottages and mini palazzos. They are now far too expensive for the Bohemian fringe who used to occupy this area and they have been replaced by latter-day yuppies with artistic inclinations. The attraction of the area is obvious as you stroll along the sidewalks. Where else in this mega-metropolis can you find the quiet, European atmosphere provided by this turn-of-the-century dream?

BACK TO NATURE

This urban carnival is hardly the place for an intense wildlife experience, but the peaceful canals at the end of the walk have a resident community of water fowl, and feeding the ducks is a popular activity for locals wanting to avoid the craziness a few blocks away.

▶ Take Dell Avenue to Washington Street and turn west toward the ocean.

5 Venice Pier

The 1,100-foot (335m) long Venice Pier anchors the south end of Venice Beach. It provides a great vantage point for a detached look back at the frantic activity of Ocean Front Walk – and it also allows fishing at no cost. Certain areas in Venice are dangerous and should be avoided.

▶ Return to Windward Avenue along Ocean Front Walk.

There's never any shortage of color or curiosities in Venice

THEME PARKS

Built in 1955, Disneyland was the world's first fantasy playground, and it led to healthy competition from neighboring Knott's Berry Farm, which grew from a 1920s roadside stand selling berries and rhubarb into a 150-acre (60-hectare) theme park, rivaling its Magic Kingdom neighbor. Hollywood got onto the bandwagon with Universal Studios, devoted to giving the public a behind-the-scenes glimpse of the world of television and film production.

Disneyland

The Magic Kingdom is the theme park to end all theme parks. The very name has become synonymous with fantasy. Even the statistics are fantastic: during the summer more than 9,000 employees look after the needs of guests; the parking lot covers 102 acres (41 hectares) and can accommodate over 15,000 cars. There are over 60 major attractions, 39 restaurants and 61 shops, visited by over 10 million people a year. In fact, its popularity is its weakness. Go during the busy season and you will spend more time in lines and traffic than meeting Mickey Mouse. The best time to visit is between Thanksgiving and Christmas, but the crowds are generally thinner from September to May – excluding holidays. Avoid weekends at any time.

You'll need more than one day to experience Disneyland. If possible, two days should be allocated, particularly during the peak season. Careful planning can help maximize your time in the park. The first rule is to arrive early. Plan to be at the gate about half an hour before the official opening time. It also pays to eat before you get there. The less time spent eating, the better. If you need to eat, try to do so outside the normal meal times, when the lines are shorter. Finally, make a plan of attack. Decide which attractions to see and make an itinerary to avoid aimless wandering.

Disneyland is divided into eight separate theme areas. Main Street U.S.A. is a replica of the archetypal American main street from the "good old

days." It forms the main entrance to the park and you will walk down it to reach the other attractions. Start your visit at City Hall to pick up maps and entertainment and dining schedules.

The Walt Disney Railroad offers an 18-minute circuit, stopping at four of the theme lands. One of four turn-of-the-20th-century trains leaves the Main Street station every five to ten minutes.

Adventureland is a world of steaming jungles and exotic sounds. Riverboats navigate a simulated jungle, and the Indiana Jones Adventure takes travelers to the Temple of the Forbidden Eye. This newest thrill ride employs computer technology to create an experience similar to being in an Indiana Jones movie.

New Orleans Square is perhaps the prettiest theme area, depicting New Orleans as it was 100 years ago, complete with strolling Dixieland musicians, French stores and sidewalk cafés. It is also home to two of the most popular attractions: Pirates of the Caribbean and the Haunted Mansion.

Critter Country is the backwoods setting for Splash Mountain, which hurls participants down a five-story mountain waterfall. The other main attraction here is the Country Bear Playhouse.

Frontierland is a re-creation of the Wild West, where the Big Thunder Mountain Railroad travels through bat-infested caverns, raging waterfalls and other hazards.

Mickey's Toontown is the closest you will get to inhabiting the set of a Disney cartoon. Everything here is off-kilter, from the buildings to the Jolly Trolley that transports visitors on a weaving route through town.

Fantasyland is dominated by Sleeping Beauty Castle. There are more attractions here than any other "land": 18 in all, and it is usually the most crowded area in the park. The Matterhorn is the highest structure in the park, usually the first visible sign of Disneyland to people arriving on the freeway. Sleds plummet from its peak on a hair-raising roller-coaster ride.

Tomorrowland has two rides that push amusement park technology to its limits. The Star Speeder lurches and banks through space, throwing passengers around as it takes wrong turns or blasts through clouds of ice crystals, and Space Mountain is a roller-coaster ride in the dark through meteor showers and gaseous nebulae.

Disney's California Adventure

This new attraction adjacent to Disneyland celebrates the State of California from wineries to Hollywood backlots, although why anyone would want to visit a pretend backlot when a half-hour drive will take you to the real things is a mystery. However, two attractions almost justify the entrance fee. Soarin' Over California is the closest you may ever come to feeling like a bird and well worth the inevitable wait in line. A Bug's Life is a remarkable 3D animation that takes you into the world of bugs in a fantasy that is pure Disney.

Knott's Berry Farm

Knott's Berry Farm has a much more down-home feel to it than Disneyland. It is almost twice the area of its Anaheim neighbor, but the lower density of the attractions makes it easy to cover

The stomach-churning roller-coaster at Knott's Berry Farm...

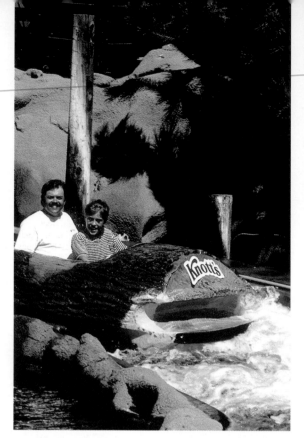

…and one of its many entertaining water rides

the park in a single day. As with Disneyland, try not to visit during holiday periods and the peak summer months. Unlike Disneyland, the Farm, as it is known locally, is based more on reality than fantasy. A refreshing aspect of the park is its commitment to culture and education. Many of the exhibits are of genuine historic value: the Old Trails Hotel in Ghost Town, for example, was relocated board by board from Prescott, Arizona. A strong emphasis is placed on the heritage of the American West, and this is successfully combined with the 168 rides to make the whole experience thoroughly entertaining. There is even a paleontologist and a naturalist on hand to answer questions relating to a couple of the attractions that are primarily just good, plain fun.

The Farm is divided into eight main areas.

California Marketplace is a large area to the left of the entrance, with stores and dining establishments that are more interesting than they sound. You can visit this area without having to pay to enter the park.

Ghost Town is an almost totally authentic group of old buildings, relocated here by Walter Knott. Unlike Disneyland, the buildings here really are as old as they look. Even the narrow-gauge railroad was brought to the farm in 1952. Knott bought the locomotives, rolling stock and even the rails of the Denver & Rio Grande, the last operating narrow-gauge railroad in America. A genuine 100-year-old stagecoach gives tours of the farm.

The Timber Mountain Log Ride is billed as the oldest log flume ride in America. The hollowed-out log boats float through a saw mill before plunging down a 70-foot (21m) waterfall. The Calico Mine Train re-creates the feeling of a real mine train in the old West. The two shows are a Wild West Stunt

Show and a classic Western melodrama in the Birdcage Theater.

Wildwater Wilderness is the smallest theme area of the farm, and the Bigfoot Rapids are its sole attraction. A sign at the entrance says "You WILL get wet" – and they mean it. This feels as authentic as any whitewater rafting trip.

For more thrills, try the Boomerang. You are dropped from an 11-story height, to be catapulted through three loops that both flip you upside down and twist at the same time. When you think it's all over, you do the same thing, except this time in reverse.

Fiesta Village is home to Montezooma's Revenge, which catapults riders to 55mph (88kph) in three seconds, loops upside down and then repeats the process. There are a number of considerably less exciting rides in this theme area, much more suitable for younger kids. Camp Snoopy is a great area for

children under six. A number of safe but fun rides, together with personal appearances by many of the characters from the Peanuts comic strip, an outdoor theater and a petting zoo, make this a perennial family favorite.

Indian Trails is a cultural exhibit devoted to Native Americans. Many tribes are represented and there are hands-on exhibits and demonstrations by a range of tribal craftsmen. There is also tradiional food, such as Navajo fry bread and buffalo stew.

Reflection Lake is the site for The Incredible Waterworks Show. This sound and light show, where hundreds of jets of water are choreographed to music, is entertaining at night, when the extravaganza is enhanced by colored lights.

Soak City

Water is the only theme at Soak City, a new attraction developed on a site directly across the road from Knott's Berry Farm.

Twenty-one major water rides follow a giant 750,000-gallon wave pool, complete with beach, a ⅓-mile-long lazy river and the Toyota Beach House, which has water squirting out in almost every direction. All this is monitored by a team of at least 50 lifeguards on duty at any given time.

Universal Studios

The romance of Hollywood never fails to draw crowds, eager to see behind the scenes and maybe spot a star. Universal Studios is a fully operational film studio and tours were offered here even in the days of silent movies. The advent of sound put an end to that, but in 1964 the idea was resurrected, allowing a tour company to drive buses through the lot. In 1965 the Entertainment Center opened, with stunt shows and screen tests, and became the model for Universal Studio tours as they are today.

Studio Tram Tour offers an overview of the studios. Try to do this early in the day, before the crowds arrive. The 45-minute ride is the only way to see the back lots where there are sets used for films such as *Spartacus*. Up on a hill is Norman Bates' house from Hitchcock's *Psycho*. (Part of the fun is matching the set to the movie.) The highlight of the tram tour is Earthquake – The Big One, that provides three frightening minutes a little too close to reality for comfort for many California residents. The tour also offers meetings with both King Kong and Jaws.

Lower Lot has three major attractions. Backdraft is a remarkable special-effects display from the film, in which you will be engulfed by flames and molten metal. To cool off take Jurassic Park – The Ride, plunge down an 84-foot (25m) waterfall and expect to get very wet. To see how all is done, go to the Special Effects Stages, where there are graphic demonstrations showing how many of Hollywood's effects are produced, including *Peter Pan*, *Seabiscuit* and *Cat in the Hat*.

Upper Lot is the main area of the studios, and The Streets of the World is the main thoroughfare. Stroll down Baker Street in London or wander through 1950s America while deciding which shows to visit next. This area has the greatest concentration of attractions. One of the most popular, with inevitable long lines is The Simpsons Ride. Eight riders in each vehicle take a thrill-packed ride alongside Homer, Marge, Bart, Lisa and Maggie in an over-the-top trip through Krustyland. The simulated speed and effects make this a rough ride.

Two attractions that provide more thrills than can possibly be good for you are Revenge of the Mummy, which takes you past terrifyingly real special effects on one of the world's fastest indoor roller coasters, and House of Horrors, which raises haunted houses to a whole new level. These are definitely not for small children.

Kids will be happier watching Shrek 4 D through the miracle of "OgreVision," and everyone will be charmed by the animal antics on the Animal Planet Live stage. For thrills without frights, Water World is a spectacular water show based on the movie, with stunts and a fiery finale. The Blast Zone is similarly wet, and kids will love the SpongeBob SquarePants characters and the opportunity to cool off on a hot summer day.

An intimate moment with Jaws!

The Inland
Empire

The Inland Empire is rarely taken seriously as a visitor destination. Its grandiose name certainly does not reflect the urban sprawl and smog that plagues this commuter outpost of Los Angeles. Compared with most of California, this is certainly a low priority destination. But where else is it possible to drive from the beaches of Los Angeles and, within a couple of hours, be skiing in high mountains in clear air above the smog level? The tour includes several places of considerable interest in the cities of the Inland Empire, and takes in the beautiful San Bernardino Mountains, which rise up to 11,499 feet (3,505m).

2 DAYS • 267 MILES • 429KM

ITINERARY

LOS ANGELES	▶ Redlands (67m-108km)
REDLANDS	▶ Big Bear Lake (59m-95km)
BIG BEAR LAKE	▶ Lake Arrowhead (27m-43km)
LAKE ARROWHEAD	▶ Silverwood Lake (20m-32km)
SILVERWOOD LAKE	▶ Riverside (35m-56km)
RIVERSIDE	▶ Chino (21m-34km)
CHINO	▶ Los Angeles (38m-61km)

ⓘ *LA INC, LA CVB, 685 South Figueroa Street*

▶ *Leave Los Angeles on I-10. Just before Redlands, the San Bernardino County Museum at 2024 Orange Tree Lane gives a good overview of how the Inland Empire has grown from cattle ranching and citrus farming days to the present bedroom communities. Directly across the freeway to the south, at 26930 Barton Road, is a branch of the Mission San Gabriel called San Bernardino Asistencia, which re-creates early 19th-century life in its two-room museum. Continue into Redlands.*

❶ Redlands

The town was once the center of California's citrus industry, and a few orange groves can still be seen around the town. The wealthy families that were attracted here by the warm climate and strong agricultural economy built many elaborate Victorian mansions and, fortunately, many of them have been carefully restored. It is worth a detour to visit Kimberley Crest House and Gardens at 1325 Prospect Street.

The French château-style mansion was built in 1897, with formal Mediterranean gardens running down the hillside below the house. Several other fine examples of Victorian architecture can be seen in the town, but most are not open to the public.

▶ *Leave Redlands driving north on Orange Street and turn right onto Hwy 38. Follow the winding mountain road for several miles until it joins Hwy 18 just before the town of Big Bear Lake. Turn left and follow Hwy 18 into town.*

❷ Big Bear Lake

Big Bear is a winter ski resort, 7,000 feet (2,133m) up in the San Bernardino Mountains. The lake extends for 7 miles (11km) and when the snow has melted it is a playground for all kinds of water sports. The air up here is clean and crisp, and the addition of rugged mountain scenery

Kimberley Crest House, a 19th-century mansion at Redlands

SCENIC ROUTES

The Rim of the World Highway past Big Bear Lake and Lake Arrowhead is a 40-mile (64km) scenic drive that wanders through the 5,000- to 7,000-foot (1,524 to 2,133m) crest of the San Bernardino Mountains, passing several quaint communities and resort areas. High forests often block the sweeping views, but the surprise view from a clearing is part of the charm of the drive. There have been serious fires in California in recent years – check locations and effects.

makes this a great escape from the Los Angeles metropolis. The town of Big Bear Lake has the feel of the European Alps, with wooden chalets tucked away in the forests, surrounded by piles of newly chopped logs for the winter. Every October a

Bavarian-style festival adds to this ambience.

▶ *Continue west on Hwy 18, the Rim of the World Scenic Byway, to Hwy 173 and turn north to Lake Arrowhead.*

3 Lake Arrowhead

This is the most picturesque area of the region. The town is almost too perfect, with exclusive resorts, fine shopping and good restaurants. Lake Arrowhead was man-made and developed as a hideaway for the rich and famous of Los Angeles, and their expensive homes can be seen around the lake shores. A 60-passenger paddlewheeler, the *Arrowhead Queen*, gives visitors a more intimate view of the lake.

▶ *Continue north on Hwy 173 to Silverwood Lake.*

4 Silverwood Lake State Recreation Area

This 976-acre (395-hectare) man-made lake has been completely undeveloped, apart from a small marina and the recreation area. There are 13 miles (21km) of trails around the lake and good fishing and swimming.

▶ *Continue west on Hwy 138 to I-15 south. Turn off I-15 onto I-215 into San Bernardino. There is little of interest here except for the Route 66 Museum, which pays homage to this famous transcontinental highway that passed through the town. Continue south on I-215 to Riverside.*

Left: Big Bear Lake, a fine ski resort

5 Riverside

The most interesting attraction here is a hotel. The Mission Inn dates back to the 1880s and is, in fact, a Spanish-style palace that sprawls across a whole city block and has entertained eight U.S. presidents. Riverside gave birth to the navel orange in the 1870s, and on the south side of town is the California Citrus State Historic Park, which comprises several acres of orange groves with exhibits on their history and cultivation. The Riverside Municipal Museum at 3720 Orange Street also traces the history of citrus-growing in the region and is housed in a 1912 post office building. The unusual Museum of Photography, at 3824 Main Street, has excellent temporary exhibits.

▶ *From Riverside take Hwy 60 west to Chino.*

6 Chino

This town is devoted to flight. At the Planes of Fame Air Museum there is a collection of aircraft from 1896 through to World War II, many flyable, and exhibits of military aviation memorabilia.

▶ *Return to Hwy 60 west and return into Los Angeles or take Hwy 71 north to I-10 west, which is considerably faster.*

An appropriate entrance to the Citrus State Historic Park

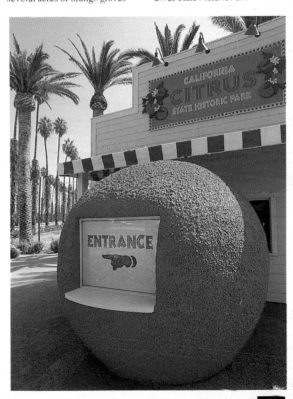

THE SOUTHWEST

San Diego is only 120 miles (193km) south of Los Angeles and is the second biggest city in the state, but it manages to retain a small-town atmosphere. This is the birthplace of California. Portuguese explorer Juan Rodriguez Cabrillo claimed the area for Spain as early as 1542, but it was Father Junípero Serra who established the first permanent settlement when he built Mission San Diego de Alcala here in 1769. It became the first of a 21-mission chain that would extend as far as Sonoma, north of San Francisco.

The early explorers were probably attracted by the mild climate and the enormous natural harbor. With an average temperature of 70°F (21°C) and average annual rainfall of less than 10 inches (250mm), the climate is almost perfect and it is a wonderland for sportsmen. Throughout the region there is year-round golf, tennis, surfing, diving, fishing and sailing. The natural deep-sea harbor is home to the 11th Naval District of the U.S., which is one of the largest fleets of fighting ships in the world.

It was not until 1848 that the city came under United States rule and there is still a strong Spanish influence, with the Mexican border and Tijuana only minutes away. Much of San Diego today has a distinctly Mexican feel, and Spanish is widely spoken around town. It's a 40-minute ride on the San Diego Trolley to San Ysidro, within walking distance of the border to Tijuana (don't forget to take your passport if you want to cross it).

Perhaps the most glorious feature of the region is the 70-mile (112km)-long strip of golden beaches, enticing coves and dramatic cliffs. Each of the more than 30 beaches has its own personality and devotees, whether you are looking for surfing, volleyball, scuba-diving or just getting a tan.

San Diego is much more than just a city. It is a vast county that includes the biggest state park in the country outside Alaska. Anza-Borrego, 90 miles (145km) northeast of San Diego, is one of the great desert areas of the state: during the spring, thousands of visitors descend on the park to witness the beauty of the desert in bloom. A range of mountains separates Anza-Borrego from the coast.

Mount Palomar Observatory

Up in the clean, clear air of these coastal mountains you can visit Mount Palomar, one of the world's great astronomical telescopes. The northern part of the county, around Temecula, has the most southerly concentration of vineyards of California's booming wine industry.

Tour 4

This tour offers a wide range of southern California's attractions, from the fascinating wildlife, protected in reserves along the stunning coast, to the historic mission district and old wooden homes of San Juan Capistrano, and taking in the very modern amusements of the beach resorts. These include Newport Beach, with its fishing boats and glorious sands, the shoppers' paradise of Fashion Island and the sublime Laguna Beach, where watersports, art galleries and hotels manage not to disturb the local dolphins and whales.

Tour 5

One of the beauties of the City of San Diego is that most of the interesting attractions are in a relatively compact area, and the driving time between them is minimal. The tour starts in Balboa Park, where there is one of the most interesting concentrations of museums in the nation. Also here is the world-famous San Diego Zoo, the finest of its kind. The route continues to the cradle of San Diego, the Mission de San Diego Alcala and on to experience the early Mexican days at Old Town San Diego. Next is the delightful, chic coastal town of La Jolla, returning past Sea World and the Cabrillo National Monument. A short ride back into town past the Maritime Museum and Seaport Village ends in the Gaslamp Quarter and the adjoining Horton Plaza complex, where it is easy to find a wide choice of places to unwind after a day's sightseeing.

Tour 6

Head inland from San Diego toward Anza-Borrego and take the Sunrise National Scenic Highway through Mount Laguna and Cuyamaca State Park to the old gold town of Julian, now famous for its apple pies. It is only 60 miles (96km) inland from San Diego, but it is like stepping back in time. Travel north past Mission Santa Ysabel to Palomar Mountain State Park and climb steep, winding roads to the world-famous Mount Palomar Observatory. Continue to the Mission San Antonio de Pala and Mission San Luis Rey de Francia before returning to the coast and the quaint town of Carlsbad. A short drive inland takes you to the San Diego Wild Animal Park, near Escondido, which is the last stop before returning south to San Diego.

The Lily Pond, Balboa Park, San Diego

Orange County
Beaches

This tour is an introduction to authentic southern California beach life, taking in bird sanctuaries and wildlife reserves, the hottest surfing spots, harbor cruises, theatrical entertainment and art festivals – with the added option of simply spending a day at the beach. For those who love the ocean, this is an ideal trip.

3 DAYS • 75 MILES • 120KM

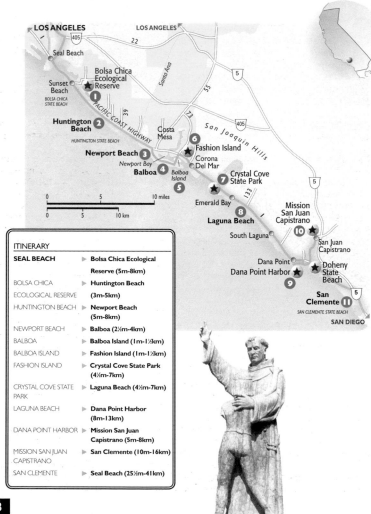

ITINERARY

SEAL BEACH	▶ **Bolsa Chica Ecological Reserve (5m-8km)**
BOLSA CHICA ECOLOGICAL RESERVE	▶ **Huntington Beach (3m-5km)**
HUNTINGTON BEACH	▶ **Newport Beach (5m-8km)**
NEWPORT BEACH	▶ **Balboa (2½m-4km)**
BALBOA	▶ **Balboa Island (1m-1½km)**
BALBOA ISLAND	▶ **Fashion Island (1m-1½km)**
FASHION ISLAND	▶ **Crystal Cove State Park (4½m-7km)**
CRYSTAL COVE STATE PARK	▶ **Laguna Beach (4½m-7km)**
LAGUNA BEACH	▶ **Dana Point Harbor (8m-13km)**
DANA POINT HARBOR	▶ **Mission San Juan Capistrano (5m-8km)**
MISSION SAN JUAN CAPISTRANO	▶ **San Clemente (10m-16km)**
SAN CLEMENTE	▶ **Seal Beach (25½m-41km)**

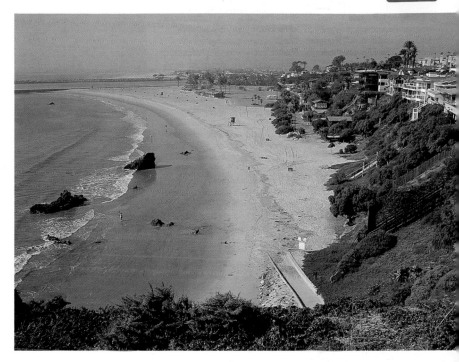

▶ Take **I-405** south from Los
Angeles and exit at Seal
Beach Boulevard. Turn right
and proceed west to the
ocean; at Pacific Coast
Highway, turn left and go
south to Huntington Beach.
The Bolsa Chica Ecological
Reserve is on the approach to
Huntington Beach along
Pacific Coast Highway.

❶ Bolsa Chica Ecological Reserve

This is a "must-see" for anyone
interested in rare birds, some of
which are endangered. Its 300
acres (121 hectares) include a
1¼-mile (2.5km) loop trail that
crosses inland over Inner Bolsa
Bay on a boardwalk, then continues to the Bolsa Chica Cliffs,
with good views of wildlife in
Outer Bolsa Bay. Bird species
that can be spotted include
herons and egrets, the endan-

Left: a statue at San Juan Capistrano
recalls Father Junipero Serra's work

gered Californian least terns (as
well as other varieties of terns),
the highly endangered Belding's
savannah sparrows, which nest
only in pickleweed, indigenous
to this reserve, light-footed
clapper rails and black-bellied
plovers. If that isn't enough,
there is also an abundance of sea
life, such as stingrays, smooth-
hound sharks and schools of
anchovies and topsmelt – all
plainly visible. Parking and
entrance are free and tours are
self-guided.

▶ Continue 3 miles (5km)
farther south along Pacific
Coast Highway to Main Street.

❷ Huntington Beach

A stroll down California's largest
concrete municipal pier, rebuilt
in 1992, gives a first-hand look at
serious surfing. On any given
day, hundreds of surfers can be
seen in the waters here, stalking
the perfect wave.

The 8½ miles (14km) of unin-
terrupted beach that comprise
the Huntington Beach area
include a paved path through

The ultimate rooms with a view,
overlooking Balboa's sweeping bay

the sand for bicycling, rollerblading, jogging or just beautiful
sunset strolls. Main Street
begins opposite the pier, heading inland, and has taken on a
refurbished look, with new
buildings housing outdoor cafés,
stores and movie theaters.

Farther inland along Main
Street, at 411 Olive Street, is the
International Surfing Museum,
where one wall is entirely
devoted to surf music, and
homage is paid to such artists as
Dick Dale and The Beach Boys.
Another exhibit describes the
early days of the surfing craze,
in Hawaii.

ⓘ Visitors Bureau, Suite 208,
301 Main Street, Huntington
Beach

▶ Take Pacific Coast Highway
south to Newport Beach exit,
on Newport Boulevard –
Balboa Peninsula/Lido Bay
Bridge. Turn right and follow
signs to Newport Pier.

3 Newport Beach

Newport Pier deserves a quick visit for its tradition of "Newport Dorymen": for 75 years these fishermen have risen before the sun to fish the waters off Newport Beach, catching rock cod, bonito, sea bass, halibut and calico bass. A walk down the pier gives a good view of the Balboa Peninsula, to the south, and the white-sand beaches of Newport. This is the location for the popular TV series *The OC*, and site maps are available at the Visitors Bureau.

▶ *Continue south along Newport Boulevard, which becomes Balboa Boulevard, and on into Balboa.*

4 Balboa

Since 1936, Balboa has been a Newport Beach institution. The Balboa Fun Zone provides hours of entertainment, with an amusement park for children complete with merry-go-round, arcades, bumper cars and a Ferris wheel, which offers a panoramic view of Newport Bay. The *Pavilion Queen*, moored at the Balboa Pavilion, is a Mississippi-style cruise boat that crosses the harbor every hour on the hour during summer. Also moored at the pavilion is *The Catalina Flyer*, a 500-passenger catamaran which ferries people over to Catalina Island, 26 miles (42km) off the Newport Coast. Here snorkeling, diving, golf, camping and tours around the island are all available, and buffalo, wild boar, deer and bald eagles roam freely. Avalon, Catalina's town, has great restaurants, nightlife, shopping and lodging.

▶ *Southern California's only ferry, which takes just three cars at a time, travels from Balboa to Balboa Island; it is reached by heading up Agate Street to Park Avenue and turning right to Marine Avenue.*

5 Balboa Island

This small haven in the middle of Newport Bay provides excellent views of the bay and the area's opulent waterfront homes. Marine Avenue is lined with beachwear stores and a wide variety of eateries, including the famous Balboa Bar and Frozen Chocolate Banana Bar.

▶ *Take Marine Avenue across the Balboa Island Bridge and up the hill to Pacific Coast Highway; turn right, continue to Newport Center Drive and turn left to Fashion Island.*

6 Fashion Island

Shopping enthusiasts can have a field day exploring Fashion Island's 200-plus stores and restaurants. Open-air concerts are given in the main courtyard of Farmers' Market every Wednesday in July and August, from 6 to 8pm, featuring artists from all over the world. The famous Hard Rock Café is a landmark, with its 30-foot (9m) neon guitar.

▶ *Take Newport Center Drive back to Pacific Coast Highway and turn left to Crystal Cove State Park, approximately 4 miles (6km) along on the right.*

7 Crystal Cove State Park

Set on rugged cliffs some 200 feet (61m) above the ocean, this park has trails leading down to the deserted beaches, where white egrets, sparrow-tail hawks, rabbits, road-runners and occasional deer can be seen. The park service maintains plantlife that is indigenous to this area and is well equipped with information boards. Try the only take-out food establishment in this area, the Orange Inn, for a great sandwich and a dateshake.

▶ *Leave the park on Pacific Coast Highway and turn right to Laguna Beach.*

8 Laguna Beach

Often referred to as the Pacific Riviera of Southern California, this resplendent seaside resort boasts rocky shoreline coves, small bays, pristine waters where dolphins, sea lions and whales swim, and protected tidepools. There are first-rate hotels and opportunities for swimming, kayaking, diving and hiking in the surrounding wilderness parks. Laguna Beach is also an artists' colony, with hundreds of galleries to browse and art festivals during the summer months. The two largest are the Sawdust Festival and the Festival of the Arts. During the annual Pageant of the Masters, famous works of art are re-created on stage by people in costumes and make-up.

As a contrast to all this activity, Laguna is blessed with immaculate beaches and coves. As many as 15 small bays make up an 8-mile (13km) stretch of the coastline – all clean and well-maintained, many containing fascinating tidepools, and some providing views of schools of dolphins swimming offshore.

i *Visitors Bureau, 252 Broadway, Laguna Beach*

▶ *Drive south on Pacific Coast Highway to Dana Point. Turn right on Golden Lantern and down to the Dana Point Harbor.*

9 Dana Point Harbor

Hundreds of pleasure craft are moored here, and a walk along the waterfront promenade passes a floating community where people live aboard their boats, before reaching the fishing fleets. A day of fishing off this stretch of shoreline brings in bonito, sea

Turn left at Pacific Coast Highway. Take the right-hand road, hugging the coast, and proceed to San Clemente. Turn right on to Avenue Del Mar.

⓫ San Clemente

This seems like a very relaxed Spanish town, in its architecture and in its atmosphere. At San Clemente Pier, bicycle and walking paths lead along the beachfront and two fine seafood restaurants are great vantage points for views of the magnificent California sunset behind

Above: the deserted sands of Crystal Cove State Park
Right: Mission San Juan Capistrano

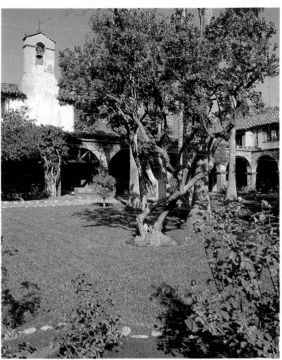

bass, rock cod and an occasional yellowfin tuna, if the waters are warm. Boats also set out from late December to March to follow the whales during their migration, and an annual whale festival takes place in February and March.

Next to Dana Point Harbor is Doheny State Park, a center for camping and water sports, with a beautiful stretch of beach and a bicycle path.

▶ *Continue to Dana Point Harbor Drive, turn right and follow this road to a traffic signal. Cross the signal heading east; this road becomes Del Obispo. Proceed east (inland) to San Juan Capistrano and turn left to Mission San Juan Capistrano.*

⓾ Mission San Juan Capistrano

This was the seventh in the chain of 21 missions, founded in 1776 by Franciscans under the leadership of Father Junípero Serra. Its 10-acre (4-hectare) site has furnished rooms, restored to look as they did some 220 years ago, and a museum with artifacts from Spanish, Mexican and Native American periods. The mission is famous for St. Joseph's Day, which marks the return of the swallows to nest. Self-guided tours are available.

Also within this area, on Los Rios Street between Del Obispo and Mission Street, is San Juan Capistrano Historic District, with Victorian homes, adobe structures and wooden cottages. The Amtrak rail station is actually a number of vintage trains connected to one another, and is the oldest depot in Southern California.

▶ *Return to Del Obispo and head west, back to the ocean.*

Catalina Island. Just south of this area is San Clemente State Beach and Park, where recreational vehicles and camping are permitted. Miles of undeveloped beaches can be enjoyed here, along with a magnificent rocky coastline.

▶ *Return to Pacific Coast Highway, heading north to Avenue Califia. Turn right to I-5. Signs indicate I-5 north to Los Angeles.*

TOUR

5

San Diego

San Diego is one of America's most pleasant cities. The climate is idyllic, never too warm and never too cold, and although the city now has sprawling residential areas, the sites that are of most interest to visitors are in a fairly compact and accessible area. The problems of urban blight and inner-city social conflicts that affect other U.S. cities are mercifully absent. San Diego can offer everything from world-class sailing to museums and the world's largest zoo. All the city's attractions can be sampled in a day, but most deserve much more time than this itinerary will allow.

ITINERARY	
BALBOA PARK ▶	**Mission San Diego de Alcala (8m-13km)**
MISSION SAN DIEGO DE ALCALA	**Old Town State Historic Park (10m-16km)**
OLD TOWN STATE HISTORIC PARK	**University of California (13m-21km)**
UNIVERSITY OF CALIFORNIA	**La Jolla (6m-10km)**
LA JOLLA	**Mission Beach (6m-10km)**
MISSION BEACH	**SeaWorld (3m-5km)**
SEAWORLD	**Point Loma (8m-13km)**
POINT LOMA	**Maritime Museum (10m-16km)**
MARITIME MUSEUM	**Seaport Village (½m-1km)**
SEAPORT VILLAGE	**Gaslamp Quarter (1½m-2km)**
GASLAMP QUARTER	**Horton Plaza (½m-1km)**
HORTON PLAZA	**Balboa Park (2m-3km)**

1 DAY • 68½ MILES • 111KM

i San Diego Visitor Information
Center, 2688 E. Mission Bay Drive,
San Diego

▶ Start in the parking lot at the
San Diego Zoo in Balboa Park,
located off Park Boulevard.

❶ Balboa Park

Balboa Park is a destination in itself. It was set aside as public parkland in 1868, and many of the buildings were added during the 1915 Panama-California International Exposition and the 1935 California Pacific International Exposition. From the zoo parking lot, walk south past the Spanish Village to El Prado, the main thoroughfare, where most of the museums are located. If time is too short to do the museums, the architecture alone is worth the walk. Plan a separate day just for museum visits.

The San Diego Zoo is far too important and extensive to see on this driving tour. It is perhaps the world's greatest zoo and you should plan to return for at least a full day's visit. The zoo covers 128 acres (52 hectares) and houses over 3,900 animals from more than 800 species. A major effort has been made to concentrate on endangered species and to develop breeding programs for these animals. The zoo is built across a steep canyon, and for those unable to cope with the strenuous walking, there is a 3-mile (5km) bus tour. Alternatively, an aerial tram called the Skyfari gives visitors a bird's-eye view above the tree-tops. Even if there isn't time to enter, the sounds of the zoo can clearly be heard as you walk down into Balboa Park.

Immediately on the left, after leaving the parking lot, you will see a collection of low, Spanish-style buildings. This is the Spanish Village, an arts and crafts complex housing the studios of 42 wood-carvers, potters, painters, sculptors, photographers and silversmiths.

Continue to Balboa Plaza, which is at the end of El Prado. The Inez Grant Memorial Rose Garden will be behind you as you look down El Prado to the landmark California Tower. You can reach the garden across the footbridge, over Park Boulevard. Next to this All-American Rose Selection Display Garden is the Desert Garden, with a wide variety of succulents indigenous to the California desert.

Walk down El Prado toward the California Tower, to the Lily Pond. During World War II this was used as a swimming pool for patients at the U.S. naval hospital. The steel frame structure behind the pond is the Botanical Building, containing

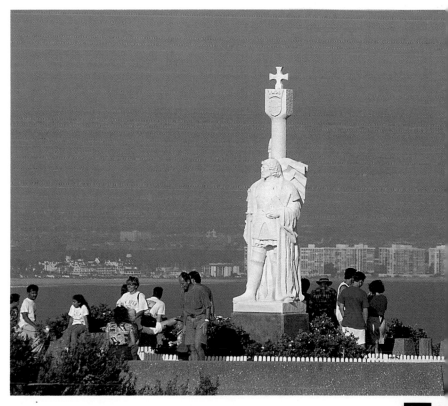

The popular Cabrillo National Monument at Point Loma

more than 500 species of tropical and subtropical plants. The framework for the building, which looks like a huge over-turned basket, was made for a station belonging to the Santa Fe Railroad, but was purchased for the 1915 Exposition.

Continue down El Prado. Past the colonnades of the San Diego Art Institute, on the left, there is an enclosed courtyard called the Alcazar Garden. This was designed for the 1915 Panama-California Exposition and was modeled on the gardens of the Alcazar in Seville, Spain, which were destroyed during the Spanish Civil War. To the left, after leaving the garden, the California Tower stands 200 feet (61m) above El Prado: it was built as the centerpiece for the 1915 Exposition. At its foot is the Museum of Man, with a fascinating collection of artifacts from the Pueblo people of the southwest and the ancient Aztec and Mayan settlements of Latin America.

Return up El Prado and turn right. On the left is the Japanese Friendship Garden, a traditional

Serenading snackers at the Bazaar del Mundo, Old Town San Diego

Japanese garden which has been adapted to the climate and topography of San Diego. It provides a perfect place for quiet contemplation. Next to the garden is the Spreckels Organ Pavilion, but unless you are in the park on a Sunday at 2pm, the world's biggest organ will be protected behind a 12-ton/tonne metal curtain.

The Aerospace Historical Center is at the end of the Pan-American Plaza, just past the Japanese Friendship Plaza. The whole history of aviation is covered in this circular building, from the Montgolfier brothers' hot-air balloon to the latest spacecraft. Every conceivable aspect of aviation is covered, including an extensive exhibit on the role of women in this field. Next door is the San Diego Automotive Museum, with a display of more than 80 vehicles, including horseless carriages, exotic cars and futuristic prototypes.

▶ *Return to the parking lot and drive north on Park Boulevard. Turn right on El Cajon Boulevard and drive to I-15 north. Exit on San Diego Mission Road.*

2 Mission San Diego de Alcala

Considering the importance of Father Junípero Serra's first mission in California, Mission San Diego de Alcala is in a curiously suburban setting. The mission is virtually the only site of interest in the valley and is refreshingly uncommercial. The original mission was built in 1769, but it was moved a few years later because of disputes between the Spanish and the Indians. The second mission was burned down by the Indians in 1775, and the present mission was constructed in 1777. It was destroyed by an earthquake in 1803, and all that remains now is a church with a bell tower and a small museum set in beautiful gardens.

▶ *Return to I-15 south, turn west on I-8, continue along Mission Valley Freeway (I-8), and turn south on I-5. Turn off on Old Town Avenue, then turn left and left again on San Diego Avenue.*

3 Old Town San Diego State Historic Park

Old Town is where San Diego began, as the first European settlement in California. The State of California bought six blocks of historic buildings in the 1960s to preserve the atmosphere of Mexican California with restored original buildings and costumed interpreters. The core of the park is a Mexican plaza, around which many of the old buildings are set. Although there are 16 historic structures, 10 of which house museums, the park feels much larger, mainly due to the presence of 33 craft and specialty shops and seven restaurants.

The commercial element of the town tends to be concentrated on the Bazaar del Mundo, a loud and garish shopping and restaurant complex immediately off the main plaza, that is supposedly an imitation Mexican street market. Fortunately, most of the visitors tend to congregate here, leaving the rest of the park relatively quiet, and preserving the historic atmosphere of the area. The most interesting buildings are the old adobe structures, most of which surround the Plaza. Casa de Estudillo, at the Mason Street end of the plaza, is the largest: this housed the 12-child family of the commander of the presidio.

▶ *Return to I-5 north and exit west on Genesee Avenue and south on Torrey Pines Road North.*

4 University of California at San Diego (UCSD)
The impressive campus of the state university stretches along Torrey Pines Road, with an eclectic collection of commissioned, site-specific modern sculpture on display in the public areas. Brochures are available at the UCSD information booths at the Torrey Pines Road North entrance. Most people, however, come here to visit the aquarium administered by the Scripps Institute. Opposite the Scripps Institute of Oceanography, turn up Expedition Way to a hillside location overlooking La Jolla

Shores Beach. Here you will find the new Stephen Birch Aquarium and Museum, featuring marine life from both the cold northern waters and the tropical oceans of the Pacific. There are also interactive exhibits and changing displays that explore the latest developments in oceanography.

▶ *Return south along Torrey Pines Road to downtown La Jolla.*

5 La Jolla
Both Prospect and Girard streets reflect the trendy, upscale

WALKING TOUR

Old Town San Diego State Historic Park gives an intimate view of early California and over the last 200 years Spanish, Mexican and American flags have flown above the town. The only way to see the park is on foot; self-guided walking tour maps are available from the Visitor Center at the Robinson-Rose House at the northwest end of the plaza.

Beautiful blue sea and top-class facilities come together at La Jolla

atmosphere of the expensive residential enclave of San Diego. According to Indian legend, Jolla means "cave" or "hole"; not surprisingly, residents tend to prefer the Spanish translation of "jewel." They also think of their ritzy neighborhood of San Diego as a separate entity, and call it "The Village." Even the post office stamps bear the name La Jolla, although it is officially part of the city of San Diego. The area is not unlike an exclusive Mediterranean resort, with the same mix of expensive houses, exquisite boutiques, gourmet restaurants and grand hotels. The cliff-lined coast adds to this overall impression, and it is worth taking the time for a short walk along the coast in front of the grand Valencia Hotel.

At 700 Prospect Street is an interesting building designed by the renowned San Diego architect Irving Gill. It houses the La Jolla Museum of Contemporary Art, specializing in the best modern art produced in California.

▶ Drive south past the
boutiques and art galleries of
Girard Avenue and turn right
onto Pearl Street. Follow Pearl
to La Jolla Boulevard and turn
left. Follow the coast to
Mission Beach.

6 Mission Beach

This is the perfect example of a
southern California beach. It is
usually humming with activity,
from surfers to volleyball players to roller-bladers, with far
more flesh on view than clothing. The boardwalk is worthy
of a short stroll, if only to enjoy
a glimpse of the beach life. At
its southern end is an amusement park complete with a
roller-coaster and an antique
carousel.

Inland from the beach is
Mission Bay, 4,600 acres (1,861
hectares) of water that form the
world's largest municipal
aquatic park. There are
27 miles (43km) of beaches,
boat-launching ramps, picnic
areas and playgrounds here,
making up one of San Diego's
major tourist attractions.

Riding along on the crest of a
wave at SeaWorld

▶ From Mission Bay take
Mission Bay Drive to
SeaWorld.

7 SeaWorld

This is the marine equivalent
of Disneyland – a fantasy land
inhabited by all forms of marine
life. Featured in this 135-acre
(55-hectare) park are six major
shows, alternately staged
throughout the day at various
stadiums and indoor auditori-
ums. Between shows, you can
touch or view live animals at 20
educational exhibits and four
aquariums. SeaWorld really
deserves a whole day to do it
justice; on this familiarization
tour, it may be better just to
note the location and return at
your leisure.

▶ Drive south on Midway Drive
and turn off on Sunset Cliffs
Boulevard. Turn left onto Hill
Street and right onto Catalina
Boulevard, which becomes
Cabrillo Memorial Drive.

8 Point Loma

The drive from Mission Bay passes the dramatic sandstone bluffs of Sunset Cliffs Park. As well as a spectacular setting, it enjoys big waves, making it very popular with expert surfers. The drive continues down the peninsula that separates San Diego Bay from the Pacific Ocean. On the way, the road passes through Fort Rosecrans National Cemetery, part of a U.S. Navy installation, where thousands of pristine white gravestones mark the resting place of San Diego's fallen troops. At the end of the road, at the very tip of Point Loma, is the Cabrillo National Monument, one of the smallest but most historic and most visited monuments in the country (it has more visitors than the Statue of Liberty). Juan Rodriquez Cabrillo's statue, a gift from his Portugal homeland, faces Ballast Point, where the great navigator landed in

1542, becoming the first European to reach California. A nearby visitor center tells the story of Cabrillo's discovery of San Diego Bay and its subsequent history. On a high bluff overlooking the monument is the Point Loma lighthouse, which was used to guide ships into the Bay between 1855 and 1891. It is open to visitors.

The most impressive aspect of Point Loma is the spectacular view – it is worth the drive for this alone. On a clear day, you can see from the mountains of Mexico, all the way up to La Jolla, and from San Diego and its bay all the way out to the Pacific Ocean.

▶ *Return along Cabrillo Memorial Drive and turn right on Canon Street and left on Rosecrans Street. Turn right again onto Harbor Drive.*

A golden city: San Diego's skyline basks in the California sun

BACK TO NATURE

Point Loma is an ideal place to watch migrating birds between mid-December and mid-February each year. There is a glassed-in observatory at the Cabrillo National Monument, for protection against winter weather. Close by is one of the best tidepool areas in California. A nature trail leads down to the pools and passes an area with a unique plant community. There are daily ranger-led tours, and information can be obtained from the Visitor Center.

SCENIC ROUTES

The drive to Point Loma provides spectacular views of the San Diego skyline. Plan the drive for late afternoon, when the sun lights up the city.

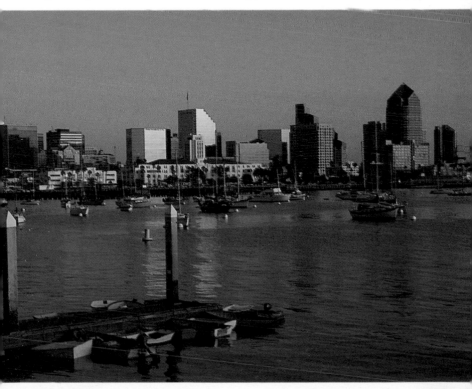

Follow Harbor Drive until it reaches the downtown area and look for the Maritime Museum on the right, opposite Ash Street.

9 Maritime Museum

The drive toward town is particularly good at the end of the day, when the high-rise buildings are bathed in warm, late-afternoon sunlight. Photographers may want to stop by the harbor to capture this classic view of the city. San Diego is very definitely a seafaring town and, apart from the strong U.S. Navy presence, sailors from all over the world congregate in this massive harbor. Sailing is one of the most popular sports in town and it was the San Diego yacht *Stars and Stripes* that brought home the America's Cup from Australia in 1987. Two nautical museums sit next to each other by the harbor. The Maritime Museum is the grand name given to three ships that are moored on the Embarcadero. The highlight of the group is the *Star of India*, a fully equipped three-masted merchant ship, built in 1863: the oldest iron-hulled ship still afloat in America. Also here is the San Francisco Bay ferry boat, *Berkeley*, which played a major role in evacuating victims of the

1906 earthquake, and a 1904 steam yacht, the *Medea*, which still makes occasional trips around the San Diego Bay. In an adjacent warehouse is the America's Cup Museum, where the story is told of this great sailing event, capable of whipping up as much patriotic fervor as the Olympic Games. San Diego hosted the race in 1992.

▶ *Continue along the Embarcadero to Seaport Village.*

10 Seaport Village

This modern shopping and dining complex, only a few minutes' walk from the very heart of downtown San Diego, is intended to depict the harborside as it was a century ago. It is difficult to believe that it could have been so well manicured back then, but it does provide a very agreeable environment for shopping with pleasant, landscaped walks overlooking the harbor. In all, 14 acres (6 hectares) have been developed, with over 60 stores and 17 restaurants. Street performers are usually out entertaining visitors and although this is a totally tourist-oriented development there is a merciful absence of T-shirt stores and other barometers of tourist culture.

SPECIAL TO...

The best way to experience San Diego Bay is on the ferry that runs between the dock at Broadway and Harbor Drive in San Diego and the Ferry Landing Market Place in Coronado. It leaves San Diego on the hour and Coronado on the half-hour, and the crossing takes 15 minutes. Coronado is a beach resort, where the main attraction is the grand old Hotel del Coronado, built in 1888 and featured in the hit film *Some Like It Hot.*

▶ *Take Harbor Drive to 6th Avenue and turn north. Turn right on Market Street and enter the Gaslamp Quarter.*

11 Gaslamp Quarter

The 16-block strip along 4th, 5th and 6th avenues from Broadway to the Waterfront is one of America's largest national historic districts. In the 19th century this was San Diego's main street area, but by the turn of the century it had become a flourishing red-light district. It sits right in the heart of San Diego and, like many inner-city areas, it has suffered years of neglect. Fortunately, none of the buildings were lost to make way for modern office blocks, and a concerted effort has been made to restore the district to its original glory, including its designation as a National Historic District. Many of the buildings have been renovated, but it has not entirely lost its seedy image: there is still a fair share of pawn shops and dilapidated buildings, but they now rub shoulders with trendy restaurants and antiques shops. At this stage of the drive it will probably be early evening – and what better place to be than this atmospheric Victorian neighborhood, filled with interesting restaurants and cafés. Hopefully, there will still be enough light to see some of the fine examples of Victorian architecture that abound in the area.

More than 100 old Victorian buildings have been lovingly restored, and a detailed map of the main points of interest is available from the William Heath Davis House, at 410 Island Avenue. This house also happens to be the area's oldest structure, a "salt box" home, shipped from New England to San Diego around Cape Horn in about 1850. Across the street, at 554 4th Avenue, is a bakery that has been in business on the site since 1875. Even when the second floor of the building was a notorious whorehouse at the turn of the 20th century, cakes and pies were still being baked downstairs. The area bordered San Diego's old Chinatown, and Wong's Nanking Café still retains the atmosphere of the period during which it was built, in 1913. Perhaps the most architecturally significant section of the quarter is on 5th Avenue, between E and F streets. Most of the buildings here were erected during the latter part of the 19th century, and include the Marston Building, the Hubbell Building, the Nesmith-Greeley Building and the Louis Bank of Commerce, which

Left: clowning around to entertain a young Seaport Villager

many people regard as the most beautiful building in the quarter.

▶ Take Broadway to G Street.

12 Horton Plaza
This colorful, modern shopping plaza, that opened in 1985, is the centerpiece of the new down-

FOR CHILDREN
The San Diego Children's Museum, at 200 W. Island Avenue, at the corner of Front Street, is full of hands-on exhibits, from poetry-writing to wheelchair basketball. There is a strong emphasis on different cultures, and the Improv Theater provides costumes and a stage for youngsters to try out their thespian talents. The more traditional pursuits of painting and modeling are also offered.

Modern architecture can be fun – as is evident at Horton Plaza

town San Diego area and is a textbook example of good design. The human scale and visually stimulating architecture combine with first-rate stores to make shopping here a totally satisfying experience. The plaza is a multilevel, open-air, six block complex of bridges, piazzas, towers, sculpture and gardens inhabited by street performers and shoppers. There are 14 different architectural styles represented, from Renaissance to Postmodern. An efficient parking garage extends under the plaza, alleviating the usual downtown parking problems. All this and parking too!

▶ Take Broadway east to Park Boulevard north and drive back to Balboa Park.

THE MISSIONS

Long before the discovery of gold, California was transformed into a European colony, as zealous Catholic missionaries spread the Christian message. Baja California (Lower California, now part of Mexico) was well established by the Spanish, who were also anxious to settle Alta California (Upper California, the present-day state). It was a dramatic, wild and magnificently beautiful corner of North America, inhabited by more than 300,000 Native Americans belonging to 105 separate nations, and a prize coveted by not only the Spanish but also the Russians and British. Spain put its faith in one man, Father Junípero Serra, who was responsible for developing a chain of missions that became the backbone of the modern state.

In 1769, when he was 55, Serra traveled for six weeks, covering 750 miles (1,207km) by donkey, from Mexico to San Diego, to build his first mission. This would be the first of a series of missions that would eventually extend up the coast of California as far as Sonoma, north of San Francisco. Serra had to fight almost insurmountable obstacles in establishing the first community. Several previous expeditions had failed to achieve their goal, and Serra's group was dogged by illness and Spanish bureaucracy, and almost ran out of supplies. Nevertheless, they struggled into San Diego in July, 1769, to erect a large wooden cross and conduct Mass in front of a group of curious Indians.

Junípero Serra had moved to Mexico from his birthplace in Mallorca when he was 37. He was a small man with a pronounced limp, resulting from an injury in Mexico for which he refused to have treatment. At the time of his death in 1784, he had traveled thousands of miles and established a further nine missions in what were then the most remote outposts of California. The second in the chain, which he built in 1771, was the Mission San Carlos Borromeo in Carmel. This was Serra's favorite mission, and it remained his headquarters until his death (he is buried at the mission chapel). Everywhere you go in California today, you see Junípero Serra's name – on schools, on highways and on monuments. His role in establishing an unshakable Catholic base to religion in the state inevitably lead to his candidacy for sainthood, and he was beatified by the Vatican in 1988.

The Junípero Serra Museum in San Diego sits high on a hill near Old Town, overlooking the site that is the birthplace of modern California. It was here, in 1769, that Serra built the first non-native settlement in California. The original mission was located here, too, but four years later it was moved to its present site for agricultural reasons. The museum documents the early history of the state and of the Indians, Spanish and Mexicans who made this area their home.

Following Junípero Serra's death, his role was taken over

Monument to faith: San Francisco de Asis (Mission Dolores)

by Fermin Francisco de Lasuen who, like Serra, had moved to Mexico in his 30s. He established a further eight missions during his 18 years in the office of President of the Missions, and he was already 66 years old when he started the project. It was Lasuen who developed the style of architecture that has come to be known throughout California as the mission style: thick, adobe walls, with red-tile roofs and shaded courtyards, surrounded by arcades.

The missions were linked by "El Camino Real" – the King's Highway. Streets bearing the same name, following the original route, can be found in most of California's coastal towns today. Highway 101 closely follows this route. The missions were built as links in a chain that extended all the way from Mexico to the north of Alta California. Each link was one day's journey from the next by horseback, and missionaries could theoretically reach the farthest outpost in Sonoma within 21 days of leaving Mexico.

Many of the first missions were destroyed by fire, and a few by earthquake, but all were rebuilt, some on

Above: a tribute in stained glass to the work of the 18th-century mission-builders

Left: Mission San Diego de Alcala

their original sites and some in new, more practical locations. Most of the missions today are restorations of the original buildings, but some still have the original decorations painted by Indian converts.

One of the most interesting of all the missions is La Purisima, north of Santa Barbara. Typically, the original buildings were destroyed by fire, and the mission was rebuilt on the present site in 1813. Even the rebuilt mission was long since destroyed, and the present buildings are reconstructions, but it has been so well done that this is now the most authentic-looking mission in the chain. Adding to its convincing physical appearance are the surrounding gardens and farmland, perfectly replicating the life of the period. All of the missions are open to the public and several also have adjoining museums that document the spread of Catholicism along "El Camino Real."

LIST OF MISSIONS

San Diego de Alcala

San Luis Rey de Francia

San Juan Capistrano

San Gabriel Arcangel

San Fernando Rey de Espana

San Buenaventura

Santa Barbara

Santa Ines

La Purisima Concepcíon

San Luis Obispo de Tolosa

San Miguel Arcangel

San Antonio de Padua

Nuestra Senora de la Soledad

San Carlos Borremeo de Carmelo

San Juan Bautista

Santa Cruz

Santa Clara de Asis

San Jose de Guadalupe

San Francisco de Asis (Mission Dolores)

San Rafael Arcangel

San Francisco de Solano

San Diego County

San Diego County is surprisingly mountainous, and the fresh mountain air provides relief from the surrounding hot deserts. Here is one of the state's most beautiful wilderness parks, the most southern wineries, a safari park and even a world famous astronomical telescope. This is a far cry from the fast life of Los Angeles, or even San Diego.

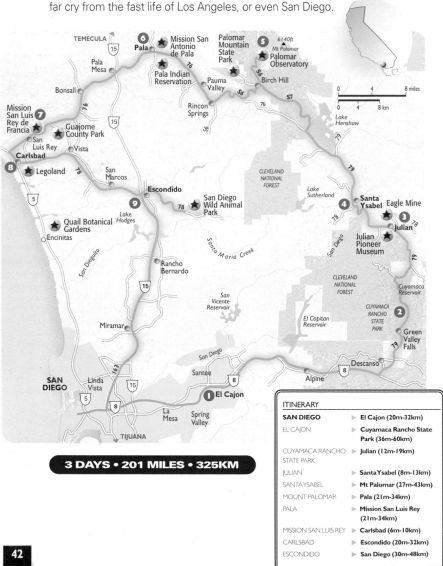

3 DAYS • 201 MILES • 325KM

ITINERARY		
SAN DIEGO	▶	**El Cajon (20m-32km)**
EL CAJON	▶	**Cuyamaca Rancho State Park (36m-60km)**
CUYAMACA RANCHO STATE PARK	▶	**Julian (12m-19km)**
JULIAN	▶	**Santa Ysabel (8m-13km)**
SANTA YSABEL	▶	**Mt Palomar (27m-43km)**
MOUNT PALOMAR	▶	**Pala (21m-34km)**
PALA	▶	**Mission San Luis Rey (21m-34km)**
MISSION SAN LUIS REY	▶	**Carlsbad (6m-10km)**
CARLSBAD	▶	**Escondido (20m-32km)**
ESCONDIDO	▶	**San Diego (30m-48km)**

i San Diego Visitor Information Center, 2688 E. Mission Bay Drive, San Diego

▶ Leave San Diego on **I-8**, heading east.

❶ El Cajon

This sprawling suburb of San Diego does not have a great deal to offer visitors, but the Heritage of the Americas Museum, on the campus of Cuyamaca College, at 2952 Jamacha Road, is worth a visit. This cultural and educational center is concerned with both the natural and human history of the Americas. Exhibits include fossils, seashells, minerals and meteorites, tribal tools, baskets, jewelry and a small art gallery. The best reason for visiting the museum, however, is the sweeping view of the campus and surrounding area from the hilltop. The Main Street of El Cajon has several fine antiques shops which are good for a browse.

▶ Continue along **I-8** to the turn off for **Hwy 79** north at Descanso Junction. Continue north directly into Cuyamaca Rancho State Park.

❷ Cuyamaca Rancho State Park

This 25,000-acre (10,117-hectare) park is only 40 miles (64km) away from San Diego, but feels much more remote. Peaks as high as 6,500 feet (1,981m) are covered in Ponderosa pines, firs, incense cedar and oaks, and at certain times of the year there are abundant wildflowers. Over 100 species of birds enjoy this habitat, as well as mountain lions, coyotes, deer, foxes and bobcats. The views from here extend from the Pacific in the west to the deserts of the east and south. The park was originally a gathering place for Indians, and during the Spanish occupation it was a ranch. Its name is the Spanish translation of an Indian word for "the place where it rains." A small museum at the visitor center has an

exhibit illustrating the Indians' resistance to 19th-century settlers' attempts at logging.

▶ Continue north on **Hwy 79** to Julian.

❸ Julian

In 1870, a gold strike put this little mountain community on the map. In the years following, some 2,000 miners extracted more than $15 million in gold ore. The Washington Mine (at the end of Washington Street) was Julian's first hard rock mine; today it is a State Historic Park (open daily). The tunnels collapsed years ago but you can still see the assay office and blacksmith's shop. Follow the signs from C Street to the Eagle Mine, which still offers tours underground. This educational, if claustrophobic, tour can be enhanced by a visit to Miners Camp, at 2605 Washington Street, where you can practice hands-on gold-panning and learn even more about the Gold Rush days.

Julian itself is a quaint, attractive town with many historic buildings along the Main Street, which still has wooden sidewalks. The Julian Hotel was built in 1887, the Julian Drug Store still has an old-fashioned

soda fountain serving sarsparilla, and an old brewery has been turned into the Pioneer Museum – almost too grandiose a term for this eclectic assortment of exhibits, which includes the first bathtub and the oldest pool table in town. It also houses a surprisingly good collection of lace. Today, Julian is known for its apples. Orchards surround the town and the apple-pie stores are a big attraction. At the Julian Cider Mill, off Main Street, you can watch the production of cider and sample honey collected from the mill's own beehives. Julian's proximity to San Diego makes it a popular weekend excursion.

FOR CHILDREN

Legoland, south of Carlsbad, has become a major attraction for younger children who are looking for a more gentle kind of theme park. There are no scary rides but lots of fun things to do including a visit to a scale model of New York made entirely from Lego.

▶ Drive 8 miles (13km) north on **Hwy 79**.

❹ Santa Ysabel

Apart from a general store dating back to 1870, the main interest here is a branch of the mission in San Diego that is still used by the local Indians. The Mission Santa Ysabel was originally built in 1818, but the present white stucco structure is a 1924 re-creation. There is a tiny one-room museum and a large Indian cemetery.

▶ Continue north on **Hwy 79** for around 11 miles (18km) and turn right onto **Hwy 57**. After another 11 miles (18km), turn right onto **Hwy 56** and make a steep climb of over 4 miles (7km) to Mount Palomar Observatory.

Julian's abundant apple crops come in handy for making apple pies

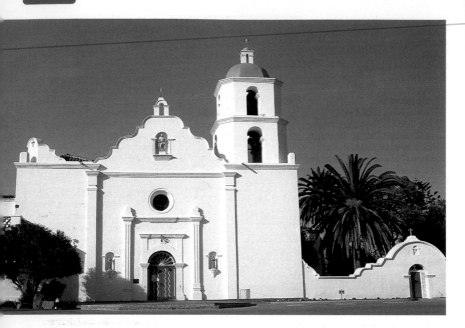

5 Mount Palomar

The 200-inch (5,080mm) reflecting Hale telescope at the Palomar Observatory is one of the biggest in the world, housed in a 13-story-high dome operated by the California Institute of Technology. A self-guiding tour explains the working of this monstrous mirror and the telescope can be viewed from the visitors' gallery. The adjoining Greenway Museum has exhibits of photographs of celestial secrets taken through this mighty lens. There are three other domes that house 48-inch (1,219mm) Oschin and 18-inch (457mm) Schmidt-type telescopes and a 60-inch (1,524mm) reflecting telescope. The interior of the observatory has to be kept at constant night-time temperatures to prevent distortion of the mirror. It can feel quite chilly after entering from the heat of the day, and a sweater can be very useful. The observatory sits at the summit of 6,140-foot (1,872m) Mount Palomar. The air up here is fresh and clear, and the scenic drive up through the chaparral and the rock-covered landscape is quite beautiful.

▶ *Return down* **Hwy 56** *and continue all the way down through almost 7 miles (11km) of hairpin bends back to* **Hwy 76**. *Stay on* **Hwy 76** *all the way into Pala.*

6 Pala

Mission San Antonio de Pala was built in 1815 as a branch of Mission San Luis Rey de Francia. It lies within the Pala Indian Reservation and is the only mission in California where the original chapel is still used primarily by Native Americans. The interior of the chapel is adorned with primitive Indian frescoes, complementing the rustic interior. Outside, the cemetery is filled with simple handmade wooden crosses marking Indian graves. Tourmaline Queen Mountain, once teeming with miners, rears up behind the mission. To see displays of some of the world's finest tourmaline, which came from this mountain, visit Gems of Pala at 35940 Magee Road, which has both exhibits and retail displays.

▶ *Return to* **Hwy 76** *and continue west to San Luis Rey.*

California's largest mission, the Mission San Luis Rey de Francia

7 Mission San Luis Rey de Francia

On the right of the highway is the largest of the California missions, built in 1798 by Father Fermín de Lasuen as the 18th in the chain. The sanctuary interior has a wooden double-dome construction with high, beamed ceilings; Indians painted the original, colorful decorations.

> **FOR HISTORY BUFFS**
>
> Three miles (5km) east of Mission San Luis Rey is the Guajome Adobe, one of the finest examples of domestic Spanish adobe architecture in California. Rancho Guajome was a mission-owned tract of land granted to Spanish-Mexican settlers for farming when Mexico gained independence from Spain in the 19th century. The 20-room Guajome Adobe now sits at the center of the 569-acre (230-hectare) Guajome County Park.

At one time it included almost 6 acres (2 hectares) of buildings and had 3,000 Indian neophytes. The mission has been beautifully restored and still operates as a seminary.

▶ *Drive west on* **Hwy 76** *and turn south on the San Diego Freeway (I–5). Take the Carlsbad exit, continue for a mile (1.5km); the town is on the west side of the freeway.*

8 Carlsbad

Carlsbad became a spa town in the 19th century, drawing the crowds to its natural well and the apparently health-giving properties of its waters. A small museum at the Alt Karlsbad Haus Gift Shop records the history of this era, when Carlsbad was a prosperous resort. Although the spring disappeared years ago, the town is still noted

---

BACK TO NATURE

Nine miles (14km) south of Carlsbad, near Encinitas, Quail Botanical Gardens has more than 30 acres (12 hectares) of rare plants. A chaparral area serves as a bird refuge and provides a great opportunity to see many different species of birds from the garden's self-guiding trails.

SPECIAL TO...

One of the more bizarre attractions in California is a few minutes' drive north of Escondido. Popular dance band leader Lawrence Welk liked the area so much that he built a resort around his mobile home, including a restaurant, a motel, a theater and a museum of Welk memorabilia. To many older Americans, who grew up with his television broadcasts, the Lawrence Welk Resort is something of a shrine. Take the Mountain Meadow Road exit off I-15 north; the resort is located at 8860 Lawrence Welk Drive.

---

for its spas, including the La Costa Hotel and Spa, frequented by the rich and famous. The cobblestone streets, quaint stores and the arrival of Legoland have once again made Carlsbad a popular destination.

▶ *Take* **Hwy 78** *east to Escondido.*

9 Escondido

In recent years, Escondido has become the center of California's most southerly wine-producing region. More than a dozen wineries have sprung up in the surrounding area, and they are all open for tours and tasting. Ferrara Winery, at 1120 West 15th Street, is the oldest in the county, and has been designated a state historical site. However, the reason most people come here is the San Diego Wild Animal Park. If you continue east through Escondido on Hwy 78 to San Pasqual Valley Road, the park is clearly signposted. It began as a breeding facility for San Diego Zoo's large animals, and its 2,100 acres (850 hectares) are now home to more than 2,500 animals from Africa and Asia, including elephants, rhinos, giraffes and zebras. The park has been landscaped to resemble the natural habitat of the animals and the experience is as close to actually being on safari as possible. A monorail makes a 50-minute circuit of the park and there is a marked walking tour. Wide expanses of land allow the animals to roam with considerable freedom, undisturbed by their human observers. A good pair of binoculars can be an extremely useful accessory here.

▶ *Return to San Diego on* **I-15** *south.*

A photo opportunity grasped at San Diego Wild Animal Park

THE DESERTS

Within a couple of hours' drive from the urban concentration of Los Angeles, you can be in the middle of an arid wilderness. The deserts of southern California are one of the great natural features of the state – though at first appearance these barren tracts of land look bleak and inhospitable, and most people drive through with never a thought of stopping. What a mistake this is! The deserts are a fragile and fascinating environment, with their own austere beauty that unfolds slowly to the visitor. Wildlife abounds, but only patience will give rewards. Bighorn sheep can still be seen in some of the more remote areas, and there are wild burros, sidewinder snakes, kit foxes and a host of cacti and other plants adapted to the harsh, dry conditions. The hand of man has unfortunately left an indelible scar on the desert. Wherever development has occurred, it seems that little care has been taken to harmonize with, or protect, the landscape. Old mining operations lie in ruins, trailer homes are surrounded by abandoned cars and machinery, and rusting tin cans and empty bottles litter the sides of highways. Fortunately, though, the fragility of the desert has not escaped attention, and with the passing of the California Desert Protection Act in 1994 most of the state's deserts are now wildlife sanctuaries. No one should leave without experiencing this desolate grandeur.

There are two distinct desert areas. The Mojave is high desert, ranging in elevation from 3,000 to 5,000 feet (914 to 1,524m). At a much lower elevation are the northern extension of the Sonora Desert, most of it within Anza-Borrego Desert State Park, and the southern extension of the Colorado Desert, culminating in Death Valley National Park. From May to October the temperatures can reach infernally high levels, especially in Death Valley, where some of the highest temperatures on earth have been recorded. Death Valley is a popular winter vacation destination, and during November hundreds of recreational vehicles descend on the valley to take advantage of the pleasant climate. In the high desert, winter usually brings snow and the temperatures can be extremely low. In both areas, early spring is the best time to visit, when the desert floor suddenly comes alive with a carpet of colorful wildflowers.

Over 1,000 years ago, the Agua Caliente Indians were attracted to the shady palm oases and freshwater springs of the desert. Today, the clean air and a dry, sunny climate have attracted world-class health spas, resorts for tennis and golf, and some of the most exclusive housing in America. Palm Springs, Palm Desert and Rancho Mirage are an extension of Hollywood, in terms of both their residents and the extravagant lifestyle that is enjoyed here.

The whole desert is punctuated with old mining operations. Gold, silver and borax were at one time profitably mined throughout the high desert region, but as the mineral deposits ran out and the mines closed, towns were abandoned, leaving a legacy of ghost towns scattered along the desert highways. Today, where irrigation is possible with water diverted from the Colorado River, agriculture has become a thriving industry and valleys full of date palms and other produce extend down to the Mexican border.

The venerable bristlecone pines

Tour 7

Palm Springs is only a short drive from Los Angeles, and it became an extension of Hollywood during the 1930s. Since those early days, even more exclusive resorts have been built and the tour continues through the fashionable desert communities of Rancho Mirage and Palm Desert to Coachella and the date palm groves that lead down to the surreal, artificial Salton Sea. A spectacular drive takes you through the desert of Anza-Borrego Desert State Park.

During the spring, this huge area, the largest state park in the contiguous United States, is a riotous explosion of color, as thousands upon thousands of desert plants burst into flower. The tour continues north through the desert, returning to Los Angeles via the alpine community of Idyllwild, sitting a mile (1.5km) high in the San Jacinto Mountains.

Tour 8

Passing through Palm Springs, the road travels east to Joshua Tree National Park, where the Mojave and Colorado deserts meet and dramatic Joshua trees are set against chaotic boulder formations. This is the southern limit of the Joshua tree but the giant, distorted yuccas can be seen all over the high desert. The tour goes through the Mojave Desert, across to Needles on the Arizona border, then back east across the northern boundary of the desert, to Barstow and San Bernadino County.

Tour 9

This tour provides an outstanding introduction to two of California's major deserts. After leaving Los Angeles, it crosses the high Mojave Desert to Owens Valley, before climbing over the Panamint Mountains and dropping into Death Valley and the lowest point in the western hemisphere.

From here the tour returns to Highway 395 and at Lone Pine there are spectacular views of Mount Whitney, the highest peak in the continental U.S. outside Alaska. Continue up to the White Mountains to see the world's oldest living trees, *Pinus longaeva*. NB There is no direct route from this tour to Sequoia and King's Canyon.

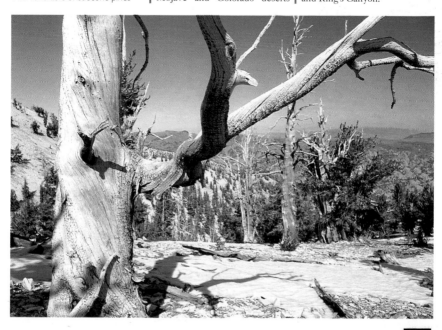

Palm Springs, Salton Sea &
Anza-Borrego

This tour shows the extremes of desert life, from the manicured golf courses of Palm Springs and Palm Desert, to the barren mountains of Anza-Borrego. Glittering resorts line the Coachella Valley, while endless pristine deserts await exploration. This region gets unbearably hot in the summer, but in winter and spring the blue skies and warm days are ideal.

ITINERARY		
LOS ANGELES	▶	**Ontario (38m-61km)**
ONTARIO	▶	**Desert Hot Springs (11m-18km)**
DESERT HOT SPRINGS	▶	**Palm Springs (14m-22km)**
PALM SPRINGS	▶	**Rancho Mirage (13m-21km)**
RANCHO MIRAGE	▶	**Palm Desert (3m-5km)**
PALM DESERT	▶	**Indio (11m-18km)**
INDIO	▶	**Salton City (36m-58km)**
SALTON CITY	▶	**Anza-Borrego (27m-44km)**
ANZA-BORREGO	▶	**Los Angeles (195m-314km)**

3 DAYS • 348 MILES • 561KM

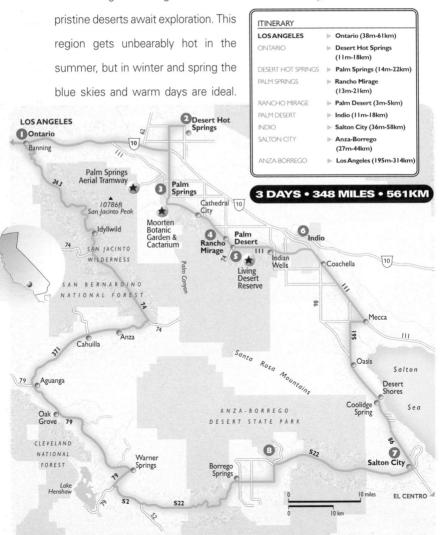

i *Palm Springs Desert Resorts Convention and Visitors Bureau, 70–100 Highway 111*

▶ *Leave Los Angeles on I-10.*

1 Ontario

This otherwise uninteresting suburb of Los Angeles has an international airport and is an important gateway to the desert regions. Once a thriving agricultural community, its only remaining vestige of this era is the Garber Olive House at 315 East 4th Street. Established in 1894, this olive-processing facility conducts tours and tastings, and is at its most active during the harvest, from October to December.

▶ *Continue east on I-10 and take the Desert Hot Springs exit.*

2 Desert Hot Springs

As the name suggests, this resort exists because of the springs – and they are hot. The water comes out of the ground at a searing 207°F (84°C) and has to be cooled before it can be used for therapeutic purposes. Two Bunch Palms is perhaps the most famous spa in town, because of its dubious past as a hideaway for Al Capone. The desert has always attracted its share of eccentrics: one of the first settlers in Desert Hot Springs was a prospector named Cabot Yerxa. He arrived in the valley in 1913 with a bottle of water and bag of food, and proceeded to build a pueblo loosely based on Indian architecture. His adobe home eventually had 35 rooms with 150 windows made from odd-shaped pieces of glass. It is now Cabot's Pueblo Museum and visitors can look at the intriguing collection Cabot gathered together, including an 8-foot (2m)-tall grizzly bear and a 20-ton carving from a giant sequoia tree that fills the four-story home. The museum is located at 67-616 East Desert View Avenue.

Flowers of the wilderness: the Living Desert at Palm Desert

▶ *Return toward I-10 but continue across the freeway to Palm Springs.*

3 Palm Springs

Palm Springs became the favorite Hollywood celebrity vacation during the 1930s, and it is easy to see why. First there is the balmy winter weather, when the temperature rarely exceeds 85°F (29°C) nor drops below 55°F (13°C). Then there is the natural mineral spring that has helped to make this the country's most famous resort. Many celebrities established homes here, including Bob Hope, Frank Sinatra and Liberace, and this brush with glamour still accounts for much of the resort's popularity. Golf courses abound – in fact, if you don't play, there is little else to do apart from sunbathe. The city is certainly pleasant, but it has the feel of a commuter suburb, rather than a major resort. Most of the action takes place along Palm Canyon Drive. This is the main thoroughfare where, at peak times, there can be bumper-to-bumper

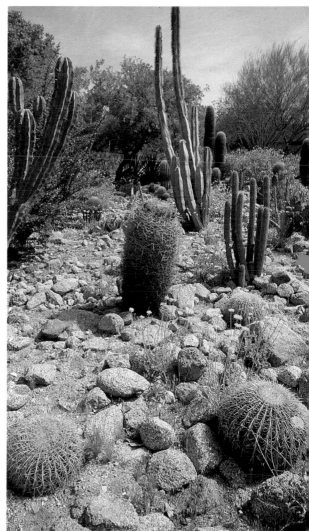

traffic. All the major stores are here, along with restaurants and the Palm Springs Follies.

The Village Green Heritage Center sits incongruously in the midst of a modern shopping development at 221 South Palm Canyon Drive. It is about the only historic site in town – and the entire history of the town is covered in three buildings.

The McCallum Adobe is the oldest building, once the home of the city founder. Built in 1884, it houses an exhibit of tools, books and clothes from the early years of the town, and has a display of photographs of Hollywood stars associated with Palm Springs. The railroad tie-house, next door, was built by

One of the Agua Caliente Indians who own most of Palm Springs

pioneer Cornelia White in 1893, and was originally part of the city's first hotel. Ruddy's General Store Museum is the third building, which re-creates a typical 1930s general store. Nearby is the Desert Fashion Plaza, an upscale shopping mall with designer boutiques and department stores. Behind it, on Museum Drive, is the Palm Springs Desert Museum. In a town that appears to be devoid of any culture, this is one of the country's best regional art museums. Even the modern red rock building, that seems to be part of the desert itself, is standing in exceptionally interesting landscaped sculpture gardens. The museum is widely acclaimed for its superb collection of modern art and a strong collection of the fine art of the American West.

FOR CHILDREN

The Oasis Waterpark is the perfect place for children to escape the heat of the desert. The 21-acre (8-hectare) resort is one of the largest in Southern California, with a wave pool and 13 different water slides. It is located at 1500 Gene Autry Trail, Palm Springs.

RECOMMENDED WALK

An area of Palm Springs called the Old Movie Colony will provide a glimpse of some of the homes owned by the great names of show business. Kirk Douglas still lives here, although most of the other stars have long since left. You can see where Elvis Presley spent his honeymoon, the house where Liberace spent his last days, and the winter homes of Douglas Fairbanks and Mary Pickford, Clark Gable and Liz Taylor. All of them are set beside easily walked streets, and a location map is available from the Palm Springs Visitor Center at 2781 North Palm Canyon Drive.

In addition, there are good natural science exhibits on the surrounding environment and Indian culture.

Way down South Palm Canyon Drive, the Moorten's Botanical Garden has displays of desert plants from all over the world. More than 3,000 varieties of plants grow among 4 acres (2 hectares) of petrified trees and dinosaur fossils. The garden is frequently filled with birds, and lizards are everywhere.

Visitors are often surprised to hear that most of Palm Springs is owned by the Agua Caliente Indians, from whom businesses rent land on 99-year leases. Their tribal lands are 5 miles (8km) south of Palm Canyon Drive, at the Agua Caliente Indian Reservation. This vast, scenic area is filled with canyons tucked into the mountains, and it abounds with hiking trails – but it is best to experience the canyons by car. Palm Canyon is the most accessible, and a parking lot at Hermit's Bench gives great views of the stands of 1,500 century-old Washington Palms that line the canyon for 7 miles (11km). A steep trail drops down into the canyon for the adventurous. Beyond Palm Canyon, Andreas Canyon has a shady grove of sycamores and cottonwoods, and there is an impressive grove of California fan palms close by.

On the northern edge of Palm Springs, at Chino Canyon, the Palm Springs Aerial Tramway takes passengers from 2,600 feet (792m) to 10,800 feet (3,292m) in less than 18 minutes. Mount San Jacinto is one of the sheerest mountains in North America and the Tramway is the largest single-span, double-reversible aerial tramway in the world. On clear days, the views from the top are awe-inspiring, and during the winter it is not unusual for travelers to leave the warm desert valley and be surrounded by snow within minutes. At the top is an observation deck and a restaurant serving lunch and dinner. There are over 50 miles (80km) of trails into the San Jacinto Wilderness State Park.

▶ *From Palm Springs, continue along **Hwy 111** to Rancho Mirage.*

4 Rancho Mirage
Golf courses and high-walled estates dominate this wealthy bedroom community. The wife of President Ford gave her name to the country's most well known drug treatment clinic, based here. Don't expect to see any celebrities going to the Betty Ford Clinic, however: it is very discreet, and impossible to approach without an appointment. The streets are named after film stars and directions tend to be along the lines of "go down Bob Hope, cross Frank Sinatra and turn right

on Jack Benny." There is nothing to stop for in Rancho Mirage – but take a drive through some of the streets to witness Californian excess.

▶ *Continue on **Hwy 111.***

5 Palm Desert
This is a mirror of Rancho Mirage, with the addition of one of the most expensive shopping streets in the world. El Paseo is the desert equivalent of Rodeo Drive in Beverly Hills.

The golf courses here are very highly rated and musical events are produced at the Bob Hope Cultural Center. The Living Desert is the highlight of this town – if you don't like shopping, that is. The 1,200-acre (485-hectare) wildlife and botanical park features rare plants and animals from deserts around the world. Among the animals are Mexican wolves, bighorn sheep, mountain lions, gazelles and

---

SCENIC ROUTES

Route 74 from Palm Desert leads up into the Santa Rosa Mountains. The tree-lined highway climbs high above the Coachella Valley, giving tremendous views of the desert communities.

Arabian oryx. The whole park is beautifully designed, and so cleverly laid out that the animals could easily be in the wild.

▶ *Continue along the Coachella Valley on **Hwy 111** to Indio.*

6 Indio
The blue-collar environment of Indio is in stark contrast to the ritzy estates of Palm Springs and its neighbors. This is the start of the Coachella Valley's agricultural region. Early in the 20th century, sophisticated irrigation

systems changed ed this arid desert into a major agricultural center producing grapefruit, cotton, alfalfa, vegetables and dates. Indio is surrounded by palm trees and is the self-proclaimed "Date Capital of the World." Along Highway 111, orderly rows of date palms alternate with roadside stands, often with elaborate Moorish facades, selling date products. The big event of the year in Indio is the National Date Festival, held in mid-February. It started in 1921 and the traditions include an Arabian Nights pageant and ostrich and camel races. Aside from dates, the Coachella Valley has a Museum and Cultural Center at 82616 Miles Avenue, housed in the 1920s adobe home and office of a local doctor. Exhibits include Cahuilla Indian artifacts, old farm and household equipment and a blacksmith's shop. Of more specific interest is a large relief map showing the development of the desert's water system, and dioramas explaining the date-growing industry.

▶ *Continue south. At Mecca turn west on **Hwy 195** and then south on **Hwy 195** to **Hwy 86**; then go south through Oasis to Salton City.*

INDIO · DATE FESTIVAL
PIGGLY · WIGGLY'S FAMOUS
DATE-SHAKES

SPECIAL TO...

Driving south through Indio and the date palm groves, roadside stands abound selling dates and the local specialty: date shakes. These date milkshakes taste better than they may sound, and give plenty of energy to fuel your continuing journey through the hot, desert valleys.

A sheet of salty water at the Salton Sea National Wildlife Refuge

7 Salton City

One of the most surreal places in California is the town of Salton City, on the shores of the Salton Sea. Planned as the next Palm Springs, it never attracted the numbers expected, so its carefully laid-out streets lead nowhere and there are more vacant lots than houses, giving the town a strange, deserted look. The marina, with its adjoining hotel, submerged in the rising waters of the lake, add to the feeling of desolation. In fact, there is a significant population, many of whom developed their land before the dream evaporated (and with summer temperatures often exceeding 100°F (38°C), evaporation is an all too common occurrence).

The 35-mile (56km)-long Salton Sea, one of the biggest salt-water lakes in the world, appeared by accident in 1905. Canals directing waters from the Colorado River to the Imperial Valley breached their banks

BACK TO NATURE

The Salton Sea is the most southerly stop on the Pacific flyway. At its southern tip, the Salton Sea National Wildlife Refuge has attracted 371 different bird species, including stilts, green-winged teal and the endangered Yuma clapper rail. One third of all North America's white pelicans winter here and during the fall the skies are full of Canada and snow geese. A 2-mile (3km) nature trail follows the shore of the lake and a lookout tower provides a perfect vantage point. To reach the refuge headquarters turn west on Sinclair Road and drive for just over 4 miles (6km).

during an exceptionally severe winter. Billions of gallons of water flooded into this once dry desert, and were trapped 235 feet (72m) below sea level, with no natural outlet. The sea has become increasingly saline over

the years, and is now more salty than the Pacific Ocean – but it still manages to support fish and other wildlife. It is an important winter recreation area for sports such as fishing, boating and water-skiing.

▶ Turn west on **Route S22** into Anza-Borrego Desert State Park. Continue into Borrego Springs.

8 Anza-Borrego Desert State Park

A thousand square miles (2,590 sq km) of desert make this the biggest State Park in the contiguous United States. An extension of Mexico's Sonora Desert, it was named after Juan Bautista de Anza, who first pioneered a route through these inhospitable surroundings in 1774. Borrego is the Spanish word for sheep, and the rare desert bighorn sheep can still be seen in some of the more remote areas of the park. The landscape is stark, but during the spring Anza-Borrego bursts into bloom as colorful wildflowers carpet the desert floor. Special wildflower maps can be picked up at the Visitor Center at Borrego Palm Canyon, 3 miles (5km) west of Borrego Springs.

▶ *From Borrego Springs take Route S22 west. Turn north on Hwy 79 then take Hwy 371 east to Hwy 74 north. Turn north onto Hwy 243 and climb the wonderfully scenic but steep road to Idyllwild, sitting high on the western edge of the San Jacinto Wilderness Area. This charming, alpine community is a sharp contrast to the desert areas that surround the San Jacinto Mountains. Continue north on Hwy 243 and join I-10 west at Banning to return to Los Angeles.*

Right: wildflowers bring a flash of spring color to the desert at Anza-Borrego Desert State Park
Below: the harsher landscape of Anza-Borrego's "southern badlands"

Mojave
Desert

This tour gives a thorough introduction to California's vast Mojave Desert, from the distinctive Joshua trees to the banks of the Colorado River and the border with Arizona. It returns through historic gold- and silver-mining country, before heading back to Los Angeles.

3 DAYS • 635 MILES • 1,022KM

ITINERARY

LOS ANGELES	▶ **Palm Springs** (107m–172km)
PALM SPRINGS	▶ **Indio** (24m–39km)
INDIO	▶ **Chiriaco Summit** (30m–48km)
CHIRIACO SUMMIT	▶ **Joshua Tree National Park** (12m–19km)
JOSHUA TREE NATIONAL PARK	▶ **Twentynine Palms** (70m–113km)
TWENTYNINE PALMS	▶ **Needles** (144m–232km)
NEEDLES	▶ **Daggett** (113m–182km)
DAGGETT	▶ **Calico** (7m–11km)
CALICO	▶ **Barstow** (11m–18km)
BARSTOW	▶ **Los Angeles** (117m–188km)

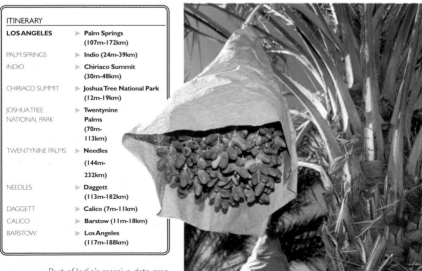

Part of Indio's massive date crop

i Hollywood Visitors Information
Center, 6801 Hollywood Boulevard

▶ Take **I-10** out of Los Angeles to
Redlands and continue to
Palm Springs. Take **Hwy 111**
into the Coachella Valley.

1 Palm Springs
(See also pages 49–51)
Both the Palm Springs Desert
Museum and the Moorten's
Botanical Garden give a good
introduction to desert natural
history, with displays of more
than 3,000 different desert
plants at the gardens and more
general natural science exhibits
at the museum.

Combine this with a visit
to the Living Desert, just
outside Palm Desert, where
there are 1,200 acres (485
hectares) of habitat for desert
animals from throughout the
world, and 6 miles (10km) of
trails to introduce visitors to
desert life.

▶ Continue on **Hwy 111** to Indio.

2 Indio
(See also page 51)
The 200,000 date palms
surrounding this town yield 40
million pounds (18 million kg) of
dates a year. Several date grow-
ers have exhibits, but one of the
best is at Shield's Date Gardens
on Hwy 111, just before entering
town. Not only can you feast on
black date ice cream and date

shakes but their slide show *The
Romance and Sex Life of the Date*
will tell you everything you ever
needed to know about this
desert fruit.

▶ Leave Indio on **I-10** and
continue for 30 miles (48km)
to the Chiriaco Summit exit.

3 Chiriaco Summit
The General Patton Museum
stands just off the freeway, on
the site that was General George
S. Patton's Desert Training
Center during the early 1940s.
The museum concentrates on

Joshua trees and rock climbers
at Joshua Tree National Park

displays of memorabilia from
World War II, but other eras of
American military history are
also covered, and include
displays of tanks and heavy
artillery. A video of General
Patton's life and career provides
a structure to the exhibits. A
relief map indicates the site of
the 11 desert training camps and,
more importantly, shows the
development of Southern
California's water system, so
vital to the area.

▶ Return west along **I-10** to the
Cottonwood Springs Road exit.

4 Joshua Tree National
Park
About 7 miles (11km) north of
the freeway is the southern
entrance to Joshua Tree
National Park. The small visitor
center at Cottonwood Springs
has a very basic display relating
to the park, but there are maps
and guide books available there.
Covering 870 square miles
(2,253sq km) in all, the park's
elevations range from 1,000 to
6,000 feet (305 to 1,829m),
making it pleasant at almost any
time of year. It rarely reaches the
unbearable temperatures of the
lower desert areas. The Joshua
tree, after which the park is
named, is a striking cactus-like
plant that only grows on high

ground between 3,000 and 5,000 feet (914 and 1,524m). It is actually a giant member of the lily family – older specimens are frequently over 40 feet (12m) tall – and got its name from the Mormon pioneers making their way across the desert. They also called it the "praying plant," because of its upstretched arms. Don't expect to see any of the trees near the southern entrance: it is far too low. The vegetation here consists of smoke trees, cottonwoods, spindly ocotillos and cholla cactus.

Drive north for about 20 miles (32km) to the Cholla Cactus Garden, an extensive area of opuntia, also called jumping cacti for the way they seem to leap to attach themselves to clothing. Directly across the road is an ocotillo patch. As the road continues north, the Joshua trees start to appear. At the first road junction, turn left onto Loop Road and drive through one of the most beautiful sections of the park. Joshua trees abound and the landscape consists of large, rounded granite boulders in an area aptly named "Wonderland of Rocks." This is a popular rock-climbing area: climbers are often seen scaling the smooth boulders. Keys Road is the next turn left; follow it to the end to Keys View, where there are sweeping vistas stretching from the Salton Sea, 235 feet (72m) below sea level, to the San Gabriel Mountains, 10,000 feet (3,048m) above sea level. Return to Loop Road and continue north, past more bizarre rock formations, to leave the park at the town of Joshua Tree.

▶ Turn right onto **Hwy 62** and drive 17 miles (27km) east to Twentynine Palms.

5 Twentynine Palms

There are far more than 29 palms in this small desert community – but not much else. The main entrance to Joshua Tree National Park is here, and the Oasis Visitor Center has good displays providing an

introduction to the flora, fauna and history of the park. At 6136 Adobe Road, the small Historical Society Museum has displays of mementos of the early days of mineral prospecting around Twentynine Palms, and explains the origins and growth of this desert settlement.

▶ Continue east on **Hwy 62** to Vidal Junction and turn north onto **Hwy 95** and drive 45 miles (72km) to Needles.

6 Needles

Sitting on the great Colorado River, which forms the boundary between California and Arizona, Needles was first settled in 1869 as a steamboat landing and supply station on the Old Emigrant Trail. The building of the Atchison, Topeka and Santa Fe Railroad in 1882 established the town, and there is a well-preserved Harvey House train depot and hotel. The town was named for the needle-like peaks that can be seen across the river in Arizona. The river is its focal point, and is a major recreational facility. Good beaches line the water and there is boating, fishing and water skiing available. One of the most spectacular boating trips is through the Topock Gorge, where the I-40 crosses the river. The gorge is 15 miles (24km) long and the river winds through steep, colorful walled canyons that are impossible to approach by road. For a change from the natural world, the casinos of Laughlin, Nevada are just 15 miles (24km) up the road. Surrounding Needles are several mountain

> **BACK TO NATURE**
>
> About 11 miles (18km) south of Needles on I-40 is the Havasu National Wildlife Refuge. This is a big attraction to fishermen, for the striped bass and trout that swim there, and it is also good for bird-watching during the winter months.

groups: Turtle, Whipple, Spirit and Hackberry, all attracting rock hounds looking for fossils, petrified wood and semi-precious stones.

> **FOR HISTORY BUFFS**
>
> Across in Arizona, only 20 miles (32km) from Needles, London Bridge spans Lake Havasu. It was moved here from London, stone by stone, in 1971. At one end is a marina; at the other, the London Bridge Resort and English Village – complete with Tudor-style shops!

> **SCENIC ROUTES**
>
> Take the Goffs exit north off I-40 just outside Needles, and drive to Mid Hills campground, where Wildhorse Canyon Road makes an 11-mile (18km) link with Hole-in-the-Wall campground. This was declared the country's first official Back Country Byway. The road passes through dramatic volcanic desert scenery scattered with several kinds of cactus, and during the spring, the desert floor is carpeted with wildflowers.

▶ Drive west along **I-40** through dramatic desert scenery to Daggett.

7 Daggett

On the south side of the road, as you drive through Daggett, a high tower something like a lighthouse can be seen glowing in the sun. This is Solar One Power Plant, an experimental solar energy plant with hundreds of mirrors directing the suns rays to a receptor at the top. The experiment has been spectacular, but not too successful. However, if the Visitor Center is open it is worth taking a tour of the plant.

▶ Return across **I-40** and drive north on Yermo Road, which *becomes Ghost Town Road after passing under I-15. Continue to the end.*

8 Calico Ghost Town

Calico was founded in 1881 after a particularly rich silver strike. At its peak, it had a population of more than 4,000 people, with two hotels, a church, a school-house and even a small Chinatown. Like many of these wooden boom towns, it was destroyed by fire – twice – and rebuilt each time. More than $13 million of silver was mined here, but when the price of silver plummeted in 1895, the town fell into ruin. In 1951, Walter Knott of Knott's Berry Farm recognized the tourist potential and restored the town. Knott's

uncle had grubstaked for the original prospectors. Today, Calico Ghost Town is a contrived tourist attraction with strong commercial overtones, but it is close enough to the main road to merit a short visit. The tunnels of the high-yielding Maggie Mine can be explored, and you can take a cable tram or a ride on the Calico-Odessa Railway; but the buildings on the main street form the core of Calico, and their stores always seem to be the main attraction.

For a more authentic and educational historic experience, visit the Calico Early Man Archaeological Site, reached along the I-15 east, taking the exit north on Minneola Road. The site was discovered by an

amateur archaeologist in 1942; Dr. Louis Leakey began excava-tions here in 1964, and since then more than 12,000 stone tools have been found, dating back 200,000 years – making this one of the oldest prehistoric tool sites ever discovered in the West. The tools can be seen in the walls and floors of the excavated pits.

▷ *Return to I-15 west and continue to Barstow.*

9 Barstow

Most people use Barstow as a rest stop on the drive from Los Angeles to Las Vegas. It was founded as a railroad town in 1886, and became an important mining center. The Mojave River Valley Museum chronicles the area's history, and also has a good collection of desert miner-als and archaeological finds from the Calico excavation site. More information on deserts is avail-able at the California Desert Information Center, at 831 Barstow Road. For many visitors, the Factory Merchants Outlet Plaza, with 50 factory stores sell-ing heavily discounted goods, 4 miles (6km) south on the Lenwood Road exit, is more than enough reason to stop here.

i *California Welcome Center, 2796 Tanger Way, Suite 106, Barstow*

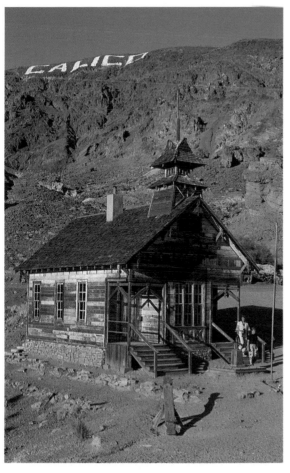

FOR CHILDREN

Returning to Los Angeles on I-15, the road passes Victorville, which is home to the log fort that is the Roy Rogers and Dale Evans Museum. Any lover of Westerns will find this treasure trove of cowboy memorabilia fascinating. Roy Rogers' faithful horse Trigger, now stuffed for eternity, presides over the collection.

▷ *Return to Los Angeles on I-15.*

A remnant of past glories: one of the survivors of Calico Ghost Town

Highest, Lowest
& Oldest

4 DAYS • 873 MILES • 1404KM

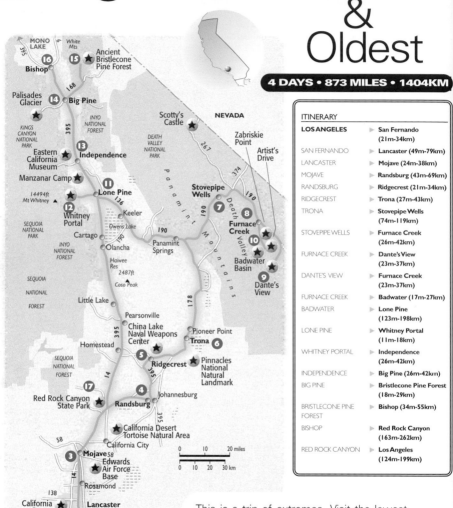

ITINERARY		
LOS ANGELES	▶	**San Fernando (21m–34km)**
SAN FERNANDO	▶	**Lancaster (49m–79km)**
LANCASTER	▶	**Mojave (24m–38km)**
MOJAVE	▶	**Randsburg (43m–69km)**
RANDSBURG	▶	**Ridgecrest (21m–34km)**
RIDGECREST	▶	**Trona (27m–43km)**
TRONA	▶	**Stovepipe Wells (74m–119km)**
STOVEPIPE WELLS	▶	**Furnace Creek (26m–42km)**
FURNACE CREEK	▶	**Dante's View (23m–37km)**
DANTE'S VIEW	▶	**Furnace Creek (23m–37km)**
FURNACE CREEK	▶	**Badwater (17m–27km)**
BADWATER	▶	**Lone Pine (123m–198km)**
LONE PINE	▶	**Whitney Portal (11m–18km)**
WHITNEY PORTAL	▶	**Independence (26m–42km)**
INDEPENDENCE	▶	**Big Pine (26m–42km)**
BIG PINE	▶	**Bristlecone Pine Forest (18m–29km)**
BRISTLECONE PINE FOREST	▶	**Bishop (34m–55km)**
BISHOP	▶	**Red Rock Canyon (163m–262km)**
RED ROCK CANYON	▶	**Los Angeles (124m–199km)**

This is a trip of extremes. Visit the lowest point in the western hemisphere, see the highest mountain in the continental United States and walk among the oldest living things on earth. The trip can be completed in four days, but as it covers some of California's most exceptional scenic sites, many people will prefer to take longer.

i *Hollywood Visitors Information Center, 6801 Hollywood Boulevard*

▷ *Leave Los Angeles on **I-5** to the San Fernando Valley.*

❶ San Fernando

The San Fernando Valley is home to many of the world's great film and television studios, including the world's biggest, Universal Studios. Here you can also find Disney, Warner Bros, Burbank Studios, NBC Studios and Columbia.

Universal was established in 1914, with the philosophy that film-making is an attraction in itself, and it has grown to become one of the major visitor attractions in America (see page 21). NBC Studios, in Burbank, is the only national network television studio to open its

The old gardens of the mission, now called Brand Park, have flowers and shrubs from all the missions in the chain. The museum theater was damaged in the most recent Northridge earthquake, but has reopened and is screening several different films, including one on the history of the mission and another on the life of Father Junípero Serra (see page 40). There is an Indian craft room and an archive center preserving historic documents of California's Catholic heritage.

▷ *Return to **I-5** and exit onto Hwy 14, the Antelope Valley Freeway. Drive past Palmdale, which is the gateway to the High Desert, and continue to Lancaster.*

Reserve and Interpretive Center is on Lancaster Road, between 130th and 170th Streets.

▷ *Continue north on **Hwy 14** for 20 miles (32km).*

❸ Mojave

The town of Mojave sits in the middle of the high desert from which it was named. A typical desert town, it has the wind-blown, desolate feeling of a frontier community. Mojave still bears traces of its own colorful history as a mining community. In the late 19th century, the famous 20-mule team hauled 200 tons/tonnes of borax on each trip from Death Valley, across 165 miles (265km) of inhos-

Taking a break on the lonesome drive across the Mojave Desert

doors to the public and allow them to witness the behind-the-scenes life of broadcasting. They also offer tickets to many of the television shows that are taped there.

Further north along the valley, at Mission Hills, just to the south of the expensive Los Angeles suburb of San Fernando, is the fourth mission to be built in as many months. Mission San Fernando Rey de Espana was founded in 1797, but was continually damaged by earthquakes, the most recent being in 1994.

❷ Lancaster

Lancaster was established in 1884, along the Southern Pacific Railroad line. It grew up on agriculture and mining but is increasingly becoming a Los Angeles bedroom community, which gives a frightening idea of just how big Los Angeles is. Every spring, the hillsides of Antelope Valley west of Lancaster are ablaze with orange, as hundreds of thousands of California poppies burst into flower, providing one of the state's great natural sights. The California Poppy

pitable desert to Mojave. There is a marker outside the Mojave County Building to commemorate the unloading site.

Just to the southeast of Mojave is the Edwards Air Force Base. This was where the first astronauts did their training, and is now the landing site for the Space Shuttle. It is still the primary location for experimental rocketry and jet aircraft testing. On Memorial Day in May, the base is open to the public, and organizes displays of some of the latest, state-of-the-art military aircraft.

TOUR
9
Highest, Lowest & Oldest

▶ *Continue north on Hwy 14 for 19 miles (30km) and turn east onto the Redrock–Randsburg Road.*

4 Randsburg

This is still an active mining town, although many of the old gold- and silver-mines have been abandoned. At one time, the Yellow Aster Mine produced more than $16 million worth of gold and some 3,000 prospectors set up camp here. It was so important that the Santa Fe Railway built a line to the camp in 1897. During the celebrations for the opening of the line, an explosion started a fire that destroyed several of the town's buildings. As often happened in the wooden gold-rush towns, the rest of the buildings went up in flames a few years later. The town was rebuilt and the last significant traces of gold, silver and tungsten were mined in the 1920s. Randsburg is a ghost town that still has a spark of life: many of the old buildings along the main avenue have been restored and now contain antiques shops and a general store.

▶ *From Randsburg take Hwy 395 north to China Lake Boulevard.*

5 Ridgecrest

Ridgecrest is the home of the China Lake Naval Weapons Center. At the Ridgecrest Maturango Museum there are displays relating to the cultural and natural history of the upper Mojave Desert, including an interesting section on ancient Indian petroglyphs. This is also a good place to pick up information on both the Mojave Desert and Death Valley areas.

▶ *From Ridgecrest take Hwy 178 east to Trona.*

BACK TO NATURE

About 21 miles (34km) from Randsburg, on the Red Rock–Randsburg Road, is the California Desert Tortoise Natural Area. Turn south on Neuralia Road just before the junction with Highway 14, follow the road to California City Boulevard and turn east to Randsburg–Mojave Road, a dirt road for about 2 miles (3km). A kiosk here gives information on the state reptile. Tortoises are most active in the spring, when they can be seen munching on the desert wildflowers.

6 Trona

Trona is an ugly community, whose main economy is the Kerr McGee Chemical Plant – not the best reason for a visit! Two miles (3km) before the chemical plant there is a turnoff to the right: follow the dirt road to the "Y" and continue to the right until you reach the Trona Pinnacles, the most impressive tufa towers in America, with more than 500 magnificent Tioga Spires, some as high as 140 feet (43m). Their strange, other-worldly appearance has earned them a career as the background for many commercials and films, including *Star Trek V*. They formed in the waters of Owens Lake and, as the water receded, these gigantic calcified towers remained. Fortunately, they are sufficiently off the beaten track to avoid vandalism.

▶ *Continue north on Hwy 178 to Hwy 190, then turn east into Death Valley.*

7 Stovepipe Wells

Death Valley, whose very name is awe inspiring, has been designated a national park – and not before time; this is one of the truly great landscapes of the

Left: windblown sand dunes near Stovepipe Wells in Death Valley

world. Entering the valley across the Panamint Mountains gives a taste for what is to come. Totally arid, austere desert mountains plunge down to Stovepipe Wells, a dusty group of buildings including a general store, motel and campground. Just past Stovepipe Wells, on the left, is an extensive area of sand dunes. These are best visited in the cool of dawn, when overnight winds will have erased the footsteps of the previous day's visitors. During the middle of the day the dunes can be unbearably hot.

FOR HISTORY BUFFS

Scotty's Castle is by far the biggest visitor attraction in Death Valley. At the far north-ern end of the valley, just off Highway 267, a flamboyant rogue and sometime prospec-tor nicknamed Death Valley Scotty persuaded millionaire Albert Johnson to build an extravagant, Spanish-style man-sion in the desert. Scotty had originally lured Johnson out here with bogus tales of a gold mine. Johnson found that the climate suited his fragile health and forgave Scotty, and the two became lifelong friends. The 25-room house has a 50-foot (15m)-high living room, a music room with a 1,600-pipe organ, and even indoor waterfalls that acted as air-conditioners in the summer.

▷ *Continue east on Hwy 190. After a few miles a dirt road exits to the right. It heads into the flat, white salt pan on the valley floor and enters The Devil's Golf Course, an area of crystalline salt formations, pushed up from hundreds of feet underground and sitting in the midst of brine pools. The salt pan here is up to 5 feet (1.5m) thick and is as pure as table salt. Hwy 190 turns south to Furnace Creek.*

---

8 Furnace Creek

The national park headquarters are at the Furnace Creek Visitor Center, which has very good exhibits, plenty of literature on all aspects of the park and an 18-minute film on Death Valley. There are also evening programs and naturalist-led walks conducted from the center.

▷ *Leaving Furnace Creek, **Hwy 190** climbs 4 miles (6km) to Zabriskie Point, which gives the best panoramic views in the southern part of Death Valley. In the light of early morning and late afternoon, it is particularly beautiful. For the ultimate view, continue for another 23 miles (37km), turning south off **Hwy 190** onto Dante's View Road.*

9 Dante's View

At the road's end, 5,478-foot (1,670m)-high Dante's View gives a 360-degree panorama of the valley. Badwater lies one vertical mile (1.5km) below as you gaze out across the desolate landscape. Take a sweater: it can get cool up here – 20° F (6°C) cooler than in the valley.

▷ *Return to Furnace Creek on **Hwy 190**. Just before entering town, take the minor road that exits to the south. Continue south past Artist's Drive to Badwater.*

SCENIC ROUTES

Just south of Furnace Creek, on Highway 178, a dirt road branches off into the Black Mountains. Artist's Drive, as it is called, makes a 9-mile (14km) loop through some of the most barren but colorful landscapes in the world.

RECOMMENDED WALK

The best walk in Death Valley is from Zabriskie Point, 4 miles (6km) east of Furnace Creek, down through the badlands, across the foot of Manly Beacon and on through the Golden Canyon. It shows the best Death Valley has to offer, and it is downhill all the way! The 2.5-mile (4km) trail takes well under two hours, but you need to arrange a ride back to the parking lot at Zabriskie Point.

---

10 Badwater Basin

The main reason to visit Badwater is the novelty value of standing in the lowest place in the western hemisphere. This murky little pond lies 282 feet

Artist's Drive, where the landscape is marked by changing shades

The jagged peak of Whitney Portal, near Lone Pine

▶ Continue on Whitney Portal Road to the end.

12 Whitney Portal

The highest peak in the United States, outside Alaska, is just 10 miles (16km) from here, but those miles are hard-earned. A very steep trail leads to the 14,494-foot (4,417m)-high summit of Mount Whitney. Most people spend a night on the mountain, and only the fittest climbers should attempt it in one day. Even if you have no thoughts of physical exertion, the views of the High Sierra make Whitney Portal worth a visit. During the fall, the trees turn intense shades of red and yellow, providing a vivid foreground for the snow-covered peaks.

▶ Return to **Hwy 395** and drive north for 16 miles (26km).

13 Independence

Excellent exhibits in the Eastern California Museum cover the history, geology and ecology of this region, and there is also a good section on the crafts of the Shoshone and Pauite Indian tribes. More recent history is covered with an exhibit on Manzanar Camp, where 10,000 Japanese-Americans were interned in 1941, following the outbreak of hostilities between the U.S. and Japan.

The climates here are extreme. The mountains receive over 48 inches (1,219mm) of snow a year, while the valley floor is semi-arid desert, with less than 6 inches (152mm) of rain a year.

▶ Continue on **Hwy 395** for 26 miles (42km).

14 Big Pine

Like most of the East Sierra towns, there is little here other than food, lodging and spectacular scenery. Just above town is the most southerly ice sheet in the United States: the Palisades Glacier, high in the Sierra Nevada.

(86m) below sea level and is surrounded by hot, hostile desert. Fortunately, Badwater is just by the side of the road, and the effort involved in achieving this goal is minimal. It is more interesting to hike a few minutes out from Badwater into the salt flats, to experience the true desolation of the valley.

▶ Return north to **Hwy 190** and follow it out of Death Valley until it becomes **Hwy 136**. Continue to **Hwy 395**.

11 Lone Pine

Sitting at the entrance to the Owens Valley, this small mountain community provides the doorstep to some of the most impressive scenery in the entire state. Drive west out of town on the Whitney Portal Road and you will arrive at the Alabama Hills. These huge, rounded boulders take on the bizarre appearance of human skulls and giant bowling balls in the early morning light. Their unique appearance has landed them many background roles in western films and TV commercials.

▶ *Leave Big Pine on **Hwy 168** east which climbs steeply for 12 miles (19km) into the White Mountains.*

⒖ Ancient Bristlecone Pine Forest

First, go to the Visitor Center at Schulman Grove for information on the trees that are the oldest living trees on earth. Reaching ages in excess of 4,000 years, they grow only at extreme altitudes, at barely one inch (25mm) a year. The thin, cold air at almost 11,000 feet (3,352m) can be uncomfortable after such a rapid rise; do not attempt anything too strenuous. The best section of the forest is 11 miles (18km) of dirt road farther on from Schulman Grove. Up above 11,000 feet (3,352m) is a barren, rocky landscape, scattered with the gnarled, twisted

shapes of the bristlecones. The landscape is so evocative of the moon that NASA used this terrain to test their lunar rover.

▶ *Return to **Hwy 395** and drive north for 15 miles (24km).*

⒗ Bishop

Bishop is the major town in this eastern corridor of California and an important center for all manner of outdoor activities, from skiing and mountaineering to fishing in the crystal-clear mountain lakes. The town is filled with motels, restaurants, stores and outdoor-adventure outfitters. Also of interest, on a more cerebral level, is the Paiute Shoshone Cultural Center and Museum, which gives an excellent introduction to the lifestyles and handicrafts of the native population.

▶ *Return south on **Hwy 395** for 140 miles (225km).*

⒘ Red Rock Canyon State Park

This little-known state park is one of the great secrets of the desert. Red, brown and gray sandstone cliffs have eroded into shapes that used to serve as landmarks for freight wagons stopping at the canyon's springs. Red Rock Canyon is more than great scenery: there are Joshua trees, cholla cacti, golden eagles, desert tortoises and coyotes. A visitor center has information and a self-guiding nature trail.

▶ ***Hwy 395** forks east. Drive south on **Hwy 14** to Mojave and continue on **Hwy 14** back into Los Angeles.*

Ancient Bristlecone Pine Forest

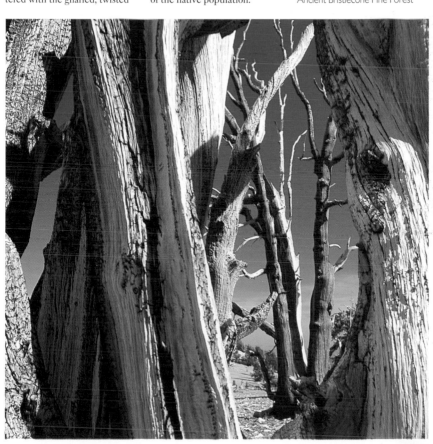

THE HIGH SIERRA

The 450-mile (724km)-long range of Sierra Nevada ("snowy mountain" in Spanish) is California's most majestic feature. It averages between 60 and 80 miles (96 and 129km) in width, starting in the north near Mount Lassen and ending in the desert near the Tehachapi Mountains. Volcanic activity started its creation some 200 million years ago. Subsequent earthquakes jolted the mountains into their dramatic peaks and valleys, which were further sculpted and polished by relentless glaciers over the last million years.

The High Sierra refers specifically to a 150-mile (241km) section of the Sierra Nevada, above the tree line from north of Yosemite Valley south to Cottonwood Pass – a series of high peaks, alpine meadows and icy lakes, which is certainly the most spectacular part of the chain. In every-day usage, the term High Sierra includes the entire range, from Lake Tahoe to the desert. The range is home to the largest and deepest alpine lake in North America, the world's biggest trees, towering water-falls, quaint old western towns and, of course, mountains. The mountains effectively divide the state – and they are big. Mount Whitney, at 14,494 feet (4,418m) above sea level, is the highest peak in the continental United States (outside Alaska), and is surrounded by sister peaks almost as high. Several mountain passes give access to the eastern slopes from the coastal region, and during the summer months these are magnificent, if somewhat tortuous drives. During the winter they are closed by deep deposits of snow, and the only reliable access across the Sierra is either via the Tehachapi Pass or Lake Tahoe. In severe conditions, even these roads can be closed for days at a time.

In the summer, the Sierra Nevada provides every kind of outdoor recreation, including fishing, boating, mountain biking, white-water rafting, rock-climbing and hiking. Every type of accommodation is available, from luxury hotels to simple cabins, but during the height of the vacation season, in the more popular areas, even campsites have to be booked weeks, sometimes months, in advance.

Tour 10

When James Marshall found gold in the waters of the Sierra Nevada's western foothills, he sparked off the 1849 Gold Rush that was to be instrumental in forming the California of today. This drive follows the trail of townships, linked by Highway 49, that reflect that era of rapid settlement and high hopes. From Chinese Camp, where thousands of Chinese miners lived harsh lives of discrimination and toil, it continues through a succession of historic gold towns. It also visits eerie underground caverns, Mark Twain's temporary cabin home, the ancient decorations of Indian Grinding Rock and even a stretch of wine-growing country, always returning to pick up the golden trail on its circuit from San Francisco.

Tour 11

Yosemite National Park is one of the most popular natural sights in America – and rightly so. This tour includes not only the highlights of the park, but also other equally exceptional destinations, making this one of the best road journeys in North America. Leaving San Francisco, the route crosses the great agricultural Central Valley before starting its climb through the southern gold country and the Sierra foothills. It passes through the old gold town of Mariposa and continues into Yosemite Valley to reveal one of America's greatest iconographic landscapes.

After leaving the valley, a visit to the Tuolomne Grove of giant sequoia trees requires only a short detour before heading over the wild, rocky landscape of Yosemite's high country. The drive then crosses the Sierra watershed and heads down to the surreal landscape of Mono Lake, before continuing north through the wild country of the eastern Sierra, to perhaps the best preserved and biggest ghost town in America. Bodie never fails to fascinate visitors, with its authentic atmosphere and remote mountain location. The return to San Francisco crosses back over the High Sierra by the Sonora Pass, and once more traverses the Gold Country and Central Valley.

Tour 12

Lake Tahoe is the jewel of the northern Sierra Nevada. After leaving Sacramento, this tour heads straight up into the mountains, and then down to this crystal-clear lake on the Nevada border.

An excursion to the less-than-natural wonders of the Nevada casinos on the lake's southern shore makes an interesting contrast to the surrounding mountain wilderness. The tour continues up the beautiful western shore of Lake Tahoe, past historic mansions and hidden coves, to Truckee, a town straight out of the Wild West, and close to the site of the last winter for many of the tragic Donner party. Only half of the 89-member group survived the harsh winter of 1846.

Once across Donner Summit, the Sierra watershed, the tour passes through two of the biggest and most developed Gold Country towns, Nevada City and Grass Valley, where, aside from charming streets lined with Victorian houses, there is one of the most interesting mine tours in California. Sacamento is a short drive back down the freeway.

Tour 13

Fresno lies at the heart of the Central Valley and, during the spring, the fruit orchards surrounding the town are ablaze with color. The tour climbs up through the foothills east of Fresno to King's Canyon National Park. Here, there are giant sequoia trees and some of the most grand, wild mountain scenery in the Sierra. Unlike Yosemite, King's Canyon National Park does not attract massive crowds, so that this is a much more authentic wilderness experience.

Sequoia National Park is next to King's Canyon and the trees here are even bigger than those next door. The world's biggest tree grows here, and whole groves of giants have been flourishing for thousands of years. Leaving the High Sierra, the tour returns to the Central Valley and the old agricultural town of Hanford, with its rich Chinese heritage, and then on to Kingsburg, established in the 19th century by Swedish railroad workers on the Southern Pacific Railroad and even today looking more Swedish than American. Fresno is a short drive to the north.

Opposite; plunging waterfalls at beautiful Yosemite National Park
Right: Placer County Courthouse, Auburn

The Gold
Country

2 DAYS • 463 MILES • 743KM

California's history was transformed when James Marshall discovered gold in the Sacramento River and began the Gold Rush of 1849. This drive follows the southern section of Highway 49 for about 300 miles (483km) through Gold Country, where the average altitude is 2,000 feet (610m) and in summer temperatures can be unbearably high. There are no hotels on the route but the area has charming bed-and-breakfast establishments and inns. At San Francisco, the Wells Fargo Museum (Montgomery Street) and the Bank of California (California Street) have memorabilia and gold specimens from the Gold Rush.

ITINERARY	
SAN FRANCISCO	▶ Chinese Camp (127m-204km)
CHINESE CAMP	▶ Jamestown (7m-11km)
JAMESTOWN	▶ Sonora (4m-6km)
SONORA	▶ Columbia (5m-8km)
COLUMBIA	▶ Moaning Cavern (9m-15km)
MOANING CAVERN	▶ Murphys (6m-10km)
MURPHYS	▶ Angels Camp (9m-14km)
ANGELS CAMP	▶ San Andreas (13m-21km)
SAN ANDREAS	▶ Volcano (35m-56km)
VOLCANO	▶ Indian Grinding Rock State Historic Park (2m-3km)
INDIAN GRINDING ROCK STATE HISTORIC PARK	▶ Jackson (11m-18km)
JACKSON	▶ Sutter Creek (2m-3km)
SUTTER CREEK	▶ Shenandoah Valley (14m-23km)
SHENANDOAH VALLEY	▶ Placerville (26m-40km)
PLACERVILLE	▶ Marshall Gold Discovery State Park (8m-13km)
MARSHALL GOLD DISCOVERY STATE PARK	▶ Auburn (18m-29km)
AUBURN	▶ San Francisco (167m-269km)

i San Francisco Visitor Information, 900 Market Street, lower level of Hallidie Plaza, San Francisco

▶ Leave San Francisco across the Bay Bridge and take **I-580** to **I-205**. Exit **I-205** on **Hwy 120** at Manteca and drive for 49 miles (79km) to reach Chinese Camp.

1 Chinese Camp

The role of the Chinese in the Gold Rush has been largely obscured, although in 1851 one in 10 of California's miners was Chinese. Most of the Chinese workers were indentured servants, and a "foreign tax" prevented any of the Chinese miners from making a significant profit from their labors. Many of them went on to build railroads, before settling in San Francisco's Chinatown. At one time, over 5,000 Chinese lived in Chinese Camp and it was the scene of a violent war between two fraternal groups. Now, all is quiet: Chinese Camp is deserted, with only a post office and gas station showing any sign of life. The past is represented by ruins of the Wells Fargo building and a 19th-century store.

▶ Drive north on **Hwy 49** for 7 miles (11km).

2 Jamestown

The first gold discovery in Tuolumne County was made here in 1848, and more gold was taken from Woods Creek than from any other stream of its size in the state. Many of the original false-front buildings are still standing and extensive restoration and preservation has resulted in a picture-perfect main street from the Gold Rush days. Commercialism has inevitably crept in, with antiques shops, restaurants and gift shops, but there is still a strong sense of the past – to the extent that Jamestown is frequently used as a backdrop for film and television. Both *High Noon* and *Butch Cassidy and the Sundance Kid* were filmed here, as were the television series *Little House on the*

SPECIAL TO...

Melt-water from the High Sierra fills the rivers flowing through the foothills, particularly in April and May. Outdoor adventure enthusiasts make the most of it, attempting to navigate their rafts through the ferocious white-water on rivers such as the American, Tuolumne and Stanislaus. A raft full of people, hurtling through the water, attempting to avoid almost inevitable capsize, is a common sight. A far safer and drier pursuit is watching the action from the river bank.

3 Sonora

Sonora is the capital of the southern Gold Rush region and the seat for Tuolumne County; it is also one of the largest and most beautiful towns on the Mother Lode. This has always been an important center and in the old days it had a reputation for lawlessness. Mexican miners, from Sonora in Mexico, founded the town, and its fine Victorian houses are interspersed with adobe buildings. Sonora soon developed into one of the wealthiest communities in the Gold Country, and still retains its

Shooting the rapids on the fast-flowing Stanislaus River

Prairie and *The Big Valley*. The Sierra Railway Company began operating from Jamestown in 1897, carrying passengers and freight throughout the gold-mining area.

Railtown 1897 State Historic Park preserves what is left of the railroad, including a roundhouse museum with a blacksmith's shop, turntables, trains, rolling stock and yard facilities. You can watch the maintenance and restoration of railroad equipment and even ride a 19th-century steam train to nearby gold towns.

▶ Continue north on **Hwy 49** for 4 miles (6km).

commercial importance. New development has destroyed the charm around the edge of the town, but it is nevertheless very well preserved and many of the fine, old Victorian mansions are still standing on Washington Street. The other building of note is the red-and-white St. James Episcopal Church, which was built in 1859 and is perhaps the most elegant structure in the foothills. The Tuolumne County Museum, at 158 W. Bradford Avenue, was originally a jail-house, dating back to 1857. (It now doubles as a tourist office.) The cells are filled with exhibits depicting the Gold Rush era, with photographs, costumed mannequins, gold specimens and antiques. The heavy equipment of gold mining, such as pelton wheels, stamp mills and arrastras, used in Sonora during the 19th century, can be seen in an outdoor display at Bradford Street Park.

▶ *Continue north on **Hwy 49** for 2 miles (3km).*

Below: Sonora, capital of the southern Gold Country, strung elegantly along its main street

RECOMMENDED WALK

One of the best preserved towns on the Mother Lode is Sonora. Known as "The Queen of the Southern Mines," its history can be traced through its architecture. The Tuolumne County Museum, at 158 W. Bradford Avenue, has a walking tour brochure that highlights about 20 points of interest in the heart of town.

4 Columbia
Once known as the "Gem of the Southern Mines," Columbia was one of the most important mining centers of the 1850s, with a population of over 15,000 and 50 saloons. In 20 years, over $87 million in gold was extracted from the local placer mines. Twelve square blocks in the old business district have been painstakingly restored to their original 1860s appearance and designated a state historic park. Most of the town is closed to cars and the tree-lined main street is the preserve of pedestrians and stagecoaches, which transport visitors in an appropriately sedate fashion. Although there is a strong commercial element in the park, with stores, restaurants and even an operating hotel, the Gold Rush atmosphere has been perfectly captured, with costumed interpreters adding to the effect. The saloon at the end of town, still serving sarsparilla, could be a Hollywood film set; and you can get a haircut at the state's oldest barber shop. Nowhere in the Mother Lode is there a more complete example of a 19th-century mining community. At the southern end of town, a grizzled old prospector gives

instruction in gold-panning, and most people leave with a few flakes of their own Sierra gold.

▶ *Take Parrots Ferry Road north out of Columbia and drive for 9 miles (14km).*

5 Moaning Cavern

The limestone in this area of the foothills is riddled with underground caverns. Moaning Cavern, to the south of Parrots Ferry Road, got its name from the sound that used to come from its entrance. A wooden staircase descends 65 feet (20m) and a steel spiral stair descends a further 100 feet (30m) into the cave. The staircases changed the acoustics of the cavern, and stopped the moaning. Just to the north of Highway 4 are the even bigger and more impressive Mercer Caverns, discovered by miner Arthur Mercer in 1885. Visitors can now tour 10 underground chambers with various extraordinary limestone and crystalline formations.

▶ *At* **Hwy 4** *drive north for 3 miles (5km) to Murphys.*

6 Murphys

Little has changed in this lively little town since it was established by two Irishmen back in 1848. In 1852, after the discovery of giant sequoia trees in what is now Calaveras Big Trees State Park, the rush of tourists through Murphys led to the building of Murphys Hotel in 1856, and the guest book is full of 19th-century celebrities such as Bret Harte, Count von Rothschild, Horatio Alger and Ulysses S. Grant. The hotel still stands among other historic buildings on the tree-lined Main Street. Across the street from the hotel, the Old Timer's Museum displays interesting Gold Rush memorabilia.

▶ *Return south on* **Hwy 4** *to Angels Camp.*

Left: a shop window reflects the 19th-century air of Columbia

7 Angels Camp

Writer Mark Twain lived in a cabin just outside Angels Camp for a few months during the 1860s, and it was here that he wrote *The Celebrated Jumping Frog of Calaveras County*, the work that first propelled him to fame. Since 1928, the annual Jumping Frogs Jamboree has taken place every May, drawing contestants from far and wide for the significant prize money. The highlight of this county fair is the frog jumping competition – now a more serious business than originally intended – in which owners take care of their frogs as if they were thoroughbred racehorses. Goliath frogs from Africa have recently caused controversy by consistently outjumping all the competition. The Angels Camp Museum at 735 South Main Street presents a static and predictable display of gold-mining equipment – a repetition of far better exhibits elsewhere along the Mother Lode.

▶ *Drive north on* **Hwy 49** *for 13 miles (21km).*

An eager contestant at the Angels Camp Jumping Frogs Jamboree

8 San Andreas

What was once just a few adobe buildings, erected by the original Mexican miners who settled here, has become a bustling, touristy little town. The Calaveras County Museum and Archives, one block east of Main Street, consists of three buildings: the IOOF Hall, the courthouse and jail. The infamous stagecoach bandit Black Bart was held in this jail awaiting trial in the adjoining courthouse. In 1883, he was sentenced to six years in prison for 28 robberies. He served his time and then disappeared. In the museum is a full-size room display of a typical miner's cabin and a Gold Rush general store. Among the memorabilia is a black-edged invitation to a public hanging, signed by the sheriff. On a similarly somber note, the pioneer cemetery to the west of town provides a fascinating insight into the brief lives of the mining community. Even to this day, obituaries are posted on the Death Tree

Giant sequoias tower over the Calaveras Big Trees State Park

outside the old post office – because San Andreas has never had a daily newspaper.

▶ *Continue on **Hwy 49** for 7 miles (11km) to Mokelumne Hill and turn east on **Hwy 26**. Follow it across **Hwy 88** onto Volcano Pioneer Road to Volcano.*

❾ Volcano

Once a town of 5,000, this old gold town, which sits in a crater-like depression, was famous for its dance halls and saloons. In fact, the town became a pioneer in many areas of California's cultural life. In 1845, California's first community theater, the Volcano Thespian Society, was

---

BACK TO NATURE

The Calaveras Big Trees State Park lies on Highway 4, 25 miles (40km) east of Angels Camp at an altitude of 4,000–5,000 feet (1,219–1,524m). Forty miles (64km) of walking trails weave through two groves of giant sequoia trees – the largest living things on earth. One tree at Calaveras is 320 feet (97m) high; another is more than 27 feet (8m) in diameter. When they were first discovered by a settler chasing a bear in 1852, they were thought to be the only examples of their kind. Subsequent press reports made these Calaveras trees a world-famous tourist destination.

---

built here. The Miner's Lending Library was the first public library in the state and the Volcano literary and debating society was also California's first. Two miles (3km) out of town, California's first observatory was built on what is now Observatory Hill. Some of the old town is preserved, but much of it disappeared in fires. During the 1850s, the McLaughlin family planted thousands of daffodils at a stagecoach stop on a hill about 3 miles (5km) north of town. Their descendants have continued the tradition and every spring Daffodil Hill still bursts into bloom, with more than 300,000 daffodils covering 4 acres (2 hectares) of land on the private farm, and now attracting hundreds of visitors to view the lovely spectacle.

> *Drive for 2 miles (3km) along the Pine Grove-Volcano Road.*

10 Indian Grinding Rock State Historic Park

Using limestone bedrock as a natural mortar, Miwok Indians pulverized acorns and other seeds into meal, eventually grinding over 1,000 cavities in the rock. These flat expanses of pock-marked rock, together with hundreds of petroglyphs, can be viewed from a self-guiding trail, which also passes a re-created Indian village and ceremonial sweat house. The adjoining Chaw Se' Regional Indian Museum includes artifacts, exhibits and audio-visual programs

> *From Pine Grove continue west on I Iwy 88 for 12 miles (19km) to Jackson.*

some other communities, although it had its share of gambling halls and bordellos, which remained open until the 1950s. Even today, there are card parlors on Main Street. The National Hotel, at the foot of Main Street, is yet another establishment that claims to be the oldest continually operating hotel in California, and on North Main Street the tiny St. Sava Serbian Orthodox Church, tucked in between trees and tombstones, is, surprisingly, the mother church for the whole United States. Jackson is the Amador County seat, and the Amador County Museum at 225 Church Street is one of the best in the region, housed in an 1850s red-brick building on top of a hill and furnished with antiques. On the grounds is a working model of the Kennedy

flumes, then over two hills to a settling pond. To get a close view of the wheel, go down Jackson Gate Road at the north end of town to Tailing Wheels Park.

> *Continue north on **Hwy 49** for 2 miles (3km).*

12 Sutter Creek

The picturesque Main Street of Sutter Creek is lined with dozens of buildings steeped in history. Most have been converted into antiques and handicraft shops, and many of the fine Victorian mansions are now bed-and-breakfast inns. A self guiding walking tour brochure and city guide can be obtained from the City of Sutter Creek at 18 Main Street. The Historic Knight Foundry, at 81 Eureka Street, is the only

11 Jackson

Many of the buildings along the narrow streets of Jackson were destroyed in a great fire in 1862 and, although they were rebuilt, somehow the town has not retained quite the same historic character as many of the other towns along Highway 49. Jackson was never as wild as

Mine, which used to operate on the north edge of town. Both the Kennedy and Argonaut Mines were at one time the deepest mines in the world. They finally closed during World War II, but still standing are the headframes of some of the buildings and a huge tailing wheel, built in 1912 to carry mine tailings into

Victorian architecture still dominates Sutter Creek's Main Street

remaining water-powered foundry and machine shop in the country. The Knight & Co. Foundry was one of many developed on the Mother Lode when it was established in 1873. At one time they produced all types of mining equipment, but they were particularly known for their water wheels. The foundry is still in operation and special ironwork for the restoration of the state capitol was produced here. Tours are offered, allowing visitors to watch foundrymen use traditional methods for preparing molten iron.

▶ *Continue north on **Hwy 49** past the quaint brick and wood-frame buildings of Amador City to Plymouth and turn east onto Shenandoah Road.*

🔢 Shenandoah Valley

This region is of growing importance as a wine-producing area. For 10 miles (16km) there are vineyards and wineries producing some of the best zinfandel wines in California. Wine has been produced here since the Gold Rush days and the D'Agostini Winery, now called the Sobon Estate, was established in 1856. The zinfandel grape is unique to California and flourishes in the heat of the Sierra foothills. Its spicy red wine is particularly prized when made from grapes off old vines and in "Amateur County" several vineyards date back more than 100 years. The nickname "Amateur County" was coined among serious winemakers because of the influx of people developing a second career in the wine business; but in recent years the Amador County wines have been able to hold their own in the best company. One of the best is Renwood Winery.

▶ *Return to **Hwy 49** and drive north for 22 miles (35km).*

🔢 Placerville

Placerville is a major stop on I-50, en route from Sacramento to South Lake Tahoe. Today, the town looks much like any other town of its size, with shopping malls, motels and fast-food restaurants lining the freeway frontage roads. Its modern appearance belies its notorious

past. Placerville was originally known as "Old Dry Diggin's," and became so lawless that criminals were hanged in pairs. As a result the name was changed to Hangtown. A dummy dangling from the second story of the Hangman's Tree Bar at 905 Main Street is a grim reminder of these not too distant times. Placerville was always a prosperous town, strategically located on the old Overland Trail, which is now I-50, and a surprising number of industrial leaders had their beginnings here. John Studebaker built wheelbarrows for miners before he turned his attention to cars; Leland Stanford, who founded Stanford University, ran a store close by in

Cold Springs; Philip Armour, who developed a canned meat empire, ran a small butcher's store in town; and railroad magnate Mark Hopkins had a store on Main Street, bringing in groceries from

Sacramento. The most interesting site is the old Gold Bug Mine, the nation's only city-owned gold mine, a mile (1.5km) from the N. Bedford exit off I-50. The 60-acre (24-hectare) Bedford Park site used to have 250 active gold mines, but all that remains is Gold Bug and its well-lit tunnels.

Wine produced in Amador County is now judged to be among the best you can get

▶ *Continue north on **Hwy 49** for 7 miles (11km).*

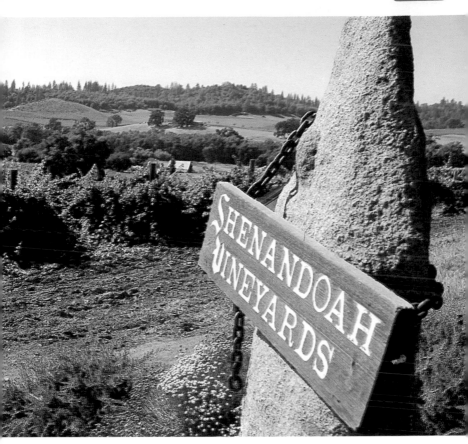

15 Marshall Gold Discovery State Historic Park

Coloma is perhaps the most historically significant town in the Gold Country. It was here that James Marshall discovered gold, at Sutter's Mill in January, 1848. Paradoxically, the town was one of the first to be abandoned, when richer deposits were found in other areas in the early 1850s. Within the space of five years the population exploded to 10,000 and then dwindled to the quiet village that it remains today. Most of Coloma now lies within the 265-acre (107-hectare) Marshall Gold Discovery State Historic Park, and the centerpiece is a full-scale replica of Sutter's Mill on the banks of the American River. Thousands of visitors re-create the experience of the Fortyniners, trying their hand at gold-panning in the American River by the old mill – those yellow flecks of metal continue to be washed down the river.

▶ *Continue north on* **Hwy 49** *for 18 miles (29km) to its junction with* **I-80**.

16 Auburn

Gold was discovered here in the spring of 1848, just a few months after the Coloma discovery. In fact, Frenchman Claude Chana, the discoverer, was a friend of James Marshall. Auburn is a major stop on the main road from Sacramento to North Lake Tahoe and, like Placerville to the south, it has developed way beyond its historic core and, some would say, has outgrown its rural charm. Fortunately, Old Town Auburn remains intact.

The landmark four-floor, red-and-white fire station dates back to 1892 and contains California's first motorized fire engine. Close by is the state's oldest continuously used post office. The narrow streets of Auburn are a magnet to antiques-hunters looking for that elusive bargain. Old Town is dominated by the yellow, domed, neoclassical Placer County Courthouse, which was built in 1852. The Gold Country Museum, at 1273 High Street, has a walk-through model of a hard-rock mining tunnel, in addition to an interesting collection of quartz and gold specimens from the local mines.

i *California Welcome Center, 13411 Lincoln Way, Auburn*

▶ *Return to San Francisco via Sacramento on* **I-80**.

GOLD

James Marshall discovered gold in the millrace of a sawmill in Coloma on the morning of January 24, 1848, and the course of California's history changed forever. Gold had always been the carrot dangling before the explorers of this frontier land: the Spanish looked in vain for El Dorado, the Golden City, during their occupation of the region. Ironically, it was pure chance that finally led to its discovery.

Within a year, thousands of fortune-seekers were heading west and starting the migration to the Golden State that continues even today. News of the discovery spread rapidly throughout the world; towns mushroomed overnight, and the population of California exploded from 15,000 to 265,000 in a period of three years. From 1849, the boom year that lent its name to the prospectors, they would always be Fortyniners. Most of the adventurers were young men, but they were soon followed by ambitious women, some of whom helped establish the Barbary Coast's notoriously bawdy reputation.

The heart of the Gold Country was along the western slopes of the Sierra Nevada foothills. The Mother Lode, the rich vein of

gold that seemed to be inexhaustible, stretched from Nevada City in the north down to Mariposa near Yosemite Valley. A string of towns survives along what is now called Highway 49, many of which have changed little since the 19th century. False-front

The dirty work that leads to the reward. Above: a statue of a gold panner in Auburn; left: a display of shining gold nuggets

buildings line the streets and old mining equipment lies rusting in open fields.

Gold was extracted from the ground by several different methods. Many prospectors just used a simple gold-pan and patiently worked in the rivers flowing from the High Sierra, hoping to strike it rich. Few did, and many of those who did succeed lost it all gambling. Panning took considerable skill, and more than a little luck. The attraction was that anyone could do it at very little expense, and thousands of people saw it as a way to rapid fortune. Latter-day Fortyniners can still try their hand at it at many sites along Highway 49. The perfect gold pan is made of steel, about 15 inches (380mm) in diameter and blackened by heat, so that the flecks of gold will be easier to see. Gravel from the stream bed is scooped up in the pan which, held in both hands, is rotated back and forth underwater to let the heavy particles of gold settle to the bottom. The dirty water is drained off and with consider-

A 19th-century illustration of gold prospectors in California able luck there may be a few grains of gold left in the gravel in the bottom of the pan.

Hard-rock mining was a much more highly organized operation, with miners toiling underground to dig out the precious yellow nuggets. At its most sophisticated, this became a huge industrial enterprise, and the Empire Mine in Grass Valley was one of the biggest, creating a vast network of tunnels under the town. This mine remained productive for over 100 years after the first discovery of the metal – and was one of the last to close. Close by, at the North Star Mine, there is a vast display of mining equipment from this era.

In the Malakoff Diggins State Park, 16 miles (26km) north of Nevada City, you can see the landscape erosion caused by hydraulic mining. Gold was literally washed out of the ground by the force of giant hoses that destroyed the landscape beyond recognition.

The boom period of the Gold Rush lasted for little over a decade, but by then the development of the northern region of California had been well established. In 1849, over 90,000 miners passed through San Francisco, which overnight became a wild frontier city. This was the only way through which the miners could travel to get to the gold fields, and the legacy of this period lives on, although most of the old buildings were destroyed in the great 1906 earthquake. Many of the workers in the mines were Chinese; throughout the Gold Country traces of their past are still evident. When the gold ran out, they settled in San Francisco and built the biggest Chinatown outside Asia. Sacramento also grew to be a major city, providing supplies for the gold fields only a few miles to the east.

As the deposits of gold ran low along the Mother Lode, new areas were explored. Gold was found as far north as Yreka, close

A monument to James Marshall at Coloma, where he first found gold

to the Oregon border, and as far south as the Mojave Desert. These fringe areas never produced the massive amounts that were found in the Sierra foothills but the old, abandoned mines can still be seen on a drive along the back country roads.

It is said that there is as much gold left in the ground in California as has been extracted. The problem is the expense of

mining it. Hundreds of weekend miners still go panning in the rivers and even some commercial mines have reopened. Many stores have California gold for sale and there is no shortage of museum exhibits, notably at the Oakland Museum and the Bank of California's Museum of Money in the American West.

Yosemite &
the High Sierra

3 DAYS • 568 MILES • 914KM

SACRAMENTO

SAN FRANCISCO — Oakland — Stockton — Pinecrest
San Francisco Bay — Hayward — Livermore — Tracy — Manteca — Escalon — Oakdale — Knights Ferry — New Melones Lake — Sonora — Twain Harte — Mi-Wuk Village — Jamestown — STANISLAUS NATIONAL FOREST — Tuolumne — Don Pedro Res — Lake McClure — Tuolumne Grove — Midpines — Mariposa — Catheys Valley — Merced — Castle Air Force Base — Kesterson Nat Wildlife Refuge — San Luis Nat Wildlife Refuge — Atwater — Planada — Gustine — FRESNO

If you only have time for one drive in Northern California, it should be this one. Yosemite National Park is one of the nation's greatest natural treasures. Combined with the surreal landscape of Mono Lake and a visit to the perfectly preserved ghost town of Bodie, the drive includes some of the best that California has to offer. As a bonus, the route crosses the Central Valley, the agricultural heart of the nation. The journey involves two high passes, Tioga and Sonora. These are both closed by snow from November until at least May each year, so the drive is only feasible during the summer months.

[i] *900 Market Street, lower level of Hallidie Plaza, San Francisco*

▶ *Leave San Francisco across the Bay Bridge and take I-580 to I-5 south. Continue south for 29 miles (47km) to the Gustine exit and drive 38 miles (61km) east to Merced.*

❶ Merced
The Central Valley has a string of large towns that are virtually indistinguishable from each other. Many people drive from Los Angeles to the north past these towns without even blinking: they are sleepy, agricultural towns, where people rise early and go to bed early and, outside the fields, nothing much happens in between. Merced is, however, a convenient rest stop on the drive to Yosemite.

[i] *California Welcome Center, 710 W. 16th Street, Merced*

▶ *Hwy 140 winds through Merced, combining with Hwy 99 for a short distance. Stay on Hwy 140 for another 48 miles (77km) to Mariposa.*

❷ Mariposa
The southern mines of the Gold Country never rivaled those of the north. Mariposa was a southern gold camp, and is one of the last towns along Highway 49. The boardwalks and false-front buildings immediately identify its lineage. At the north end of town is a two-story courthouse that has been in use continuously since 1854. The Mariposa County History Center, at 12th and Jessie streets, has a group of reconstructed interiors, including a sheriff's office and a miner's cabin. The California State Mining and Mineral Museum, 2 miles (3km) south of town, has a collection of over 20,000 gems and minerals, along with dioramas of mine interiors and a working model stamp mill.

▶ *Continue along Hwy 140 for 30 miles (48km), climbing through steep, pine-covered valleys and increasingly rugged mountain terrain.*

❸ Yosemite National Park
This must be America's favorite

The soaring rocks of Yosemite Valley, where most visitors stay popularity is reflected in the numbers of people visiting. At certain peak times the park is actually closed because it has reached capacity. If at all possible, try to visit outside of major holiday periods and during the week. Over 3 million people visit Yosemite every year and 70 percent of them arrive during the summer. Most, however, never venture out of the 7 square miles (18sq km) of Yosemite Valley, which leaves 1,200 square miles (3,108sq km) of splendid solitude. If you are planning to spend the night there, reservations must be made as early as possible. Rooms and even campsites are often booked months ahead. However unpleasant the crowds may be, the park is always a rewarding visit. The road continues down into the heart of the valley, where everything is larger than life: granite cliffs towering 3,000 feet (914m) into the air, waterfalls cascading down nearly 2,500 feet (762m) – the second highest falls in the world. Yosemite Village is the main center of the valley, and the park headquarters and visitor center are located here, along with restaurants, a hotel and a post office. There are also a few shops, including the Ansel Adams Gallery, where the work of the great landscape photographer is available for purchase.

▶ *The road loops around the valley, passing most of the main landmarks, and 6 miles (10km) from Yosemite Village* **Hwy 120** *branches off to the right. Take this road up to Crane Flat and turn right, to reach a large parking area (on the left), where there are signs to Tuolumne Grove.*

4 Tuolumne Grove
A 1-mile (1.5km) hike down an easy trail leads to the Tuolumne Grove of giant sequoias, the

Winter lends its own special beauty to Yosemite National Park

most accessible grove in the park. The trees are not the biggest, and there are only 25 of them, but they are, nevertheless, an impressive sight.

▶ *Continue east on the Tioga Road, originally built by the Great Consolidated Silver Company in 1883 and dividing Yosemite National Park in two. The road passes through increasingly dramatic landscape, with polished granite slabs and massive, smooth, granite domes towering above the road.*

5 Olmsted Point
At marker T-24, 28 miles (45km) east of Crane Flat, Olmsted Point provides one of the most remarkable scenic outlooks in the park. There is a unique view of Half Dome and Cloud's Rest and, to the east, sweeping views of Tenaya Lake and the domes and peaks of Tuolumne Meadows. Spend a while here and watch the fat marmots and little golden-mantled ground squirrels come out of the rocks, hoping for some crumbs from passing sightseers. Two miles (3km) down the road, Lake Tenaya looks inviting on a hot day. Be warned, though: the water is usually very cold. Sailboarding and windsurfing are allowed on the lake and there is usually a park ranger on hand to give information on regulations. The lake is in a wonderfully dramatic setting.

▶ *Continue east for 8 miles (13km) to Tuolumne Meadows.*

6 Tuolumne Meadows
This is Yosemite's high country. A beautiful sub-alpine meadow sits at 8,600 feet (2,621m), with the Tuolumne River winding through it. At 2½ miles (4km) long, it is the largest meadow of its kind in the Sierra Nevada, and is stunningly picturesque. This idyllic wilderness is only

55 miles (88km) by road from Yosemite Valley, but it is a world apart. It is almost a crime to pass through it without leaving the car – and, if time permits, there are numerous hiking trails. A ranger station just past the gas station and store can provide maps and information.

▶ *Continue east to the Tioga Pass, at an elevation of 9,945 feet (3,031m). East of Tioga, the road drops steeply through deep gorges, with views over the Eastern Sierra and Mono Lake. In Lee Vining, a one-street town at the foot of the Tioga Road, the Mono Lake Committee Information Center has displays on the geology of the region and the ecology of Mono Lake.*

SCENIC ROUTES

A circuitous 30-mile (48km) drive out of Yosemite Valley follows Wawona Road to Wawona Tunnel, where a parking area provides the classic view of the valley from Bridalveil Falls to El Capitan. Continue through the tunnel and up to Glacier Point Road, and follow the road to the end for absolutely incredible views of the entire valley, including Half Dome and the 13,000-foot (3,962m) peaks of the High Sierra.

---

7 Mono Lake
Once known as the "Dead Sea of California," the million-year-old Mono Lake is a large alkaline inland sea. Far from dead, however, Mono Lake is home during at least part of the year to more than 300 bird species, including almost the entire breeding population of California gulls. Most striking are the lake's vast, surrounding salt flats and unusual formations of tufa – freeform pillars of calcium carbonate, originally created under water where calcium-rich fresh spring water flowed into the salty lake. These 200- to 900-year-old bone-white

spires are now exposed to view, due to Los Angeles' thirst for new water sources. Since 1941, when Mono Lake's feeder streams were first tapped, the lake level has fallen more than 45 feet (14m), increasing the salinity and wreaking havoc on the wildlife populations. The best place to explore Mono Lake's tufa towers is the south tufa area, off Highway 120: drive south from Lee Vining along Highway 395 for 5 miles (8km) and turn east onto Highway 120. Continue for another 5 miles (8km), past interesting volcanic formations, to a dirt road that leads down to the lake.

▶ *Return to **Hwy 395** and drive north for 20 miles (32km) to **Hwy 270**. Turn right and a narrow road leading to Bodie is paved for all but the last 3 miles (5km).*

8 Bodie
The one-time gold-mining town of Bodie is California's largest ghost town, an evocative and ramshackle collection of wood-frame buildings, high in the Eastern Sierra. The 170 remaining buildings are preserved in a state of arrested decay: they will not be restored, but are not allowed to deteriorate further. Bodie was one of the wildest and most lawless towns in the West, with a population of over 10,000. Visitors can take a self-guiding walking tour and peer into the weathered homes, store and saloons that remain. Through the windows you can even see furnishings and personal belongings that were left when the town was finally abandoned.

▶ *Return to **Hwy 395** and drive north through Bridgeport to **Hwy 108**. This road takes you west over the 9,624-foot (2,933m) Sonora Pass, traversing beautiful, high alpine scenery before descending to the Gold Country towns of Sonora and Jamestown (see pages 67–8). Take **Hwy 120** west back to **I-205** and then **I-580** back to San Francisco.*

Lake Tahoe &
the Northern Gold
Country

This is San Francisco's mountain playground: during the summer, water sports, hiking and fishing are popular; in December, skiing takes over. The tour is not recommended in winter, due to sudden and frequent storms. From Lake Tahoe, the drive passes through two of the most interesting towns of the northern Gold Country, before returning to Sacramento.

2 DAYS • 269 MILES • 433KM

ITINERARY		
SACRAMENTO	▶	Placerville (44m-71km)
PLACERVILLE	▶	**South Lake Tahoe (62m-100km)**
SOUTH LAKE TAHOE	▶	**Tallac Historic Site (3m-5km)**
TALLAC HISTORIC SITE	▶	**Emerald Bay (3m-5km)**
EMERALD BAY	▶	**Sugar Pine Point State Park (12m-19km)**
SUGAR PINE POINT STATE PARK	▶	**Truckee (32m-51km)**
TRUCKEE	▶	**Nevada City (54m-87km)**
NEVADA CITY	▶	**Grass Valley (4m-6km)**
GRASS VALLEY	▶	**Sacramento (55m-89km)**

[i] *Sacramento Visitor Information Center, 1608 I Street, Sacramento*

▶ *Leave Sacramento on I-50 east and drive 44 miles (71km) to Placerville.*

1 Placerville
(See page 72)
Once known as Hangtown, a hotbed of crime, Placerville is now a substantial and thriving center, where the Gold Rush era is evoked in the underground tunnels of the city-owned Gold Bug Mine.

▶ *Continue east on I-50, climbing to Echo Summit at 7,382 feet (2,250m). During the winter, this section of the road is frequently closed for several hours at a time. Once over the summit, the road drops down to Lake Tahoe, 6,225 feet (1,897m) above sea level, 22 miles (35km) long and 1,645 feet (501m) deep – the biggest alpine lake in the nation, with enough water to cover the entire state to a depth of 14 inches (356mm). However much snow and ice covers the surrounding mountains, the lake itself*

never freezes because of its great depth. The I-50 continues into the town of South Lake Tahoe into the most heavily populated part of the lake.

2 South Lake Tahoe
For the next few miles, up to the Nevada border, the road is a continuous strip of motels, gas stations, restaurants and shopping centers. Apart from rest stops, the Historical Society Museum, at 3058 State 50, is worth visiting for an introduction to the area's past and to pick up maps and a guide to the lake's historical landmarks. The other reason for driving this section of road is to experience the decadent world of Nevada's casinos. Within inches of the state border, at Stateline, casinos spring up like mushrooms: a totally artificial world, incongruously set in the middle of a wonderful natural landscape.

▶ *Return west along I-50 and turn onto Hwy 89 and drive north for 3 miles (5km).*

Heading for the slopes along Heavenly Valley, South Lake Tahoe

3 Tallac Historic Site
Nineteen historic summer homes are spread over 74 acres (30 hectares) on the shore of Lake Tahoe, testifying to its past as the playground for California's rich and powerful. Several of the houses have been fully restored, including the 1884 Pope House, brown-shingled Valhalla and Lucky Baldwin's Baldwin Estate, which houses the Tallac Museum, where exhibits tell the story of this elite retreat. There are special events throughout the summer, including Sunday chamber music, a bluegrass festival in August and a weekend jazz festival series in late summer.

▶ *Hwy 89 winds north, climbing through rugged, boulder-strewn, pine forest scenery to a point overlooking the lake and specifically Emerald Bay.*

4 Emerald Bay
This is perhaps the most picturesque site on the lake. A perfect cove, enclosed by pine forests, has the lake's only island, Fannette. A 1-mile (1.5km) hike down from the parking lot leads to a 38-room granite mansion

The well-named Emerald Bay, and Lake Tahoe's only island, Fannette

called Vikingsholm, which is considered to be the finest example of Scandinavian architecture in the western hemisphere. It was built for half a million dollars in 1928–9, and includes elements of everything from 11th-century castles to sod-roofed homes. An easier way to see Vikingsholm and its fjord-like bay is by boat – a very big boat, a stern-wheeler that departs from South Lake Tahoe.

After climbing back up to the parking lot, if you have any energy left, take a short walk up to Eagle Falls, directly across Highway 89 from the vista point. The falls cascade over a series of granite steps with Emerald Bay glistening below.

Emerald Bay State Park sits on the lake shore and is contiguous with the D.L. Bliss State Park. Much of the shoreline does not have public access, but these parks provide for camping, fishing, swimming and boating. Lester Beach, at Bliss, is particularly popular, and fills up early on summer weekends.

▶ Continue north on **Hwy 89**.

5 Sugar Pine Point State Park

The rocky lakeshore at Sugar Pine Point offers sunbathing and hiking, including a hike to its only operational lighthouse, but the Ehrmann Mansion is the main attraction. Built in 1903, by wealthy San Francisco banker Isaias Hellman, the stone-and-wood baronial dwelling is the best example of the summer homes of the wealthy.

▶ Continue north on **Hwy 89** to Tahoe City. Visit the Gatekeeper's Museum State Park, at 130 W Lake Boulevard, where the museum emphasizes the area's native cultures and natural history. Continue north on **Hwy 28** to Kings Beach and **Hwy 267** to Truckee.

6 Truckee

Truckee developed as a result of the transcontinental railroad, and the railroad is still dominant in the town's life, with a major line passing through the center of town. The false-front Main Street has a definite frontier-town feel: Charlie Chaplin chose this as the location for his classic film *The Gold Rush*. Aside from

tourists, little has changed since the Gold Rush days.

Two miles (3km) west of Truckee, on I-80, is Donner Memorial State Park. It was here, in the winter of 1846, that 89 pioneers of the Donner Party were trapped by massive snow falls. Almost half the party died, and a monument to them rests on a 22-foot (7m)-high stone base – the depth of the snow that dreadful winter. The Emigrant Trail Museum tells the story of the Donner Party, the construction of the railroad and the natural history of the region.

▶ Drive west on **I-80** over Donner Summit at 7,239 feet (2,206m) and down through pine forests into the northern Gold Country. Turn off **I-80** onto **Hwy 20** and continue to Nevada City.

7 Nevada City

Historically, Nevada City has been host to innovators and innovations. World-class soprano Emma Nevada and Andrew Hallidie, inventor of the cable-car, were both born here. Nevada City created new and radical mining techniques, including hydraulic mining, and social engineering had its part: U.S. Senator A. J. Sargent, a local resident, prepared legislation that led to American women's suffrage. Meetings held here ultimately established both the University of California and Pacific Gas & Electricity, the world's largest utility company. Nevada City was once the third largest town in California, and even today it is grand by Gold Country standards, though it keeps a small-town charm. There are gas lights in the streets and balconied stores; and in the fall, the town blazes with sugar maples.

Nevada City's most unusual legacy is 16 miles (26km) out of town, on the North Bloomfield Road. The Malakoff Diggins State Historic Park includes a massive mine pit with colorful crags and spires, created by hydraulic mining in the 1870s. It also offers good hiking, camping and the Gold Rush ghost town of North Bloomfield.

[i] *Chamber of Commerce, 132 Main Street, Nevada City*

▶ *Take* **Hwy 49** *south to Grass Valley.*

8 Grass Valley
Like Nevada City, this is a big town, compared with the southern Gold Country settlements. The mines along this northern route were a far cry from the simple mining operations of the southern Mother Lode, where a gold pan and rocker were as

sophisticated as it got. This was big industry: large corporations moved in and mined gold on a vast scale, leaving beneath Grass Valley over 367 miles (590km) of mining tunnels. On the edge of town, on East Empire Street, is the Empire Mine State Historic Park. This was the richest hardrock mine in California, productive until 1956. It is thought that

there is four times as much gold still in the ground as was mined – but it is too expensive to dig it out. The mine stands in a 784-acre (317-hectare) estate, and many of the original buildings are still in perfect condition. Separated from the ugly mining operation by careful landscaping is Bourn Cottage, the elegant country seat of William Bourn, owner of the mine and one of the richest men in California.

Downtown Grass Valley's Cornish pasty shops are a legacy of the Cornish miners who came over from England in the early 20th century.

▶ *Take* **Hwy 49** *to Auburn and turn south onto* **I-80** *back to Sacramento.*

One of downtown Nevada City's fine Victorian buildings

Deep Valleys
& Big Trees

2 DAYS • 219 MILES • 353KM Yosemite always steals the spotlight from other High Sierra destinations, but the King's Canyon and Sequoia national parks, only a few miles farther south, offer as much natural spectacle – without the crowds. This tour starts in the agricultural city of Fresno, in the Central Valley, and climbs up to these two pristine wilderness areas, before returning to the valley. On the way back, it passes through the 19th-century railroad town of Hanford, and Kingsburg, which still holds on to its Swedish roots. The tour is not possible during the winter, when heavy snow closes the General's Highway, which connects King's Canyon and Sequoia national parks.

ITINERARY	
FRESNO	▶ **King's Canyon National Park (52m-84km)**
KING'S CANYON NATIONAL PARK	▶ **Giant Forest (29m-47km)**
GIANT FOREST	▶ **Crystal Cave (10m-16km)**
CRYSTAL CAVE	▶ **Hospital Rock (14m-23km)**
HOSPITAL ROCK	▶ **Visalia (43m-69km)**
VISALIA	▶ **Hanford (20m-32km)**
HANFORD	▶ **Kingsburg (29m-47km)**
KINGSBURG	▶ **Fresno (22m-35km)**

i *Fresno Convention and Visitors Bureau, 848 M Street, Fresno*

▶ *Start at Fresno.*

❶ Fresno

This is the gateway to the three Sierra Nevada national parks, and most visitors see it as little more than that. Fresno is a big, sprawling, agricultural center, established during the 19th century, and is now the eighth largest city in California. There is more to see here than may at first be apparent. Fresno calls itself the "Raisin Capital of the World" and the Edwardian mansion of the father of the raisin industry, Theodore Kearney, is open for tours on weekends. It is set on spacious grounds, 7 miles (11km) west of town, at 7160 West Kearney Boulevard.

Closer to town, Baldasare Forestiere spent 40 years digging out an underground home by hand at 5201 West Shaw Avenue, two blocks west of Highway 99. The Forestiere Underground Gardens are open to the public, and there is a self-guiding tour of the family's sky-lit living area and the 10-acre (4-hectare) maze of patios and passageways that were completed in 1946.

The Fresno Metropolitan Museum of Art, History and Science features a large Asian art collection, as well as the Salzer collection of European and American still-life paintings. There is also a selection of Ansel Adams photographs of Yosemite.

Every spring, the fruit orchards surrounding Fresno burst into flower, and the 67-mile (108km) Blossom Trail passes some of the more spectacular displays. Beehives are placed under the trees to produce honey from specific blossoms: as the blossoms peak, so do the bees – watch out! A map of the Blossom Trail is available from the Visitors Bureau.

The beautiful Blossom Trail in the fruit orchards around Fresno

❷ King's Canyon National Park

King's Canyon is split into two quite distinct areas. Tiny General Grant National Park was created in 1890 to protect the General Grant grove of sequoias. In 1940, it was incorporated into the King's Canyon National Park, which includes the wild, mountainous country to the east.

Visitors enter King's Canyon through the Big Stump Entrance Station on Highway 180; 3 miles (5km) farther on is Grant Grove Village, the most developed area of the park. At the Grant Grove Visitor Center there is an exhibit on the logging history of

---

FOR CHILDREN

Children can be amused for hours at 157-acre (63-hectare) Roeding Park, at 894 West Belmont Avenue in Fresno. Not only does it house Chaffee Zoological Gardens, with over 700 animals, including elephants and an Australian outback; it also incorporates a Playland and a Storyland, with a fairytale theme, featuring a castle.

▶ *Leave Fresno on Hwy 180 east and drive for 49 miles (79km) through Centerville, before starting the climb up to King's Canyon and the Big Stump Entrance Station.*

RECOMMENDED WALK

Most of the hikes in King's Canyon are serious undertakings, but one relatively easy way to get a feel for this magnificent wilderness is to follow the 1-mile (1.5km) walking trail through Zumwalt Meadow. Leaving from Cedar Grove, the trail crosses King's River by a suspension bridge, as it winds above and around Zumwalt Meadow.

Visitors to the Giant Forest are dwarfed by the mighty sequoia

It was established in 1890 to protect the groves of giant sequoia, which grow only in California; in fact, more grow here than in any other part of the state. Lodge Pole Visitor Center is the first stop, where there are good displays about sequoias and the geological history of the park; 4 miles (6km) beyond it is the Giant Forest, home of the world's largest living thing: the General Sherman Tree, 275 feet (84m) high, 103 feet (31m) in circumference. The volume of the trunk alone is 52,500 cubic feet (1,485cu m). The 2-mile (3km) Congress Trail begins near this mighty tree and goes past many other huge specimens. Booklets explaining the sites are available at the trailhead.

Back on the General's Highway you can turn left onto Crescent Meadow Road, which passes the Auto Log, a massive fallen tree through which a tunnel has been made. Farther on is Moro Rock. Steps lead 300 feet (91m) to the 6,000-foot (1,829m) summit of this massive

sequoias, the wildlife and early Indian inhabitants of the region. Two groves of sequoias grow in this, the most accessible part of the park. The General Grant Tree is the third largest tree in the world – 267 feet (81m) tall, with a base circumference of 107 feet (32m), and it was alive during the Bronze Age, mote than 3,000 years ago. Close by is the Redwood Mountain Grove of smaller but, nevertheless, very impressive sequoias.

▶ *Turn onto the General's Highway. Follow this around to Sequoia National Park, which is contiguous with King's Canyon and does not involve passing another entrance station.*

3 Giant Forest
Sequoia was the first national park in California, and second in the nation, after Yellowstone.

boulder, which gives sweeping views of the park and, smog permitting, the Central Valley.

▶ *Return to the General's Highway and drive 5 miles (8km) to the signed turnoff to the Crystal Cave.*

4 Crystal Cave
A narrow, winding road descends 2,000 feet (609m) to the Marble Fork Kaweah River Bridge and then from the parking area, down a short, steep trail. Several chambers are open to the public, including the Organ Room, the Marble Hall and the Dome Room. The temperature inside is a constant 48°F (9°C), which can feel decidedly chilly after the hot Sierra sun.

▶ *Return to the General's Highway, which now becomes Hwy 198, and drive 6 miles (10km) to Hospital Rock.*

5 Hospital Rock
This old village site of the Potwisha Indian tribe is marked by a large boulder covered in pictographs. A nearby rock has more than 50 mortar holes, used by Indian women to grind acorns into flour.

▶ *Continue along Hwy 198 and leave Sequoia National Park by the Ash Mountain Entrance Station. The road descends to Visalia.*

6 Visalia
Visalia, the oldest city between Stockton and Los Angeles, was founded in 1852. It quickly became an important agricultural center, and the lavish homes that were built during this period can be seen on a self-guiding walking tour through the historic district. Maps are available from the Chamber of Commerce, at 720 W. Mineral King Avenue. For most visitors Visalia provides a convenient base for exploring the national parks, but there are a few sites of interest within easy reach. The Tulare Historical Museum, about 8 miles (13km) south of town, traces the history

---

SCENIC ROUTES

Highway 180 continues down into King's Canyon leaving the national park soon after Grant Grove Village. From here, it drops 2,000 feet (609m) to the valley floor, in a spectacular, winding descent through impressive mountain scenery into the gorges of the King's River. On the deep valley floor, about 20 miles (32km) after Grant Grove, a road on the right is signposted to marble-walled Boyden Cavern, where there are beautiful stalactite and stalagmite formations. Continue for 10 miles (16km) through the narrow gorge of the south fork of King's River to Cedar Canyon, the end of the road for vehicular traffic. Mountains rise 6,000 feet (1,829m) above the valley floor, which is the staging point for excursions into the back country. Here there are some 700 miles (1,126km) of trails.

of the area from the time when it was covered by one of the largest bodies of water west of the Mississippi. The museum is at 444 W. Tulare Avenue, off Highway 137, west of Highway 99. Mooney Grove Park is 5 miles (8km) south of town, covering 155 acres (63 hectares), with a lake, valley oaks and date palms.

▶ Return to Visalia and take Hwy 198 west to Hanford along 11 miles (18km) of dead straight road.

7 Hanford

Hanford is an atypical Central Valley town. It has charm, history, interesting architecture and even a nationally noted restaurant. Founded by the Southern Pacific Railroad in 1877, it was named after the popular paymaster, who paid the workers in gold. Courthouse Square is the core of historic

A hazy view of the Central Valley from the Giant Forest's Moro Rock

Hanford, built in the late 19th century and overlooking a picturesque town square that has been lovingly restored and now houses boutiques, gift shops and a restaurant. Close by are other architectural gems, including a fine art deco movie theater and The Superior Dairy, an old-fashioned ice cream parlor in business for over 60 years. Hanford once claimed one of the largest Chinese communities in California: 800 Chinese families were brought by railroad at the turn of the century. All that is left now is China Alley, a few blocks east of downtown. The 1893 Taoist Temple still stands here, and can be toured by request, and next door is the Imperial Dynasty Restaurant, operated by the Wing family for more than a century and serving some of the best – and most expensive – Chinese cuisine in California.

▶ Return east on Hwy 198 and take Hwy 99 north to Kingsburg.

A Swedish coffee pot sits above the railroad station in Kingsburg

8 Kingsburg

Kingsburg was established in 1875 as a railroad town, and its Swedish immigrant population earned it the name Swedish Village. Many buildings are half-timbered, with dormer windows and steep, wood-shingled roofs.

▶ Return to Fresno on Hwy 99 north.

CENTRAL VALLEY

The Central Valley of California is one of the most productive agricultural regions of the world. Peach trees, apricots, walnuts, oranges, cotton and acres of vineyards stretch as far as the eye can see. The rich soil of the valley supports a myriad crops that are watered by the rivers, lakes and reservoirs generated by the snow melt in the High Sierra to the east.

Before agriculture, gold was the valley's fortune. During the 19th century, the area provided access to the Mother Lode, which ran up its eastern flank. Sacramento became the major supply center to the mines, and rapidly developed into a prosperous city. As the Gold Rush petered out, agriculture took hold, and within a few years the revenues from agricultural produce were rivaling those from the dwindling supplies of gold.

The 18,000-square-mile (46,620sq km) valley extends for almost 500 miles (804km) from Chico, north of Sacramento, the state capital, to Bakersfield in the south. It has never been a tourist destination – and that is much of the area's charm. Along the valley are old agricultural towns with colorful pasts; some have a rich legacy of Chinese culture, established in the 19th century, when Chinese laborers came to work on railroads and in the fields. Mexicans have had a more recent influence. In the south, around Bakersfield, oil has eclipsed agriculture as the dominant industry, and nodding oil pumps sit amid fields of cotton on the valley floor. But the greatest interest is in the towns and cities, and in the wildlife that flocks here on major migratory flight paths across North America.

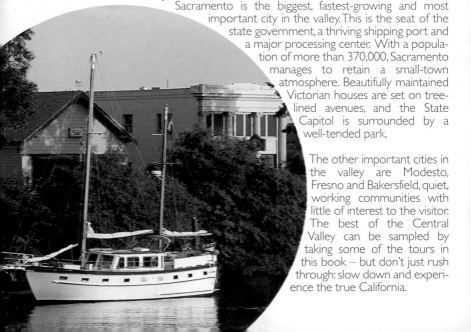

Sacramento is the biggest, fastest-growing and most important city in the valley. This is the seat of the state government, a thriving shipping port and a major processing center. With a population of more than 370,000, Sacramento manages to retain a small-town atmosphere. Beautifully maintained Victorian houses are set on tree-lined avenues, and the State Capitol is surrounded by a well-tended park.

The other important cities in the valley are Modesto, Fresno and Bakersfield, quiet, working communities with little of interest to the visitor. The best of the Central Valley can be sampled by taking some of the tours in this book – but don't just rush through: slow down and experience the true California.

Tour 14

After leaving San Francisco across the Golden Gate Bridge – where you can enjoy stunning views of the city from across the bay – this tour travels down through the chic, waterfront town of Sausalito, where there is more of a Mediterranean than an American air. The route then skirts around the northern edge of enormous San Francisco Bay, past the naval shipyards of Vallejo to the railroad museum at Suisun City.

The Sacramento Delta is a complex labyrinth of waterways, ideally explored by houseboat. Narrow country roads pass along the levees (raised embankments) through old towns such as Walnut Grove and Locke, built around 1915 by members of a Chinese association who were working in the area. It remains a Chinese community to this day. A winding country road meanders past these towns before reaching Sacramento, the state capital. On the return journey, the route passes Davis, home of UC Davis, the state's foremost university for veterinary science, and the Air Museum at Fairfield Air Force Base, before continuing past Benicia, a sleepy backwater town that once knew headier days as the state capital. Across the water, in Martinez, was the home of the great environmentalist John Muir, and close by is the now-forgotten town of Port Costa, suspended in time on the edge of the delta. The return to San Francisco takes you across the Richmond–San Rafael Bridge, and back again to the Golden Gate Bridge.

Tour 15

This tour starts, appropriately enough, at Sutter's Fort, the first settlement in Sacramento, dating back to 1839. Next to the fort is the State Indian Museum. Wide, tree-lined avenues lead down past the elegant, Victorian Governor's Mansion, which was most recently used by President Ronald Reagan. A short distance away from the Governor's Mansion is the impressive State Capitol building, which has been faithfully restored to its original splendor.

Continue past the Crocker Art Museum, which has the distinguished claim of being the first art museum in the west, and houses an impressive collection of Californian art. Carry on to Old Sacramento, an area that covers 28 acres (11 hectares) and is made up of fully restored Gold Rush-era buildings, alongside the Sacramento River. Railroad enthusiasts are sure to appreciate the California State Railroad Museum, which is the crowning glory of Old Sacramento, and is generally considered to be one of the finest rail museums in the entire world.

Just across the Sacramento River you can visit another museum with international claims. The most complete collection of Ford cars in the world is on display at the Towe Ford Museum.

Opposite page: a tranquil scene on the Sacramento Delta waterways, near Walnut Grove
Right: the carefully restored State Capitol Building, the center of California's government

Sacramento
Delta

The two major rivers of Northern California, the Sacramento and the San Joaquin, flow together near Sacramento, creating a delta region of bridges, waterways and mists. Sam Goldwyn thought the Sacramento Delta looked more like the Mississippi than the real thing, and filmed *Huckleberry Finn* there. This drive passes through the heart of the delta, stopping at several waterfront towns, in a part of California that's escaped the modern world.

2 DAYS • 222 MILES • 259KM

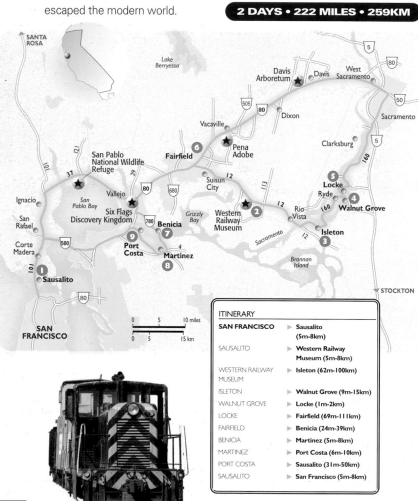

ITINERARY		
SAN FRANCISCO	▶	**Sausalito** (5m-8km)
SAUSALITO	▶	**Western Railway Museum** (5m-8km)
WESTERN RAILWAY MUSEUM	▶	**Isleton** (62m-100km)
ISLETON	▶	**Walnut Grove** (9m-15km)
WALNUT GROVE	▶	**Locke** (1m-2km)
LOCKE	▶	**Fairfield** (69m-111km)
FAIRFIELD	▶	**Benicia** (24m-39km)
BENICIA	▶	**Martinez** (5m-8km)
MARTINEZ	▶	**Port Costa** (6m-10km)
PORT COSTA	▶	**Sausalito** (31m-50km)
SAUSALITO	▶	**San Francisco** (5m-8km)

i San Francisco Visitor Information Center, Benjamin Swig Pavilion, Hallidie Plaza, Market and Powell streets, CA 94101

▶ Leave San Francisco via Lombard Street, past a seemingly endless strip of motels, and join **Hwy 101** en route for the Golden Gate Bridge. (Northbound traffic is toll-free.) Cross the bridge and stop briefly at Vista Point, on the north side, which, on a clear day, gives sweeping views of San Francisco and other Bay Area cities. Take the Alexander Avenue exit immediately after leaving Vista Point.

Houseboats tied up to the garden gates at Sausalito

popularity does create parking problems, and the meter wardens are particularly vigilant, even on weekends. Follow

FOR CHILDREN

The Bay Area Discovery Museum nestles below the Golden Gate Bridge, at the former army garrison of Fort Baker in Sausalito. It is one of the best hands-on children's museums in the country, with exhibits ranging from an interactive computer room and a maze of optical illusions to a Port of San Francisco activity center, complete with fishing boat and fish market.

Hwy 37, which follows the edge of San Pablo Bay, giving sweeping views across the marshes of the north bay. After passing Six Flags Discovery Kingdom, turn on to **I-80** north and drive to the **Hwy 12** exit to Suisun City. Take **Hwy 12** east, past Suisun City to the Western Railway Museum, which is located just outside Rio Vista.

② Western Railway Museum

Although its address is Suisun City, the museum is quite far out of town; its collection of over 100 streetcars and railroad cars, owned by the Bay Area Electric Railroad Association, is spread out over 25 acres (10 hectares). There are examples of trains

① Sausalito
Wind down Alexander Avenue to the Mediterranean-like waterfront of Sausalito. This is perhaps the most attractive town around San Francisco Bay, with steep streets tumbling down to the harbor, which is packed with sailboats and has fabulous views across the water to San Francisco. The town's

Bridgeway through town and turn right on to Marinship Way to visit a working scale model of the San Francisco Bay which, although it is at one-thousandth scale, still covers 1½ acres (0.6 hectares).

▶ Return to Bridgeway, turn right and join **Hwy 101** north. Continue north and exit on

from around the country, including a New York "L" train and even a Blackpool tram from England. On weekends during the summer there are rides on old electric trolleys, and a 12-mile (19km) round trip behind a vintage diesel locomotive.

▶ Continue east on **Hwy 12** through Rio Vista. Once across *the Sacramento River, turn north on **Hwy 160**, which winds up through the marsh-lands of the delta.*

> *Continue north along **Hwy 160** to Walnut Grove.*

boardwalks along Main Street, and the Dai Loy Museum, a former gambling house that closed in 1950, displays old gaming paraphernalia and games, such as fan-tan and Flying Bull. Close by is Al's Place, a bar and restaurant called Al the Wop's in less sensitive times, which is usually crammed with locals: an essential part of any Locke experience.

> *Continue north on **Hwy 160**, winding along beside the Sacramento River through the delta countryside to Sacramento. Join **I-50** west to **I-80** and turn south. Drive past the university town of Davis to the Fairfield exit.*

SPECIAL TO...

East Brother Light Station sits on an island in the San Pablo Bay, just off Point Richmond. The old beacon, built in 1873 and in operation for almost 100 years, is still a working lighthouse, but it doubles as one of the most unique bed-and-breakfast inns in the state, with four rooms decorated with period furnishings.

3 Isleton

At one time, 90 percent of the world's canned asparagus came from this little delta town, which billed itself as the "Asparagus Capital of the World." Sixty years on, it is a shadow of its former self. The old tin-sided buildings remain, and can still evoke an atmosphere of the days when a flourishing Chinatown jostled for room with the gambling dens and brothels along Main Street. Most buildings stand vacant, but the Quong Wo Sing Company store still survives, having been owned by the same family for four generations.

4 Walnut Grove

Sleepy little Walnut Grove is the only town south of Red Bluff to occupy both banks of the Sacramento River. Once it was a lair for riverboat bandits, but it is now an agricultural community that fills up on weekends with people boating on the delta. The charming stores and houses date back to 1915, when the town was rebuilt after a fire.

> *Cross the river just north of town. Locke is below the levee.*

5 Locke

Members of a Chinese association that worked on the levees, railroads and farms in the surrounding area built this rustic community in 1915, soon after the Chinatown in neighboring Walnut Grove had burned to the ground. At its height, more than 2,000 people lived there, but today little other than the Main Street survives, with fewer than 100 residents. Listed in the National Register of Historic Places as the only rural community in America built and occupied by the Chinese, the town is overflowing with atmosphere. Chinese families still occupy the old buildings lining the

6 Fairfield

Fairfield is an air force town, as well as being home to the Anheuser-Busch Fairfield Brewery, at 3101 Busch Drive, which offers one-hour guided tours of the brewing facility.

> *From Fairfield, take **I-80** south to **I-780** and follow it to the Benicia exit.*

7 Benicia

It is difficult to understand how this quiet delta town could ever have had delusions of grandeur. In 1847, when it was founded, the city fathers envisaged Benicia as the capital of California – and it did, indeed, hold that position in 1854; but its exalted status only lasted for 13 months. The Benicia Capitol still stands, a refined, brick building operated as a State Historic Park, with a restored interior, down to the candles on every desk of the senate chamber. During its period as capital, Benicia did achieve an impressive number of firsts for the state: the first public school, the first law school, the first chamber of commerce, the first railroad ferry in the West and the first steamboat built by Americans in California. One of

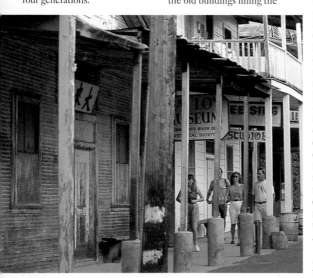

A unique Chinese community still thrives in the delta town of Locke

the town's more bizarre historic attractions is the Camel Barn Museum, scene of a brief experiment using camels to transport military supplies across the Southwest in the 1860s.

▶ *Return to I-780 and turn south onto I-680 and exit on to Hwy 4 west. Exit at Martinez.*

8 Martinez

Scotsman John Muir has attained almost mythical status among American environmentalists. He did more for the preservation of California's wilderness than any of his contemporaries, as co-founder of the Sierra Club, founder of five national parks and the U.S. Forest Service, and

Above and left: the exterior and interior of the Benicia Capitol, legacy of a brief, distinguished past

an indefatigable writer. From 1890 until his death in 1914, he lived with his wife in the elegant 1882 Victorian farmhouse at 4202 Alhambra Avenue. It is now the John Muir National Historic Site. Muir did most of his conservation writing while he lived here and the restored study, Muir's "scribble den," is littered with notes, manuscripts and editions of his books. The 17-room house has been restored to its original appearance and on the grounds is the Martinez Adobe, built by Don Vincente Martinez in 1844 as part of the old Rancho Las Juntas.

▶ *From Martinez take McEwen Road to Port Costa.*

9 Port Costa

Port Costa sits opposite Benicia, on the left bank of the Carquinez Strait, where fresh

water from the rivers meets the salt water of the bay. Early this century it was a major grain-shipping port but now, like so much of the delta, it has become a sleepy backwater at the end of a country lane. Old buildings are being taken over by artists and antiques shops, but the charm of the town relies heavily on the almost total lack of gentrification. On the corner of Erskine Street and Canyon Lake Drive is Muriel's Doll House, a museum housing the antique and hand-made dolls that were collected by Muriel Whitmore for "loving and sharing."

▶ *Leave Port Costa on the Crockett Road, which follows the Carquinez Straits. At I-80 turn south and exit on Cutting Boulevard, which leads to the San Rafael Bridge. Cross the bridge and return to San Francisco on Hwy 101 south across the Golden Gate Bridge. Immediately before crossing the bridge, a road exits to the Marin Headlands. Several parking areas give fine views of both the bridge and the city of San Francisco.*

Sacramento

3 HOURS

Since 1854, Sacramento has been California's capital, fighting off challenges by Benicia, San Jose and Monterey. The discovery of gold first gave the city its prominence, but agriculture soon became the industrial base for the economy. More recently, military installations and the aerospace industry have contributed to its importance. In 1963, a deepwater channel to San Francisco Bay was completed, making Sacramento a major inland port. All that apart, it is a very pleasant place, and although the city is primarily the state's administrative center, it has many important visitor

attractions. This walking tour starts appropriately at Sacramento's first settlement, at Sutter's Fort, and continues to the 19th-century Governor's Mansion, the State Capitol and the Crocker Art Museum. It ends in Old Sacramento, featuring four blocks of restored Gold Rush-era buildings that now house stores, restaurants and several interesting museums.

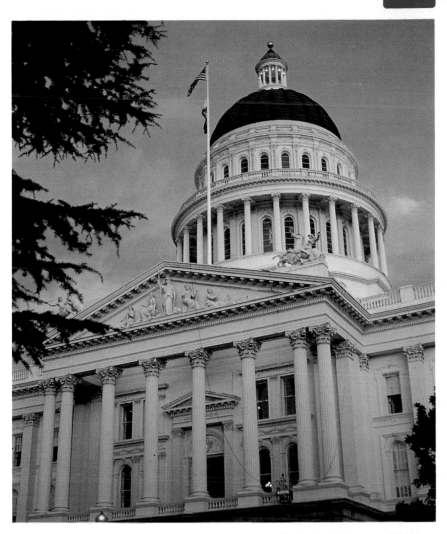

ℹ️ *Sacramento Visitor Information Center, 1608 I Street, Sacramento*

▶ *Start at 27th and L streets.*

❶ Sutter's Fort

Captain John Sutter, an immigrant from Switzerland, established California's first inland settlement at the confluence of the American and Sacramento rivers, where the Mexican government had given him a 50,000-acre (20,235-hectare) land grant in 1839.

An adobe fort was the first building erected; now restored, it stands among residential streets – a far cry from the pioneer days. On weekends, costumed interpreters add to the atmosphere. The California State Indian

SPECIAL TO...

The Central Valley is a major almond-growing region and at 1701 C Street you can visit the Blue Diamond Almond Packing Plant and see how the nuts are sorted, cracked, sliced, halved and roasted. This is the largest almond-packaging plant in the world – and the tours are free.

Looming over Capitol Park: the 19th-century State Capitol

Museum is on the grounds of Sutter's Fort and depicts California's Indian cultures, with displays of baskets, clothing, jewelry and art.

▶ *Walk down L Street to 15th and the black granite panels of the California Vietnam Veterans Memorial, engraved with 5,822 names of the state's dead and missing, in Capitol Park. Return one block to 16th Street, turn left and continue to H Street.*

2 Governor's Mansion

Ronald Reagan was the last governor of California to live in the Governor's Mansion, now open to the public. Furnishings and personal items of the state's former governors are displayed in this splendid Victorian building, which is filled with antiques. Some of the more interesting items include a 1902 Steinway piano and Persian carpets bought by Mrs. Earl Warren in 1943. The gardens contain plants dating back to 1877.

▶ *Walk down H Street and turn left on 12th Street. This goes through the heart of downtown Sacramento. Turn right on L Street, then left on 10th Street, into Capitol Park.*

3 State Capitol

A 210-foot (64m)-high dome on top of this grandiose neoclassical government building towers over Capitol Park. The dramatic, white structure was erected between 1860 and 1874, and modeled after the nation's

A glimpse of the glorious Gold Rush days at Old Sacramento

Capitol in Washington D.C. Since then, it has undergone extensive renovation, and there are free tours of the main building and seven historic museum rooms, which re-create the early days of the California legislature.

▶ *Leave on Capitol Mall and walk down it to 3rd Street, not forgetting to look back for a great view of the State Capitol. Turn left on 3rd Street and continue to O Street and the Crocker Art Museum.*

4 Crocker Art Museum

This is the oldest public art museum in the West and it

FOR HISTORY BUFFS

An example of virtually every car that Ford manufactured between 1903 and 1953 is on display at the Towe Ford Museum of Automotive History of California, at 2200 Front Street, close to Old Sacramento. A vast warehouse is crammed with the world's largest collection of Ford vehicles.

---

contains an extensive display of fine and applied art from Northern California and Europe. The collection has been increasing since its foundation in 1873, and is housed in the former mansion of Edwin Crocker. The building dwarfs the collection with hand-carved walls, parquet floors and the grandest of grand ballrooms.

▶ *Walk down O Street to the Sacramento River, turn right and continue to Old Sacramento.*

5 Old Sacramento State Historic Park

This 28-acre (11-hectare) national historic landmark has more than 100 restored buildings, complete with wooden sidewalks, giving a remarkably good idea of how Sacramento must have looked during the height of the Gold Rush.

The B.F. Hastings Building, at J and 2nd Streets, is a good place to start. It was once the western terminus of the Pony Express, and now houses the Wells Fargo Museum, with exhibits on that legendary delivery service.

Above: replicas of the old paddle-wheelers ply the waters of the Sacramento River and relive the days when they were a common-place sight
Right: shining machinery from the age of steam, displayed in the splendid California State Railroad Museum

The Eagle Theater, built in 1849, is the oldest in California, and still stages Gold Rush era shows. The showplace of the development is the California State Railroad Museum one block to the north, the largest museum of its kind in the world. In the three-story, glass-and-steel structure are no fewer than 27 restored locomotives and more than 40 interpretive exhibits that set out to recapture the romance of steam. On summer weekends, you can take a 6-mile (10km) train ride pulled by a historic locomotive from the museum's Central Pacific Depot.

In the 19th century, hundreds of paddlewheel riverboats used to ply the Sacramento River and one of the best examples, the *Delta King*, is permanently docked along Old Sacramento's waterfront. Cruises are offered on the riverboats.

▶ *Take a cruise along the river on one of the replica paddle-wheelers, or return along L Street to Sutter's Fort.*

THE SAN FRANCISCO BAY AREA

San Francisco is everyone's favorite city. With its cable cars, Golden Gate Bridge and sophisticated European ambience, it rarely fails to meet the expectations of millions of visitors. It has an intimate scale rarely found in American cities due, in part, to its geography: built on a series of hills on a peninsula, it covers only 46 square miles (119 sq km) and has a population of less than 800,000.

The climate is wonderful: it rarely gets too hot and almost never freezes. Most of the time, the air is clean and clear, but it does get cold, particularly in the summer, when the famous sea fogs roll in from the Pacific. The only people wearing shorts at this time of year are tourists!

Within two years of James Marshall discovering gold in the Sierra Nevada mountains, in 1849, San Francisco grew from a population of 900 to 25,000. Forty years later, it had exceeded 300,000. This cosmopolitan community, drawn by the lure of gold, set its future pattern as one of the most international cities imaginable, with a Chinatown bigger than many towns in China, large Japanese, Filipino and Vietnamese communities, a Spanish-speaking Mission District that provides a home for families from Mexico and Central America, and a very strong Italian presence in North Beach. Even a French neighborhood has evolved in the downtown area, with Parisian-style bistros, cafés and bookstores. Along with this ethnic diversity comes a tolerance that has embraced the Beatniks of the '50s, the flower children of the '60s, and now the largest gay population in the United States.

San Francisco is the jewel in the crown of the Bay Area, which has a population of over 6 million, making it the fourth largest metropolitan area in the U.S. From the Wine Country in the north, to the beaches and redwood forests in the south, all in one of the most exquisite natural settings on earth, this region is exceptional. It is also the perfect base for visits to the great natural attractions of Northern California, including Yosemite Valley, the giant coastal redwoods on the North Coast and the thermal wonders of Lassen Volcanic National Park.

Tour 16

If you only have one day to see San Francisco, take this drive, which passes virtually every major site in the city. The route is well marked and easy to follow, but though the journey can easily be completed in one day, not much time will be available for visiting sites. There is so much to see along the way that this drive should be considered a sampler, to search out the more interesting places for a return visit at your leisure.

Tour 17

Although San Francisco dates back only to the mid-19th century, its colorful past has created a wealth of historically interesting sites. Walking here is always a pleasure, and there is no shortage of charming rest stops on the way through diverse cultural neighborhoods. The tour passes through the biggest Chinatown outside of Asia, North Beach, relics of the 1906 earthquake, haunts of the gold miners of 1849, and a glimpse of the world of Dashiel Hammet and Sam Spade.

Tour 18

San Francisco is a city of hills, and a network of steps connects many of the major thoroughfares. This is one of the few American cities where the pedestrian can feel at home, and the steps of San Francisco represent the ultimate walk in the city. Rarely used by tourists, they meander through residential districts, falling steeply between flower-covered gardens and giving a glimpse into the real San Francisco, that can only be experienced on foot.

Tour 19

No visit to Northern California would be complete without experiencing the world-famous vineyards of Napa Valley and the Wine Country. The drive from the metropolitan area to the closest vineyards takes little more than an hour, but it is well worth continuing north to Calistoga, and over to the vineyards of Sonoma for a taste of the real thing.

Although a day trip will give you a pretty good feel for the area, it really deserves more time, and has more than enough attractions to keep even the most jaded visitor happily occupied. The route is scattered with bed-and-breakfast inns and fine restaurants – giving no excuse for returning to the city too quickly.

Tour 20

The excursion to Monterey begins with a scenic introduction to Northern California's rugged coastline. Highway One hugs the coast as it passes through Half Moon Bay on its way to Santa Cruz, with mixed agricultural and natural landscapes along the way. From Santa Cruz, the road makes its way through more agricultural land before eventually arriving at Monterey Bay.

San Francisco Peninsula has become one of the richest areas in America, mainly due to the phenomenal growth of the hi-tech industry. The return journey up the east side of the peninsula is a dramatic contrast to the rugged Pacific coast. This is the home of Hewlett Packard, Apple Computers, Stanford University and a whole host of other household names in the computer industry.

The browsers' delight: City Lights bookstore, in North Beach, was the U.S.'s first paperback book shop

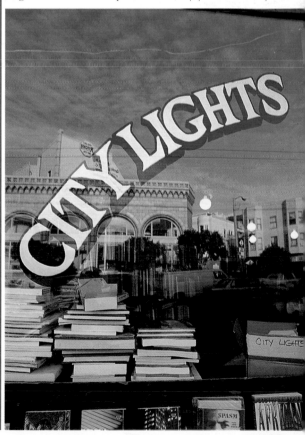

Forty-Nine-Mile
Drive

1 DAY • 49 MILES • 79KM

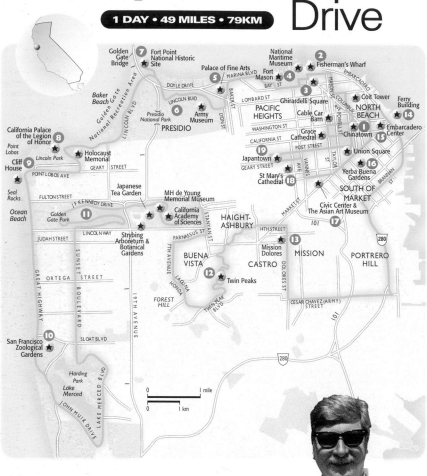

Golden Gate Bridge ⑦ Fort Point National Historic Site
Palace of Fine Arts ⑤ Fort Mason ④
National Maritime Museum ② ★ Fisherman's Wharf
DOYLE DRIVE
MARINA BLVD
BAY ST
LOMBARD ST
Ghirardelli Square ③ ★ Coit Tower
Ferry Building
Baker Beach Area
LINCOLN BLVD
PACIFIC HEIGHTS
Cable Car Barn
NORTH BEACH
Presidio National Park ⑥ Army Museum
PRESIDIO
WASHINGTON ST
CALIFORNIA ST
Grace Cathedral ★
Chinatown ①
Embarcadero Center ⑮
California Palace of the Legion of Honor ⑧
Point Lobos
Holocaust Memorial
POST STREET
Union Square
Cliff House ⑨ Lincoln Park
POINT LOBOS AVE
GEARY STREET
Japantown ⑲ ★
Yerba Buena Gardens ⑯
Seal Rocks ★
FULTON STREET
Japanese Tea Garden
St Mary's Cathedral ⑱
SOUTH OF MARKET
Ocean Beach
Golden Gate Park ⑪
J F KENNEDY DRIVE
MH de Young Memorial Museum
California Academy of Sciences
HAIGHT-ASHBURY
Civic Center & The Asian Art Museum ⑰
JUDAH STREET
LINCOLN WAY
Strybing Arboretum & Botanical Gardens
PARNASSUS ST
14TH STREET
Mission Dolores ⑬
MISSION
PORTRERO HILL
BUENA VISTA
CASTRO
Twin Peaks ⑫
FOREST HILL
ORTEGA STREET
CESAR CHAVEZ (ARMY) STREET
San Francisco Zoological Gardens ⑩
SLOAT BLVD
Harding Park
Lake Merced
JOHN MUIR DRIVE

0 ___ 1 mile
0 ___ 1 km

The best that San Francisco has to offer is covered
by this well-marked drive through the city, passing virtually every major site worth seeing. It is
best to plan the drive to avoid the congested
downtown area during rush hours, and
to spend more of your time at the
sites farthest away from town.
Look for the "49-Mile Drive" blue-and-
white seagull signs.

i *San Francisco Visitor Information Center, Benjamin Swig Pavilion, Hallidie Plaza, Market and Powell streets*

▶ *Start in Union Square, which is the center of the hotel and shopping district. Take Post Street to Grant Avenue, turn left and drive through the Chinatown Gate to California Street.*

❶ Chinatown

The junction of California and Grant is the heart of the biggest Chinatown outside Asia. Old St. Mary's Church (see page 111) is on the right – be sure to look out for cable cars: this is on the cable car line, and they always have right of way.

RECOMMENDED WALK

San Francisco's Chinatown has not changed very much over the past 100 years. Its streets are not designed to take present-day traffic and the congestion can be dreadful. The only way to see this area is on foot. An underground parking lot on Kearny Street, at Clay, has an elevator that delivers you right into Portsmouth Square, the social center of Chinatown, which is the ideal place to start an exploration of the neighborhood. Visit when it is most lively, in the middle of the day.

▶ *Continue up California Street to Nob Hill, pass between the Mark Hopkins Hotel on the left and the Fairmont on the right. Continue past the Flood Mansion (see page 109) and turn right in front of Grace Cathedral (see page 109) onto Taylor Street. Turn right on Washington Street and continue to Kearny Street. There is an underground parking lot here; the elevators exit*

Two features of Fisherman's Wharf
Left: a chef displays his catch
Right: boats line the wharf

right in the square. Turn left on Kearny and left again onto Columbus, and continue through North Beach (see page 110) to Grant Avenue. Turn right and continue as far as Lombard Street. Turn left onto Lombard Street: straight ahead are the hairpin bends of "The Crookedest Street in the World." Turn right on Powell Street and follow it to Jefferson Street. Turn left and follow Jefferson through Fisherman's Wharf.

❷ Fisherman's Wharf

Locals dismiss Fisherman's Wharf as one big tourist trap, but if you can overlook the amusement arcade, museums, and the plethora of T-shirt and sea-shell jewelry stores, there are still a few authentic corners. A small fishing fleet still operates out of the harbor at the foot of Jones Street. Their catch is sold to local restaurants, and at the junction of Jefferson and Taylor streets, old Italian families still operate crab stands, selling freshly cooked Dungeness crab and sourdough bread. Pier 45 is still a working wharf and gives a feeling of what this area was like before the T-shirts arrived. Pier 39 is a different story: this old steamship wharf is now a two-level shopping and restaurant complex. The street performers here provide some of the best free entertainment in town, and the views from the end of the pier are some of the best in the bay. Aquarium of the Bay is the latest major attraction, where a 700,000-gallon (3 million-liter) saltwater tank allows visitors to

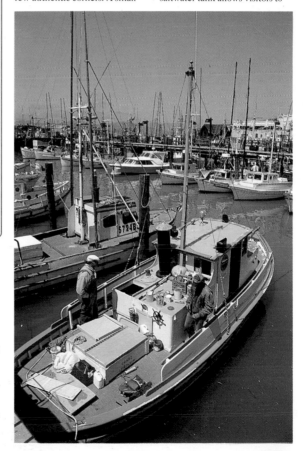

see the marine life from below the water, through a large, acrylic tunnel. On Pier 45 at the end of Taylor Street the Musee Mecanique houses one of the world's largest collections of mechanically operated, antique machines all in working order. Across the street, as it opens out into Aquatic Park, is the Hyde Street Pier, which is part of the National Maritime Museum. Seven historic ships are anchored here, including the *Eureka*, an 1890 ferryboat, and the *Balclutha*, a Scottish merchant ship built in 1886 that rounded Cape Horn no fewer than 17 times carrying coal, wine and hardware from Europe. Also here is the three-masted schooner *C A Thayer*, which carried lumber down the California coast.

machines working, and even sample the goods. Opposite Ghirardelli Square, the National Maritime Museum has a display of model ships, photographs and various nautical memorabilia.

▶ *Turn up Polk Street and right onto Bay Street. Continue to Laguna Street, turn right and Fort Mason is straight ahead.*

❹ Fort Mason
This collection of old warehouses and wharves is now home to around 50 non-profit organizations, including Greenpeace, and three small museums: the Mexican Museum, the Museo Italio-Americano, and the San Francisco Craft and Folk Art Museum. The S.S. *Jeremiah*

O'Brien, preserved as the National Liberty Ship Memorial, is also moored here. It is the last survivor of 2,751 Liberty Ships, launched during World War II. Amazingly, it took only 57 days to build.

▶ *Continue along Marina Boulevard, past Marina Green, where kite-flyers and joggers outnumber pedestrians. The Marina District was badly affected by the Loma Prieta earthquake in 1989, although little evidence of the disastrous fires is visible today. At the end of Marina Boulevard, turn left onto Baker Street.*

Home, sweet home: Ghirardelli Square was a chocolate firm's base

---

FOR HISTORY BUFFS

The infamous island of Alcatraz can be reached by a short ferry crossing from Fisherman's Wharf. It was named by Spanish explorer Juan Manuel de Ayala in 1775, and in 1854 the very first Pacific Coast lighthouse was built on the island. In 1859, a fort built for 300 troops, and a prison for the army followed in 1912. It became the notorious civil prison in 1934, and operated until 1963, housing some of the most desperate criminals in America, including Al Capone, "Machine Gun" Kelly and Robert Stroud, the "Birdman of Alcatraz."

▶ *Turn left on Hyde and right onto Beach.*

❸ Ghirardelli Square
At the junction of Larkin and Beach is one of San Francisco's most attractive shopping and restaurant developments. Ghirardelli Square was originally the home of Ghirardelli chocolate, which is still highly regarded as one of the best in the U.S. You can still see the antique chocolate-making

Sole survivor of the Panama-Pacific Exposition: the Palace of Fine Arts

5 Palace of Fine Arts

In 1915, the Panama-Pacific Exposition extended all the way across what is now known as the Marina District. Today, there is only one remnant: the Palace of Fine Arts. The building was designed by eminent San Francisco architect Bernard Maybeck. Originally a stucco construction, it deteriorated so severely that in the 1960s the building was completely rebuilt in concrete. Set by a small lake, that is permanent home to several families of swans and geese, the palace houses an auditorium and the Exploratorium, a children's science museum.

FOR CHILDREN

The Exploratorium, at the Palace of Fine Arts, is a hands-on museum for children of all ages, with more than 600 exhibits. The prestigious *Scientific American* magazine has rated it as "the best science museum in the world."

▶ Return to Marina Boulevard and enter the Presidio on Lincoln Boulevard.

6 The Presidio

Established by the Spanish in 1776 and taken over by the U.S. in 1846, these 1,440 acres (583 hectares) of wooded hills were an army base until 1995, when the army handed over the Presidio to the National Park Service. This landscaped corner of San Francisco is now part of the Golden Gate National Recreation Area. Still here is the Presidio Army Museum, protected by antique cannon and housing a collection of military uniforms and weapons. One of the more unusual sights at the Presido is an extensive pet cemetery, with headstones eulogizing the dear, departed, furry friends of the soldiers.

▶ Continue on Lincoln Boulevard and turn right to follow Long Avenue to the end.

7 Fort Point

The only brick fort to be built west of the Mississippi nestles under the girders of the Golden Gate Bridge. It was completed in 1861, to deter incursions into San Francisco Bay, but is now so dwarfed by the bridge that it looks like a pretty futile deterrent. In its day, however, the fort was an impressive building. Rooms off the courtyard are filled with exhibits covering many aspects of U.S. military history, and costumed interpreters are on hand to answer questions.

▶ Return to Lincoln Boulevard and turn right. Continue through the beautiful

tree-filled landscape of the Presidio and make a quick detour to Baker Beach. From here, there are wonderful views of the Golden Gate Bridge and Marin Headlands. Lincoln Boulevard passes through the exclusive residential neighborhood of Seacliff and becomes El Camino del Mar. Follow this through Lincoln Park to the Palace of the Legion of Honor.

8 California Palace of the Legion of Honor

This newly remodeled museum is not only one of the most attractive in the city, it also houses one of the most interesting collections of art, and has the most commanding views, from its location above Land's End in Lincoln Park. The collection was started by Alma Spreckels,

The Cliff House, latest in a line of majestic buildings set on this spot

whose husband Adolph was a sugar magnate. She met Rodin on a visit to Paris and developed a lasting interest in his work, which now forms the core of the collection. Styled after the Palais de la Légion d'Honneur in Paris, the building was donated to the city by the Spreckels family in 1924. The collection has expanded from its original focus of French art and now covers an eclectic range of work, from medieval to contemporary paintings. Included in the collection is the Achenbach Foundation for Graphic Arts, which holds 100,000 prints and 3,000 drawings ranging from Albrecht Dürer to Georgia O'Keeffe.

▶ *Leave the museum down Legion of Honor Drive. Turn right onto Geary Boulevard and, after 39th Avenue, fork right onto Point Lobos Avenue.*

9 The Cliff House
On this far western point of San Francisco, jutting out into the Pacific, the Cliff House sits majestically, overlooking the crashing ocean waves. The original Cliff House was built in 1858, and became a favorite

society restaurant, hosting dinners for no fewer than three U.S. presidents. It was bought in 1881 by philanthropist Adolph Sutro, who laid a railway line to make the restaurant accessible to the ordinary people of San Francisco. A fire destroyed the building in 1894, but Sutro rebuilt it as an eight-story concoction with fancy spires that earned it the name French-Château-on-a-Rock. Next door were the Sutro Baths, a remarkable salt-water bath house that spread over 3 acres (1 hectare). Both the Cliff House and the Baths survived the 1906 earthquake and fire, but the Cliff House burned to the ground the following year. The Sutro Baths survived until yet another fire destroyed them in 1966 – the ruins can still be seen from the latest and considerably less grand incarnation of the Cliff House, which houses two restaurants and a bar, with great views of Seal Rock and its colony of California sea lions.

▶ *Continue down the Great Highway along the coast to Sloat Boulevard.*

10 San Francisco Zoological Gardens
Recent renovation has returned this zoo to its position as one of

the top six in the nation. Most of the cages have been replaced with natural habitat enclosures, using psychological barriers to separate man and beast. The zoo was developed in an area of sand dunes close to the Pacific Ocean and, during the summer, fog can blanket the area, making this a decidedly chilly excursion. Its collection of more than 1,000 animals and birds includes snow leopards, white tigers, pygmy hippos and an excellent gorilla habitat.

The Primate Discovery Center has 16 endangered species of monkey and a nocturnal gallery. Within the zoo is a separate Children's Zoo, where all the animals can be petted and fed.

▶ *Continue south and join Skyline Boulevard, turning off onto John Muir Drive. Drive around Lake Merced, turning north onto Lake Merced Boulevard. Continue around to Sunset Boulevard and drive north through this residential district into Golden Gate Park.*

11 Golden Gate Park
The 1,017 acres (411 hectares) of parkland that stretch all the way across the western half of San Francisco are the work

of 19th-century horticulturalist John McLaren, who turned an expanse of rolling sand dunes into one of the great urban parks of the world. This is a major recreation area for the local population, with a boating lake, a lake for sailing model boats, rhododendron dells, a casting pond for fishermen, and even a buffalo paddock and working windmill.

On weekends, John F. Kennedy Drive, the main road through the park, is closed to vehicles and opened to jugglers, roller-skaters, skateboarders and anyone else who needs open space and an enthusiastic audience. Follow the 49-Mile Drive signs and, after making a circuit of Stowe Lake, you will enter

BACK TO NATURE

The Strybing Arboretum, in Golden Gate Park, is a 70-acre (28-hectare) park within a park, containing more than 6,000 species of bushes and trees. There is a Cape Province Garden with South African plants, a New World Cloud Forest, and imaginative ideas such as a Biblical Garden, where only plants mentioned in the Bible grow. All the plants are labeled, and the avid horticulturalist should find plenty to occupy a long visit.

The Japanese Tea Garden on Stowe Lake, Golden Gate Park

in the West. It is housed in a new building that is on the cutting edge of sustainability, with solar panels, a "living" roof and water reclamation. Inside is a three-story rain forest in a 90-foot (27m) dome, a colony of penguins and a Philippine coral reef. It is the only place in the world with an aquarium, a planetarium and natural history museum all under the one roof.

▶ *Leave Golden Gate Park on Stanyan Street and drive south to Parnassus Street. Turn right and continue to 7th Avenue, then turn left and continue onto Laguna Honda. Follow Laguna Honda past the hospital to Woodside and round to Twin Peaks Boulevard.*

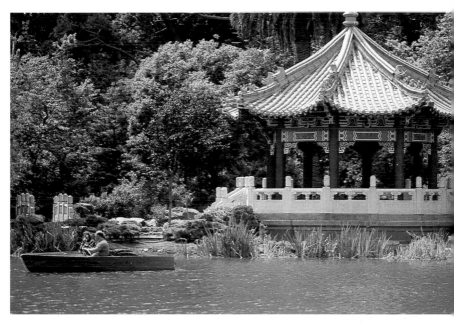

the Music Concourse, where the park's main attractions are based.

The M.H. de Young Memorial Museum reopened in late 2005 after extensive renovation. The building integrates art, architecture and landscape, and houses an eclectic collection, ranging from four centuries of American art to tribal arts from Africa and Oceania.

Next to the de Young is the Japanese Tea Garden, the oldest public Japanese garden in California. It is laid out in traditional style, with curved bridges, ponds, waterfalls, stone lanterns, a Buddhist pagoda and Japanese tea served in the tea house by kimono-clad women.

Across the concourse is the California Academy of Sciences, the oldest scientific institution

🔢 Twin Peaks
The television and radio antennae crowning Twin Peaks, visible from all over the city, are surrounded by a 65-acre (26-hectare) park, and the 910-foot (277m)-high summit gives some of the best views of San Francisco and the Bay Area. The views at night are magical – but this is not the safest place to be in the dark.

San Francisco spreads out beneath the winding road to Twin Peaks

SCENIC ROUTES

This drive is, in itself, one great scenic experience, but the section on Twin Peaks gives particularly fine panoramic views of the whole city and the bridges that link it to Marin County and the East Bay.

▶ *Drive down Twin Peaks Boulevard and turn right on 17th and left on Roosevelt. Continue down to 14th Street and turn right onto Dolores. Drive four blocks to Mission Dolores.*

13 Mission Dolores
Completed in 1791, this was the sixth of the 21 missions to be established by Father Junípero Serra. The adobe walls are 4 feet (1.2m) thick, and the roof timbers are lashed together with rawhide strips. It is so solidly built that the 1906 earthquake had no effect on the building, and it is now the oldest in the city. The price of construction was high: as many as 5,000 native Indians building the mission died from diseases caught from the Europeans. They are buried in a mass grave in the adjoining cemetery. The mission lies in the shadow of the Basilica built next to it in 1913.

▶ *Continue down past the palm trees lining Dolores Street through the edge of the Mission District. Turn left onto Caesar Chavez Street and drive east under the Hwy 101 freeway to Indiana Street. Turn left and drive onto I-280 freeway. Take this to the Brannan Street exit. Brannan Street crosses the revitalized SoMa (South of Market) district, site of the Moscone Center and the Museum of Modern Art.*

Continue along Brannan to the Embarcadero, given a face-lift after the Embarcadero Freeway was demolished following the Loma Prieta earthquake. Follow the Embarcadero round to the Ferry Building.

14 Ferry Building
Neither the 1906, nor the 1989, earthquake could shake this symbol of old San Francisco. It was built in 1903 and the 235-foot (72m)-tall clock tower is a well-loved fixture. The Ferry Building has undergone a complete renovation and is now a mecca for foodies. Specialty food shops and restaurants are complemented by the San Francisco Farmers' Market on Tuesdays, Thursdays and Saturdays. A resurgence in ferry use has occurred in response to impossible commuter traffic, and you can once again travel in style from the San Francisco Ferry Building to the docks in Marin County and Oakland.

15 Embarcadero Center
Directly across from the Ferry Building a series of high, monolithic office buildings dominate the skyline. The Embarcadero Center houses a three-level shopping mall, offices and a couple of major hotels. This is the center of the business district and parking is usually impossible, but the center has an extensive underground parking lot. An observation deck is on the 41st floor of Embarcadero One.

▶ *Continue on the Embarcadero and turn left onto Broadway, and left onto Battery Street. Drive through the historic Jackson Square district (see page 110) and continue to Market Street. Drive down Market Street and turn down Fourth Street.*

The Ferry Building
clock tower

16 Yerba Buena Gardens
This complex includes the magnificent San Francisco Museum of Modern Art, the Center for the Arts at Yerba Buena Gardens, the Sony Metréon Entertainment Complex, and the Museum of Cartoon Art. At the heart of all of this culture is an esplanade of gardens and outdoor public art.

▶ *Return to Market and drive down to McAllister Street. Turn right to the buildings of the Civic Center, including the impressive City Hall.*

17 Asian Art Museum
The old City Library opposite City Hall is now the Asian Art Museum, the collection of the former International Olympic Committee president Avery Brundage. With nearly 12,000 outstanding Asian works of art, spanning 6,000 years, it's the largest in the U.S.

▶ *Take McAllister to Van Ness; turn right then left on Geary Boulevard to Gough Street.*

18 St. Mary's Cathedral
This modern, white marble edifice is a remarkable architectural feat. The enormous roof was built without columns, so that views of San Francisco can be seen from all four sides. Stained-glass windows curve down and reflect on to the 7,000 free-hanging polished aluminum rods of the baldachin. The original cathedral was destroyed by fire in 1962.

▶ *Continue down Geary Boulevard to Webster Street. On the right is an ugly, modern development: the Japanese equivalent of Chinatown.*

19 Japantown
Unfortunately, Japantown has none of the color and atmosphere of its Chinese counterpart. Nihonmachi Mall, on Buchanan Street, is the most pleasant corner. Pass under a *torii* gate to a cobblestone pathway that meanders past fountains: on either side of the path are delightful little shops, selling everything from *shojii* screens to antique kimonos.

▶ *Return to Union Square on Post Street.*

Historic
San Francisco

Although the city is new by European, or even East Coast, standards, a lot has been compressed into a short time. The 1906 earthquake had a major impact on the downtown area, and this walk takes a look at the few buildings of note that withstood it, and the development that followed the devastating fire. Two major ethnic areas, Chinatown and North Beach, are also explored. Some of the route coincides with cable car lines – a fun alternative to walking. Cafés are part of the city's life, and there are plenty along this route.

4 HOURS

i San Francisco Visitor Information
Center, Benjamin Swig Pavilion,
Hallidie Plaza, Market and Powell
streets

▶ *From Market Street walk up
Powell Street for two blocks,
following the cable car line, to
Union Square.*

❶ Union Square

This has long been considered
the center of the city. The grand
St. Francis Hotel overlooks the
square, and the hotel lobby is a
celebrated place for meeting
people. Many of the most prestigious department stores
surround the square, along with
high-fashion boutiques and art
galleries. (The landscaped
square itself attracts a clientele
that is unlikely to be welcomed
in any of the surrounding
outlets.) Overlooking all this
activity is a statue of *Victory* on
top of a 97-foot (29m) granite
column, erected in 1903, that
miraculously withstood the 1906
earthquake. The underground,
multilevel parking lot beneath
the square was the first of its
kind, built in the early 1940s.

▶ *Continue up Powell, across
Sutter Street, which is known
for its exquisite fashion
boutiques, art galleries and
antiques shops, and up a steep
hill to California Street. Turn left
and walk up two more steep
blocks to Huntington Park.*

❷ Nob Hill

Several great hotels sit up here
presiding over the city. This has
always been the best address in
town, and many prominent 19th-
century businessmen lived here.
All but one of their mansions
were destroyed in the 1906
earthquake. The brown,
ominous-looking Flood Mansion
remains, occupied by the exclusive, all-male Pacific Union
Club. The other businessmen
have had their names adopted
by the hotels: Stanford Court,
The Huntington, Mark
Hopkins.

Overlooking the square is
the great, neo-Gothic Grace

Grace Cathedral is a striking landmark among the city's office blocks

Cathedral, the third largest
Episcopal cathedral in the country. Construction was started in
1910, but it was not until 1964
that the cathedral was dedicated.
The main entrance doors are
replicas of the Ghiberti *Doors of
Paradise*, originally cast for the
Cathedral Baptistery in
Florence. Inside, the morning
sun casts a spectacular palette of
color across the cathedral, as it
passes through the many
stained-glass windows. The east
rose window was created from
more than 3,800 pieces of glass.

▶ *Walk down Taylor to
Washington Street, past
expensive apartment blocks.
Turn right onto Washington
Street and left at Mason.*

❸ Cable Car Barn

This building on the corner of
Mason and Washington is the
heart of San Francisco's
legendary cable car system,
housing the main control center.
You can see the actual cables
running at precisely 9.5mph
(15kph) over 14-foot (4m)
pulleys called "sheaves."
There is a good exhibit of old
photographs, drawings and
models, and some of the
original cars built in 1873, by
Andrew Hallidie.

▶ *Continue walking down
Washington Street and turn
right onto Stockton Street.*

❹ Chinatown

Stockton Street is the true heart
of the biggest Chinatown
outside Asia. Walk one block to
Clay Street; on the left corner,
above the main post office, is the

Old St. Mary's Church, built by
Chinese laborers in Chinatown

> SPECIAL TO...
>
> What visit to San Francisco
> would be complete without a
> ride on a cable car? The tour
> follows different cable car lines,
> so hop on and rest your feet
> for a few blocks.

1857 Kong Chow Temple, a
typical example of the mixed-
use buildings in this neighborhood. Continue around the
corner on Clay and enter narrow
Waverly Place, on the left. Half
way down on the left, on the top
floor of No. 125, is the oldest
temple in San Francisco: the
Tien Hou, built in 1852. The
temple is open to the public –
but it's a long flight of stairs.
Continue down Waverly Place,
turn left onto Washington, right
onto Stockton Street and
continue to Columbus. This
section of Chinatown is the most
authentic: most people in the
street are Chinese, English is the

> FOR CHILDREN
>
> At 56 Ross Alley, in the heart of
> Chinatown, the Golden Gate
> Fortune Cookie Factory bakes
> thousands of cookies a day.
> You can watch the cookie
> dough being prepared and the
> fortunes being inserted as they
> go into the cookie-making
> machine that nearly fills the
> tiny bakery.

second language, and the stores
sell all manner of food stuffs
from fresh fish to exotic fruit
and vegetables.

> ▶ At Columbus, turn left and
> walk for two blocks through
> North Beach.

5 North Beach
This is still a distinctly Italian
neighborhood, in spite of
encroachment by Chinatown. In
the 1950s it was the bohemian
center of San Francisco, when
Jack Kerouac and other Beat
Generation poets would congregate in the Italian coffee bars.
Columbus Avenue is the main
street through North Beach, and
coffee bars remain an
important cultural gathering
place. Continue walking to
Washington Square, where old
men sit on benches conversing
in Italian, overlooked by the
twin spires of St. Peter and St.
Paul Church, which took 15
years to build, from 1922. Turn
right on Filbert Street and walk
up to Grant Avenue, then turn
right and walk back toward
Chinatown. Grant Avenue was
the first street in the 1834
Spanish settlement called Yerba
Buena. It was named Dupont
Street until the 1906 earthquake
destroyed it, by which time it
had earned itself such a notorious reputation for debauchery
that the rebuilt version was
named Grant, in an effort to
conceal its scandalous past.
Along this section, Grant is full
of small stores and coffee bars
such as the splendidly Italian
Café Trieste, on the corner of
Vallejo Street.

> ▶ Continue walking down Grant
> and across Broadway to
> Pacific. Turn left on Pacific and
> walk across Montgomery
> Street to the Jackson Square
> district.

6 Jackson Square
Jackson Square is actually a few
blocks of 1850s brick buildings,
saved from the ravaging fires
following the 1906 quake by a
mile-long (1.5km) hose, bringing
water from Fisherman's Wharf.
In 1971, it became the city's first
designated Historic District, and
today the buildings house exclusive antique furniture stores, law
firms and advertising agencies.
To get a feel for the area, walk to
Sansome Street, exploring some
of the narrow alleyways that give
the area its character.

> ▶ Return to Montgomery Street.

7 Financial District
Montgomery Street is the "Wall
Street of the West." This deep
canyon of office and bank buildings extends for several blocks.
At 600 Montgomery is one of
San Francisco's great landmarks:
the Transamerica Pyramid, built
in 1972, with a distinctive 853-
foot (260m) profile that is now as
much part of the city as the
Golden Gate Bridge.

After the offices close this
area tends to be deserted and
offers few attractions for the
visitor.

> FOR HISTORY BUFFS
>
> The Wells Fargo History
> Room, at 420 Montgomery
> Street, traces the story of the
> company that became the
> greatest banking and transport
> company in the West. The rich
> history of Wells Fargo is illus-
> trated with memorabilia,
> including one of the legendary
> stagecoaches often featured in
> western movies.

> ▶ One block past the
> Transamerica Pyramid is
> Commercial Street.

8 Pacific Heritage Museum

The old Bank of Canton building, at 608 Commercial Street, houses the Pacific Heritage Museum, which explores the links between the countries on the Pacific Rim with a series of changing exhibits. This was also the site of the city's first U.S. Branch Mint which, in 1875, was replaced with a new U.S. Subtreasury. The brick walled vault contains an exhibit of coins, bullion bags and other memorabilia, all of which attest to the fortune in gold that started coming down from the Sierra foothills.

▶ *Return to Clay Street, turn left and cross Kearny to Portsmouth Square.*

9 Portsmouth Square

It is difficult to believe that this was once San Francisco's waterfront. Water is no longer in sight, and the square is now a social center for Chinese men who come here to gamble or practice tai chi. Walk up one block to Grant Avenue and turn left. This section of Chinatown caters more to tourists, with stores selling cheap toys from Hong Kong, oriental jewelry and other knick-knacks.

▶ *Follow Grant Avenue to the corner of California Street.*

10 Old St. Mary's Church

At the corner of California Street is Old St. Mary's Church, which has been a Chinatown landmark since 1854. It was built mainly by Chinese laborers, using granite from China and brick from New England that had been shipped around Cape Horn. This was the first Catholic church in the city, which, at the time, served a predominantly Irish population. An inscription on the tower beneath the clock has the message: "Son, observe the time and fly from evil" – which was reputedly directed at the many brothels that stood across the street during the Gold Rush days.

▶ *Continue along Grant, and through the Chinatown Gate. Grant suddenly changes to an upscale shopping street. Continue to Maiden Lane and turn right.*

11 Maiden Lane

This attractive alley was once a notorious collection of bordellos. The earthquake and fire solved that particular problem, and in its present incarnation, designer boutiques sit next to pavement cafés. During the day, Maiden Lane is a pedestrian-only area and makes a welcome relief from the traffic of Chinatown

and Union Square. Look for No. 140, the Circle Gallery, which was designed by Frank Lloyd Wright in 1948, as a prototype of the Guggenheim Museum in New York.

▶ *Turn left on Stockton Street and walk past Union Square down to Market Street. Turn right on Market and walk one block to Hallidie Plaza.*

Soaring between conventional high-rises and traditional San Francisco architecture, the Transamerica Pyramid is an instantly recognizable city feature

Steps of
San Francisco

There's no better way to see San Francisco than to wander up and down the steps of the two most prominent hills, catching spectacular glimpses of the city and bay between the homes and gardens clinging onto steep slopes. There are several places along the way to stop and rest, including many of North Beach's Italian coffee houses. Parking is notoriously difficult, but on Vallejo Street, close to Powell, there is a public garage that almost always has space available, at a moderate cost. Otherwise, public transport and taxis run to the Broadway and Columbus intersection.

2 HOURS

i *San Francisco Visitor Information Center, Benjamin Swig Pavilion, Hallidie Plaza, Market and Powell streets*

▶ *From the public garage, turn left on Vallejo, turn right on Columbus and walk down to Broadway.*

❶ Condor Club

This was the heart of the sleazy adult entertainment center of the city. A small plaque on the wall recognizes it as the first topless (and bottomless) club in America. It is once again a "Gentleman's Club."

▶ *Turn left down Broadway, past the remnants of the sex industry, and turn left again up Kearny Street. These are the first steps: the street seems to rise almost vertically. At Vallejo Street, turn right and descend down flower-strewn steps to Montgomery Street.*

❷ Montgomery Street

This is the "Wall Street of the West" as it passes through the Financial District, but up here it is a hillside vantage point with bird's-eye views of the Bay Bridge through the gaps between buildings, until it becomes too steep to continue. A staircase links the street to its upper section. Look back toward the Financial District for dramatic views of the Transamerica Pyramid.

▶ *Continue until the street divides and take the right fork to Filbert Street.*

❸ Filbert Steps

The Filbert Steps are the most beautiful in the city, descending very steeply past charming cottages, with gardens overflowing with flowers, in a very intimate neighborhood. Breathtaking views over the bay can be enjoyed here.

▶ *The Filbert Steps end at Levi Plaza.*

Above left: Coit Tower

❹ Levi Plaza

A new landscaped office and shopping complex has been developed here by the Levi Strauss Company, of jeans fame, attracting people from the surrounding advertising agencies to relax in the sun and eat their bag lunches. There are several good restaurants close at hand.

▶ *Continue left down Sansome Street to Greenwich Steps.*

❺ Greenwich Steps

All the altitude lost has now to be regained, and the Greenwich Steps climb through charming residential buildings to Coit Tower. At Montgomery Street turn right to reach the pink

Julius Castle, a well-known restaurant.

▶ *Continue up the steps on the left to the tower.*

❻ Coit Tower

This San Francisco landmark was built in 1934, with money bequeathed by Lily Coit to beautify the city. Lily was crazy about firefighters, and the tower is said to represent a fire hose. There are sweeping views of San Francisco Bay from the parking lot, and an elevator goes to the top of the tower for an even

Viewing the city from the restful vantage point of Coolbrith Park, on Russian Hill higher viewpoint. More interesting are the WPA murals on the inside of the tower, part of the 1930s Federal Arts Project, covering nearly 4,000 square feet (370sq m) of wall space.

▶ *Descend Telegraph Hill to the steps on Filbert Street, that start by a tiny green and yellow house at No. 115. Continue down to Washington Square.*

7 Washington Square

Chinatown is steadily encroaching on the old Italian neighborhood of North Beach, but Washington Square and its surroundings manage to hold on to the area's Italian heritage. It is surrounded by coffee shops and Italian restaurants; Mario's Bohemian Cigar Store, on the corner of Union and Columbus, is perhaps the most authentic North Beach coffee house left. Unfortunately, the landscaped square has become a refuge for homeless people (who often appear more threatening than they really are). St. Peter and St. Paul Church, dominating the square, was the first Italian parish church in America.

FOR HISTORY BUFFS

North Beach Museum, at 1435 Stockton Street, on the second floor of the Eureka Bank, documents the history of both North Beach and Chinatown in an exhibit of old photographs. Particularly interesting are the photographs of the bohemian period of North Beach, when the Beat poets made their mark on the world.

▶ *Cross the Square diagonally to Union Street. Continue right on Union and turn left on Taylor. A short way up Taylor, on the right, is a wooden stairway. This is the start of Macondray Lane.*

8 Macondray Lane

Steep wooden steps give way to a cobbled lane that winds past old San Francisco mews-type houses, lovingly and expensively restored. This is one of the most delightful residential areas of the city. Macondray Lane was immortalized as Barbary Lane in Armistead Maupin's "Tales of the City" series.

▶ *At Jones, turn left and left again on Vallejo.*

9 Coolbrith Park

Walk up to tiny Coolbrith Park, which cascades down the hillside. A small, grassy area here accommodates not much more than a dozen sunbathers. Once again, the views over the bay and the Financial District are magnificent.

SPECIAL TO...

Walk along Leavenworth Street to Lombard Street and look up at "The Crookedest Street in the World." This section of Lombard was far too steep for vehicles to climb, so in the 1920s a series of eight extreme hairpin bends was constructed to overcome the 27-degree slope.

▶ *Continue down the steps, past a riot of colorful blooms, and return to the public garage on Vallejo.*

The leafy verges and cobblestones of exclusive Macondray Lane

Wine
Country

2/3 DAYS • 184 MILES • 295KM

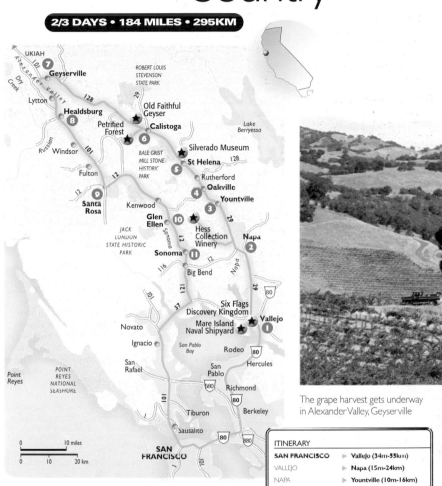

The grape harvest gets underway
in Alexander Valley, Geyserville

Some of the world's greatest wines are produced in two valleys that are just a one-hour drive north of San Francisco. This tour visits the most interesting sites in the Napa and Sonoma wine areas. The elements that help create great wine – the right soil, warm days and cool nights – also create very pleasant countryside.

i San Francisco Visitor Information Center, Benjamin Swig Pavilion, Hallidie Plaza, Market and Powell streets

▷ *Leave San Francisco across the Bay Bridge and take I-80 north. The buildings of UC Berkeley can be seen from the freeway. Continue north on I-80 over the Carquinez toll bridge to the Columbus Parkway exit. Turn west onto Marine World Parkway.*

1 Vallejo

For over 150 years, Vallejo has been synonymous with the Mare Island Naval Shipyard, which was established in 1854. Over the years more than 520 ships have been built here, including USS *Saginaw*, the first U.S. warship in the Pacific, and the 1920 battleship *California*, the largest naval craft built on the West Coast. The Vallejo Naval and Historical Museum, in the old Vallejo City Hall building at 734 Marin Street, has exhibits on the history of Mare Island, with relics, model ships and murals.

FOR CHILDREN

Today, most people go to Vallejo to visit Six Flags Discovery Kingdom, a 160-acre (65-hectare) wildlife park and oceanarium. Killer whales, dolphins, sea lions and tigers are all the stars of their own shows, and a range of interactive attractions includes Butterfly World, a tropical area filled with a dazzling array of free-flying butterflies; Elephant Encounter; and Lorikeet Aviary, where the brightly colored birds sometimes interact rather too closely with the visitors. A clear, underwater tunnel passes through the Shark Experience, giving a fascinatingly intimate view of the world of these denizens of the deep. Eighteen rides have been added to the park, including eight roller coasters.

▷ *Continue west on Marine World Parkway and turn north onto Hwy 29, then Hwy 12, which is followed through sprawling, unattractive development into Napa.*

2 Napa

The town from which this world-famous valley gets its name was not the expected romantic image of the Wine Country (see also pages 120–1). It was a blue-collar town offering little reason to stop here until COPIA: The American Center for Wine, Food & the Arts opened on the banks of the Napa River in 2001. Since then the town has been transformed, attracting exceptional restaurants. The Oxbow Market is the latest addition, with two resort developments close behind.

A century ago, this was a bustling port; the Napa River was the main transportation route to the valley, and river cruises show the town from the best perspective. Close to the river is the historic downtown area, and Main Street has many fine, restored Victorian buildings.

SCENIC ROUTES

To avoid congestion on Highway 29, follow the alternative route along the Silverado Trail, that parallels Highway 29 and passes through some of the most beautiful vineyards in the Napa Valley. It also passes some of the best wineries, such as Stag's Leap, Mumm Napa Valley and Clos du Val. Zinfandel Lane, at the northern end of the Silverado Trail, connects back to Highway 29, just to the south of St. Helena.

▷ *Leave Napa on Trancas Street and drive west across Hwy 29 to Redwood Road. Continue for 8 miles (13km), climbing Mount Veeder to the Hess Collection Winery, one of the more remote wineries in the valley, but well worth the drive, for its location, for the*

collection of contemporary art housed in its multilevel gallery, and for the self-guiding tour of the winery. Drive back down to Hwy 29 and turn north and exit at Yountville. Try to avoid Hwy 29 on weekends, when the traffic can be impossible.

3 Yountville

George Yount, the first white settler in the valley, is buried in the Pioneer Cemetery, off Jackson Street, near the land on which he planted the valley's first vines in the 1850s. Yountville has grown to be an important town with many very fine restaurants, Vintage 1870, a shopping complex housed in an old red-brick winery, and a number of antiques shops. Despite appearances to the contrary, Yountville is a large center and an important source of affordable housing for people working in the valley. Domaine Chandon is the American outpost of the French champagne house Moët et Chandon. It offers one of the best tours, demonstrating the production of sparkling wine; there is also a small museum and one of the area's outstanding restaurants. For a taste of old Napa, visit Trefethen Vineyards, reached via Oak Knoll Avenue, just south of town. The redwood winery was built more than a century ago and sits splendidly in the midst of the vineyards.

SPECIAL TO...

The most peaceful and unusual way to see the Napa Valley is from a hot-air balloon. Several companies offer flights, which generally last for about an hour, and go wherever the wind takes them. They always leave in the very early morning, when the air is cool, and float over the vineyards as the first rays of sun strike the vines.

▷ *Continue north for 3 miles (5km) to Oakville.*

A bird's-eye view of the Napa Valley vineyards, by hot-air balloon

taken by expensive boutiques and galleries. Two blocks west of Main Street, the modern St. Helena Public Library houses the definitive collection of literature of the Napa Valley Wine Library Association, and the Silverado Museum. Robert Louis Stevenson spent his honeymoon in a cabin on Mount St. Helena and lived there during 1880–81. He wrote about the experience in *Silverado Squatters*. The museum has a large collection of over 8,000 items relating to Stevenson's life and first editions of his work.

Just north of town, on the west side of Highway 29, the ornate, Victorian Rhine House of Beringer Vineyards can be seen at the end of an imposing drive. Established in 1876, it is the oldest Napa Valley winery in continuous operation, and the mansion is now on the National Register of Historic Places. Half-hour tours of the winery end with a tasting in the mansion.

A few minutes farther north is the three-story Greystone building, built in 1888 and, until recently, owned by the Christian Brothers. Once a winery, it now houses the West Coast facility for the Culinary Institute of America. Directly across the road is the Charles Krug Winery, built in 1861; tours of the property look at both old and new winemaking techniques.

▶ *Continue north on **Hwy 29** to the sign for the Bale Grist Mill State Historic Park. Dr. Edward Bale, a London surgeon, built a small flour mill on Mill Creek in 1846. The wheel and mill have been restored and can be reached from the parking lot. Continue north to Dunaweal Lane, where a cable car transports visitors up to Coca Cola's Sterling Vineyards. Across the road is one of the newest wineries, Clos Pegase, housing a vast art collection. Continue north on **Hwy 29** to Calistoga.*

4 Oakville

North of Oakville is one of the most celebrated wine-growing areas in California. The soil of the Rutherford Bench produces some of the finest Cabernet Sauvignon grapes in the world and, not surprisingly, some of the greatest wineries are to be found here. Oakville is little more than a cluster of houses, but the Oakville Grocery rivals any big city grocery with its wide range of gourmet produce. Opposite the grocery is arguably the most significant winery in America. Robert Mondavi changed the face of winemaking when he opened it, raising the level of viticulture to new heights. His innovative methods have influenced a generation of wine-producers. In the 1980s, he established a partnership with the late Baron Rothschild, of Mouton Rothschild fame, to produce Opus One, a new breed of premium American wine. The tour of the Mondavi Winery gives one of the best overviews of the state-of-the-art winemaking process in the valley.

Traveling on toward Rutherford, St. Supery offers one of the most educational tours available. Their wines may not be the equal of the finest in the region, but they have a modern winery designed specifically to allow visitors to see and understand the whole production system. The most interesting exhibit is a contraption that reproduces the distinctive "nose" of different varieties of wine.

▶ *Continue along **Hwy 29** to St. Helena.*

5 St. Helena

To many, this is the heart of the Napa Valley. St. Helena is an attractive, small town that has been at the center of the wine business for more than a century. The 1890s look of Main Street is carefully maintained, although some residents are concerned that the small-town stores serving local needs are being over-

6 Calistoga

Although only a few miles north of St. Helena, Calistoga has a much more down-home feel. The town was founded on a thermal stream in 1859 by Sam Brannan, who intended to make it a resort spa. Brannan's cottage still stands on Washington Street, next to the Sharpsteen Museum, and is furnished with period antiques. His dream came true, and Calistoga has become a popular spa destination, with hot springs appearing all over town. If you want a mud bath, a herbal wrap or just a plunge in a mineral pool, someone, somewhere in town will provide exactly what you need.

Just to the northwest of town, on Tubbs Lane, is "Old Faithful of California," one of only a few geysers in the world that erupts at regular intervals. A nominal entrance fee gives access via a run-down group of buildings that shield a piece of wasteland, out of which the 100-foot (30m) jet of water shoots every 40 minutes.

About 5 miles (8km) farther west, at 4100 Petrified Forest Road, a short trail leads through the fossilized remains of the ancient redwoods that have become a California landmark. Volcanic ash from an eruption of Mount St. Helens blanketed the area 3 million years ago, covering all the redwoods. Over the centuries, silica and other minerals from the ash infiltrated the trunks and gradually turned them to stone.

▶ *Return east along Petrified Forest Road and turn north onto* **Hwy 128**.

7 Geyserville

(See also page 156)
The tiny town of Geyserville, in the heart of Sonoma County's Alexander Valley, at the foot of Geyser Peak, is second only to Napa for the quality of grapes. Compared with the Napa towns, though, Geyserville has little interest for visitors. This is a wine-producing area, pure and simple. The striking architecture of Chateau Souverain appears across Highway 101, to the west of town; the winery offers chamber music and jazz concerts during the summer, but little else is offered to entertain visitors other than tours and tastings at the wineries.

▶ *Take* **Hwy 101** *south to Healdsburg.*

8 Healdsburg

(See also pages 149 and 156)
St. Helena must once have been like this. Healdsburg's town center is arranged around a charming, Spanish-style plaza, shaded by palms, redwoods and other trees – perfect for a summer picnic. Friendly little stores provide all you need for a delightful day out in the Wine Country. The extensive Sonoma County Wine Library includes the collection of the Vintners Club Library of San Francisco, and is housed in the new Healdsburg Regional Library at Center and Piper streets. At 221 Matheson Street, the Healdsburg Museum is dedicated to the preservation and exhibition of northern Sonoma County history. Housed in the old Carnegie Library, it has strong collections of Pomo Indian artifacts and every Christmas season there is a popular toy and doll exhibit.

The town stands at the confluence of three major wine areas: Alexander Valley, Dry Creek and Russian River. All three produce distinctly different wines. Over 50 wineries lie within the immediate vicinity of Healdsburg, most of them producing extremely good wines. Deciding which to visit is an enviable dilemma. Clos du Bois is here in town, at 5 Fitch Street, in an uninspiring building; since 1974 their wines have given more than their share of inspiration.

Just north of town, at 16275 Healdsburg Avenue, Simi Winery produces outstanding Cabernet Sauvignon and visitors can get a tour of their state-of-the-art facilities. Pinot Noir lovers should head west to the Russian River area along Westside Road, where Arista and Rochioli produce very drinkable big, soft reds.

▶ *Drive south on* **Hwy 101** *for 14 miles (22km) to Santa Rosa.*

9 Santa Rosa

After a tour through all the small towns of the Wine Country, arriving in Santa Rosa is like reaching the big city: this is the biggest town in Sonoma County, with a population of well over 100,000. As one of the fastest-growing towns in Northern California, it has its share of shopping malls and suburban sprawl, and looks like any ordinary, modern city.

What would have been the historic downtown area was destroyed by the 1906 earthquake, but an area called Railroad Square, west of Highway 101 between 3rd and 5th streets, is part of a restored 1920s shopping district with gift and antiques shops and cafés. One of the more unusual sites in town is the Church of the One Tree, at 492 Sonoma Avenue: a Gothic-style church, complete with 70-foot (21m) steeple, built entirely from a single redwood felled near Guerneville in 1875.

Old Faithful, near Calistoga

Sonoma Plaza, where independence was declared in 1846

The church was immortalized by Robert L. Ripley in his long-running *Believe It or Not!* comic strip, that became an American institution. Ripley hailed from Santa Rosa. Across the street is the Luther Burbank Home and Memorial Gardens.

i *California Welcome Center, 9 Fourth Street, Santa Rosa*

▶ *Take College Avenue to **Hwy 12** east. The urban sprawl of Santa Rosa soon gives way to the hills and wineries of the Sonoma Valley. Kenwood is the first settlement on the road south, and has one of the best restaurants in the area, the Kenwood Restaurant. Continue south on **Hwy 12** for 3 miles (5km) to the exit to Glen Ellen on Arnold Drive.*

🔟 Glen Ellen

Glen Ellen is a quaint little village that grew up around a sawmill built by General Vallejo in the 19th century. A narrow-gauge railroad reached Glen Ellen in 1879, and San Franciscans came to visit the saloons and brothels that opened up around town. One of these visitors was writer Jack London, who decided to stay. His home, Beauty Ranch, is now the Jack London State Historic Park, an 800-acre (323-hectare) park reached from London Ranch Road, right in the center of Glen Ellen. London settled on his Glen Ellen Beauty Ranch permanently in 1909 and the white-frame cottage where he wrote many of his books has been restored, as has the log cabin he built in memory of his days in the Klondike. More interesting are the ruined remains of the Wolf House, which was to be the dream home of London and his wife, Charmian, until it mysteriously burned down, days before they were due to move in. The massive stone walls that remain give a good idea of the original grandeur of the house.

London died at the early age of 40, soon after this disaster. His widow built the House of Happy Walls, now a museum dedicated to London's memory. London is buried close by, under a grove of oak trees.

On the left, returning down London Ranch Road, is Benziger Winery, whose vineyards were established by Julius Wegener. He had received the land as payment from General Vallejo for constructing his home in Sonoma. Mike Benziger came across the estate and persuaded his father, Bruno, a master marketeer, to buy it. The winery soon became the second largest in Sonoma Valley, its Glen Ellen label wines representing good value and establishing an unassailable position in the marketplace. The family have sold the label and now concentrate on their own Benziger wines. The winery offers tram tours of the property and a section of the vineyard has been set aside to demonstrate different viticultural techniques.

▶ *Return along Arnold Drive. Just before **Hwy 12**, turn left on Dunbar Road. A short way down, Shona Gardens, open only by appointment, has an extensive collection of sculpture in stone and metal by members of Zimbabwe's Shona people. Turn south on **Hwy 12** to Sonoma.*

🔟 Sonoma

Sonoma was the birthplace of the California wine industry. Hungarian Count Agoston Haraszthy planted the first experimental vineyards, from which a vast wine industry developed at Buena Vista Winery. Daily tours and tastings are offered, as well as an historical presentation and an art gallery. The other major winery in this town is Sebastiani, which has the world's largest collection of carved wooden wine casks on display.

▶ *Leave Sonoma on **Hwy 12** south; turn west on **Hwy 121** and west again on **Hwy 37**. Take **Hwy 101** south to San Francisco.*

RECOMMENDED TRIP

Nine miles (14km) north of Napa, in the town of Yountville, is a museum dedicated to the culture, art and history of the Napa Valley. The centerpiece of the Napa Valley Museum is a state-of-the-art exhibit – "California Wine: The Science of An Art," with 26 video-disc players, nine micro-computers, 24 monitors and 11 audio speakers. The museum is located at 55 Presidents Circle and is closed on Tuesdays. For information call 700/944–0500.

WINE

When a Stag's Leap Wine Cellars' 1973 Cabernet Sauvignon won first place in a blind tasting in Paris, competing against the finest French wines, California wine had well and truly arrived, 200 years after the first vineyards had been planted.

Spanish missionaries introduced the first grapevines to San Diego in 1769. The vineyards extended northward with the establishment of the missions, but it was not until the Gold Rush that wine-making came into its own. Buena Vista Winery was founded in Sonoma in 1857 by Count Agoston Haraszthy, a Hungarian considered by many to be the father of the California wine industry. Over the next two decades, European immigrants built wineries throughout Napa, Sonoma, Santa Clara and the Central Valley.

The most important element in wine-making is

"terroir," a combination of soil type, climate and elevation. California provides exactly what is needed to produce the finest wine grapes possible, but its early wines were humble table wines, produced by European families who had been drinking these simple accompaniments to their meals for generations. California wine-making never really developed beyond this before 1920.

The industry ground to a halt during the 13 years of prohibition and by 1933, when the law was repealed, it was in complete disarray. Some of the

more enterprising wineries moved into production of communion wine, but many ceased operation completely.

Nevertheless, techniques and vine stocks improved over the ensuing years, to such an extent that, in the early 1970s, California wines could compete with the best in the world.

California wine-makers are now very innovative, and are continually pushing the limits of their skills. New grape varieties are always being tested; the finest wines are still produced from the white Chardonnay grape and red Cabernet Sauvignon, but outstanding wine is produced from virtually every variety of grape available, including Sauvignon

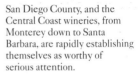

Blanc, Pinot Noir, Chenin Blanc, Riesling, Merlot, Sangiovese and California's very own Zinfandel, which can have a light, almost Beaujolais-like quality, or can be big, alcoholic and chewy, like a massive Rhone wine.

The undisputed center of the California wine country is Napa Valley. In this narrow valley there are 273 wineries, some dating from the 19th century. Every inch of territory is covered in vineyards, producing some of the very best wines in the world. Several of the great French wine producers have acknowledged the exceptional quality of California wines and have established their own wineries in the valley: Moët et Chandon, Tattinger and Mumm all have their own champagne houses

here, and the great Chateau Mouton Rothschild has joined forces with Robert Mondavi to produce Opus One, a Medoc-styled wine made to exacting standards in an amazing modern winery.

Other areas now rival Napa, and Sonoma County, long thought to be a poor relation of Napa, is producing wines that are the equals of their neighbors. The Russian River area, in particular, has exactly the right cool climate to produce exceptional Pinot Noir grapes, and the resulting wines from Dehlinger, Rochioli and Gary Farrell, among others, are difficult to beat.

The Wine Country extends as far south as

San Diego County, and the Central Coast wineries, from Monterey down to Santa Barbara, are rapidly establishing themselves as worthy of serious attention.

Central Valley is the biggest producer of wine grapes in the state. Millions of gallons of wine are produced annually from its enormous supply. The wines are certainly no competition for the great wines of France, or of Northern California, for that matter, but they are enjoyed in copious amounts throughout the world. Ernest and Julio Gallo are the undisputed leaders in the field; their winery looks more like a heavy industrial plant than the romantic image of a rustic building among the vineyards. Fortunately, even the Gallos are moving into the premium wine arena, producing high-quality wines for an increasingly discerning market.

California viniculture benefits from the marriage of scientific experimentation and the gut reaction most great wine-makers have for their craft. Unfortunately, the scientific element has had disastrous ramifications. The University of California at Davis, near Sacramento, has the world's most advanced course in eneology. Academics here developed a new improved root stock for vines, code-named AXR-1, which was widely adopted by the wineries. No one realized that it could not resist the dreaded phylloxera louse that almost destroyed the French wine industry in the 19th century. In Napa Valley alone, hundreds of acres of vines have had to be uprooted and burned, resulting in the loss of thousands of gallons of wine.

Most California wineries encourage visits from the public and have tasting rooms; many also offer winery tours. For any true wine-lover, visiting California is like going to heaven.

Reaping the rewards of a perfect climate: Alexander Valley's harvest

San Francisco Peninsula &
Monterey Bay

From San Francisco south to the lively college town of Santa Cruz, and on around the Monterey Bay to the city of Monterey, this Pacific coast tour passes strawberry and flower fields, lush apple orchards and a spectacular, deserted shore, revealing California's agricultural riches and undeveloped beauty.

2 DAYS • 261 MILES • 420KM

ITINERARY

SAN FRANCISCO	▶	**Half Moon Bay** (30m-48km)
HALF MOON BAY	▶	**Santa Cruz** (51m-82km)
SANTA CRUZ	▶	**Monterey** (43m-69km)
MONTEREY	▶	**Felton** (47m-76km)
FELTON	▶	**Big Basin Redwoods State Park** (15m-24km)
BIG BASIN REDWOODS STATE PARK	▶	**San Francisco** (75m-121km)

A dizzy view of a spectacular route: Highway 1, at Half Moon Bay

i San Francisco Visitor Information Center, Benjamin Swig Pavilion, Hallidie Plaza, Market and Powell streets

▶ *Leave San Francisco on 19th Avenue, which crosses Golden Gate Park, and turn right at Sloat Boulevard. Pass the San Francisco Zoo and turn left onto the Great Highway, which becomes Skyline Boulevard. To the right are the cliffs of Fort Funston, a popular lift-off point for hang-gliders. Continue south to Hwy 1 and pass through Pacifica, one of California's newest towns, established in 1957, and a popular surfing community on the coast. The road becomes a series of breathtaking hairpin bends as it navigates steep cliffs with sweeping views of the ocean opening out around every curve. Take care at Devil's Slide, where the unstable hillsides periodically collapse into the sea, particularly after heavy rain. Continue to Half Moon Bay.*

Left: a dish fit to grace any giant's supper table – a monster Half Moon Bay pumpkin

❶ Half Moon Bay

Halloween is the big event for this small coastal town, when thousands of visitors come to the annual Art and Pumpkin Festival. During the rest of the year the attractions include craft and antiques shops, cafés and bakeries, and several restored 19th-century homes converted into bed-and-breakfast inns, in addition to the miles of rugged coastline and sandy beaches.

▶ *Continue south on Hwy 1 through Pescadero, founded by the Spanish in 1856, and now an artichoke-growing center. Past Pigeon Point Lighthouse, built in 1871 and, at 115 feet (35m), one of the tallest on the West Coast, the shoreline is increasingly deserted. At Año Nuevo State Reserve there is a large elephant seal reserve and an easily accessible beach with millions of fossilized sea shells embedded in the rocks. Just before Santa Cruz, the Natural Bridges State Beach is a good place to witness the migration of thousands of monarch butterflies; nearby, on Delaware Avenue, the Joseph M. Long Marine Laboratory of the University of California has an aquarium, touch-tank and sea lion enclosure.*

BACK TO NATURE

The northern elephant seal was close to extinction in the late 1950s, when the Año Nuevo State Reserve was established. This massive and decidedly ugly marine mammal made a spectacular recovery, and a large breeding colony of more than 3,000 can been seen from December to April at this site 18 miles (29km) north of Santa Cruz. The males, which can weigh up to 3 tons, leave after the pups are born, but at any time of the year there will be females with their offspring, basking in the dunes.

❷ Santa Cruz

Laid-back, counter-cultural values have become the trademark of this college town; in many ways, Santa Cruz today bears similarities to San Francisco's Haight-Ashbury in the 1960s. The presence of the University of California infuses the town with a high proportion of young people hell-bent on partying and surfing – all contributing to its relaxed atmosphere. Last century, this was logging country, but in the early 1900s the town developed into a

The Giant Dipper, Santa Cruz, has been turning stomachs for 70 years

holiday resort, and in 1904 the now famous Boardwalk was built. Along Santa Cruz beach, the Boardwalk is the ultimate seaside entertainment center and the only original boardwalk amusement park still operating on the West Coast, with an antique merry-go-round, a 1924 wooden Giant Dipper roller-coaster that has carried more than 25 million passengers, a Ferris wheel, bumper cars and, of course, arcade games and cotton candy.

Lighthouse Point, at the western end of the bay, is a popular surfing area, and the sea is usually teeming with an army of wet-suited figures hoping to catch a big wave. On the ground floor of the lighthouse is the tiny Surfing Museum, with a collection of old photographs and antique surf boards. Santa Cruz surfers have had their share of shark attacks, and the teeth marks in some of the displays graphically illustrate the ever-present danger.

The university was founded in 1965, and is spectacularly situated on 2,000 acres (809 hectares) of the Cowell Ranch, overlooking Monterey Bay. The Arboretum is particularly interesting for its Mediterranean garden and its outstanding collection of plants from Australia and South Africa. Many of the specimens are the only examples to be found in America.

▶ *Continue south on* **Hwy 1** *through Aptos and Watsonville, surrounded by strawberry fields and orchards, to Moss Landing. Colorful boats fill this weather-beaten little fishing harbor and close by is Elkhorn Slough National Estuarine Research Institute, where 1,400 acres (566 hectares) of salt marsh and tidal flats form one of the few undisturbed coastal wetlands remaining in California, home to more than 150 species of birds, including golden eagles. Continue south, skirting Castroville, the "Artichoke Capital of the World" and passing the cheap motels that line the road at Seaside, into Monterey.*

8 Monterey

Until the middle of the last century, Monterey was the most important town in California. Discovered by Cabrillo in 1542 (but not settled until 1770), it was first the Spanish capital of Alta California; it became the Mexican capital in 1822, and the American capital in 1846. The discovery of gold in 1848 moved interest away from Monterey to San Francisco. Whaling and then fishing became the main industries, until, more recently, tourism took over.

Fishing is still important, and at the Municipal Wharf commercial fishing boats unload their catches of tuna, swordfish, squid, salmon, halibut, cod, shark and anchovy – which are then cleaned, packed, and sent off to market.

Fisherman's Wharf was built in 1846 for ships bringing goods around Cape Horn, and was used by whalers and sardine fishermen before becoming a tourist attraction with shops and fish restaurants. Several boat tours of Monterey Bay leave the wharf and the seals, sea lions and sea otters provide non-stop entertainment. Across from the Wharf is the Custom House, California's oldest public building, erected in 1827. It was here that the American flag was raised for the first time in 1846, by Commodore Sloat. Inside is a display from a cargo ship of the 1830s.

Monterey's other great legacy from the height of the sardine fishing industry is Cannery Row. At its peak, the row housed 16 canneries that packed over 240,000 sardines, but the area went into steep decline after the sardine supplies mysteriously disappeared in 1948, and the fishing canneries closed. Thanks to John Steinbeck's novel *Cannery Row*, the street has seen a dramatic resurgence. It bears little resemblance, now, to the author's depiction, and the old buildings that remain house galleries, cafés and wine-tasting rooms. The highlight of the street is, without doubt, the Monterey Bay Aquarium, one of the largest and finest in the world, where 6,500 forms of marine life fill over 100 display tanks in a series of buildings that aim to capture the atmosphere of the original Cannery Row. There is a three-story mature kelp forest exhibit, a below- and above-water sea otter exhibit and a 90-foot (27m)-long tank replicating life in Monterey Bay. In the latest exhibit, visitors view the 35-foot (10m) tall Outer Bay through the largest window in the world. The "indoor ocean" has more water than all the other aquarium exhibits combined.

RECOMMENDED WALK

The Path of History, through downtown Monterey, includes several good examples of the Monterey style of architecture. Stop at the visitor center at the Custom House, near Fisherman's Wharf, for a map and to pay a single, nominal entrance fee to all the buildings on the walk; these date from as early as 1770, and several were built during the mid-19th century, including California's first theater.

▶ *Return to Santa Cruz and take Hwy 9 north off Hwy 1.*

4 Felton

Up in the Santa Cruz Mountains, just before Felton, is the Roaring Camp and Big Trees Narrow Gauge Railroad, on which an 1880s steam train carries passengers on a 6-mile (10km) trip through redwood groves. In Felton is a covered bridge, dating from 1892, typical of the old California bridges, most of which have long since disappeared.

▶ *Continue north on Hwy 9.*

5 Big Basin Redwoods State Park

Beyond Felton is the Big Basin Redwoods State Park with several stands of 2,000-year-old redwoods in its 17,000 acres (6,880 hectares). The park extends as far as the Pacific Ocean, but its western side is accessible only from Highway 1. This vast area of forest offers genuine wilderness hiking; once off the main road it is difficult to believe that one of the most densely populated areas of California is only a few miles to the east. There is a profusion of campsites and dozens of walking trails.

▶ *Follow Hwy 9 across Skyline Boulevard to Saratoga and continue along Saratoga Avenue to join I-280 north. I-280 passes through Silicon Valley, where many of the world's high-tech company*

FOR CHILDREN

Children love the spooky atmosphere of the Winchester Mystery House, built at San Jose (off I-280) by Sarah Winchester, the eccentric heiress to the Winchester rifle fortune. She believed that she would live as long as the house continued to grow. When she died in 1922 there were 160 rooms covering 6 acres (2.4 hectares). Doors open onto blank walls, stairways lead nowhere, and ghost stories abound.

---

headquarters, including those of Apple, can be seen lining the freeway. From Los Altos the road climbs back to San Francisco, passing through some of the bay's most exclusive residential areas.

Enjoying life at Monterey, above the water at Fisherman's Wharf ...

... and under the water, at the aquarium in Monterey Bay

SCENIC ROUTES

Freeways are not normally the route chosen by anyone looking for great scenery, but I-280 is an exception. Known as the Junipero Serra Freeway, it cuts through the most beautiful part of the peninsula, from San Jose to downtown San Francisco.

THE CENTRAL COAST

Between San Francisco and Los Angeles, California Highway 1 hugs the coast, passing through some of the most dramatic scenery and interesting towns in the state. Fog-shrouded cliffs, crashing surf and wind-blown cypress trees have become symbols of this remarkable shoreline, and this is certainly the best way to drive between the two cities, if time allows. The road is narrow, long and tortuous, but the views are worth it.

Great scenery is not the only reason to visit the area. Several charming towns punctuate the coast, offering a variety of attractions; and perhaps the most intriguing place to visit along the route is Hearst Castle, at San Simeon. The area has also developed a well-earned reputation for its wines. Over the coastal range, the warm inland valleys offer perfect growing conditions for many varieties of grape, producing wines rivaling those of Napa Valley. The inland region lays claim to some of the most fertile soil in the nation, and around Salinas, the birthplace of writer John Steinbeck, fields of vegetables stretch as far as the eye can see.

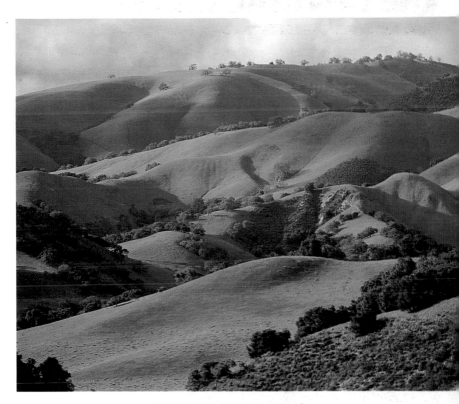

Tour 21

John Steinbeck is most famous for his books about the Monterey Peninsula, particularly Cannery Row. This tour starts in the town of Monterey and heads south through Pebble Beach, Carmel and Point Lobos, through increasingly spectacular coastal scenery to Big Sur. Farther south, at San Simeon, William Randolf Hearst built the most opulent and extravagant residence in California: Hearst Castle, complete with 38 bedrooms, 14 sitting rooms and two libraries. Four different tours are offered by the State Park Service. Continue through the artist's colony of Cambria to San Luis Obispo; from here, the route returns north on the eastern side of the coastal range, passing through regions of vineyards and continuing past several missions built by Father Junípero Serra. Pastoral Carmel Valley leads back to Carmel and Monterey Bay.

Above: the lovely, gentle rolling landscape of Carmel Valley
Left: The jewel in Santa Barbara's crown – the 1929 County Courthouse

Tour 22

The fabulous Getty Villa is the first stop on this drive from Santa Monica along the Pacific Coast Highway. Past Malibu and Ventura, the road winds along the coast to Santa Barbara, one of the most beautiful towns in the country, sitting on a curving, sandy bay with the Santa Ynez Mountains as a backdrop. It then passes over the mountains into the Santa Ynez Valley, and into a world of horses and wine (singer Michael Jackson's Neverland is here), before dropping into Solvang which is as close to Denmark as you can get in America. The return to Santa Barbara takes you through La Purisima Mission State Historic Park, and the colorful flower fields of Lompoc.

The Steinbeck
Loop

3 DAYS • 346 MILES • 557KM

ITINERARY

Monterey Bay and Big Sur are set in one of the world's most dramatic and beautiful coastal areas. Coupled with the extravagant splendor of Hearst Castle at San Simeon, and the missions along "El Camino Real," this tour represents some of the best California has to offer. It begins at Monterey, one of California's first and most successful settlements, where a walking and bike path follows the coastline for 3 miles (5km), passing rocky beaches and rich tidepools.

i Monterey Peninsula Visitor and Convention Bureau, P.O. Box 1770

▶ *Leave Monterey on Ocean Drive and continue past Point Piños Lighthouse and the Del Monte Forest at the Pacific Grove Gate to Pebble Beach.*

BACK TO NATURE

Every October, thousands of orange and black monarch butterflies congregate in a grove of trees at the end of Lighthouse Avenue in Pacific Grove, known as Butterfly City, U.S.A. They come from as far as Alaska and Mexico to spend winter together on the Monterey Peninsula.

❶ Pebble Beach

This private community lies within the Del Monte Forest and the famous 17-Mile Drive passes some of the most photographed seascapes in America. Aside from beaches and Monterey pines, there are six world-class golf courses, two deluxe resorts and palatial residential estates. Wildlife abounds here and sea lions, sea otters, cormorants and a host of other sea birds are everyday sights. Many of the gnarled and wind-sculpted Monterey pines have reached stardom in their own right: most photographed is the Lone Cypress standing alone on a rocky outcrop above pounding surf. The only negative aspect to Pebble Beach is a fairly hefty entrance charge.

▶ *The southern gate at Pebble Beach exits in Carmel.*

❷ Carmel-by-the-Sea

Carmel is usually described as quaint, and with good reason: it is a picture-perfect little town full of art galleries, antiques shops, designer boutiques and tea shops. If anything, it is almost too perfect: the tree-lined streets seem to be out of Disneyland, rather than a real community, and there are bans

Standing firm above the sea: the Lone Cypress, Pebble Beach

on traffic lights, neon signs and hot dog stands. Carmel is, nevertheless, a very popular, if expensive, destination, and having had Clint Eastwood as its mayor has certainly helped its popularity. At the edge of Carmel is Mission San Carlos Borromeo del Rio Carmelo (usually known as Carmel Mission). This extremely well-restored piece of California's Spanish history is the final resting place of its founder, and the architect of the California mission chain, Father Junípero Serra. It is one of the most beautiful of the 21 missions and houses an interesting museum devoted to Serra.

The only other site of note is the Tor House, built by poet Robinson Jeffers with his own hands, from rocks carried up from the beach, and now open for visits. The white sands of Carmel beach below Tor House provide a very pleasant stroll back into town.

▶ *Leave Carmel and turn south on* **Hwy 1**. *After 4 miles (6km) turn right into Point Lobos State Reserve.*

3 Point Lobos State Reserve

This beautiful 1,276-acre (516-hectare) reserve, reputed to be the setting for Robert Louis Stevenson's *Treasure Island*, boasts tall stands of cypress trees, hidden coves, pristine beaches and strange sculpted rocks, redesigned by the crashing waves of the Pacific Ocean.

The area was immortalized by the great photographer Edward Weston and is a shrine to landscape photographers throughout the world. Marine life is abundant here, and the great success story is a thriving colony of sea otters that not too long ago were on the verge of extinction.

▶ *Continue south on* **Hwy 1** *for 20 miles (32km).*

4 Big Sur

This wild section of coastline along Highway 1 is the jewel in the crown of California's coast. Big Sur is the name of a specific village on the coast, but it more generally refers to the stretch of coast between Carmel Highlands and Bixby Bridge. Dramatic cliffs rise from the Pacific Ocean; grassy promontories covered by wildflowers jut out over the surf; towering redwoods rise over coastal streams. Highway 1, the Cabrillo Highway, was carved and blasted out of the western slopes of the Santa Lucia Mountains over 100 years ago and, fortunately, the area has remained

unspoiled. There are a few stores and restaurants, notably Nepenthe, built as a honeymoon cottage by Orson Welles for his wife, Rita Hayworth; and close by is the Henry Miller Memorial Library, where Miller made his home in his later years when he wrote *Plexus* and *Nexus*.

The Julia Pfeiffer Burns State Park is home to the most southerly grove of giant coastal redwoods, along with cascading waterfalls, hiking trails and spectacular views along the coast.

▶ *Continue south on* **Hwy 1** *for 64 miles (103km) to San Simeon.*

5 Hearst Castle

The gilded towers of newspaper magnate William Randolph Hearst's fantastic creation can be seen on a hilltop overlooking San Simeon. After one of the most magnificent natural sights of California comes what must certainly be the most extravagant man-made example.

A rich man's castle – William Randolph Hearst's opulent home

Outpost of an ancient volcanic range – Morro Rock

Hearst, with his architect Julia Morgan, took almost 30 years, from 1919 to 1947, to complete his fantasy castle. With more than 100 rooms, it would cost $400 million to build today. The architecture is an eclectic mix of Italian, French, Moorish and Spanish styles, and the interiors are an equally bizarre mix of antiques from around the world. At one time, wild animals roamed the gardens in what was then the world's largest private zoo. In 1941, Hearst's life was immortalized in the Orson Welles film *Citizen Kane*, and the house was frequented by many Hollywood personalities, including Charlie Chaplin, Greta Garbo and Clark Gable. But the bubble suddenly burst when Hearst died in 1951. Within six years the family had to donate the property to the State of California in return for a $50 million tax write-off. Hearst Castle is now a State Historic Monument, second only to Disneyland in popularity. The property is so vast that four different tours are offered of the house and gardens, and reservations are highly recommended, especially in the summer.

▶ *Continue south on Hwy 1 for 9 miles (14km).*

6 Cambria
Nestled in a valley lined with pine trees, Cambria is an artists' settlement with a somewhat contrived atmosphere, created with half-timbered buildings and many quaint gift shops pandering to tourists. If you can get past the tourist face of the town, there really is a thriving community of artists, and several of the galleries are worth browsing. The best bet, however, is to take a walk on one of the beaches searching for jade pebbles, or to observe the large sea otter colony offshore.

▶ *Continue south on Hwy 1 for 16 miles (25km).*

7 Cayucos
This old fishing town was founded in 1867 by Portuguese fishermen, as a shipping point for dairy and beef products. It is noted for its long fishing wharf and the gentle waters of Estero Bay.

▶ *Continue on Hwy 1 for 6 miles (10km).*

8 Morro Bay
Dominating the view as you drive down Highway 1 is the silhouette of Morro Rock, an enormous volcanic peak marking the westernmost point of a range of nine extinct volcanoes, created 20 million years ago and known as "The Sisters." This 576-foot (175m)-high sentry served as a landmark for Spanish explorers; today it is a protected nesting site for peregrine falcons. Beneath the rock stretches a 5-mile-long (8km) beach, with 85-foot-high (26m) white sand dunes that serve as the habitat for a wealth of bird and plant life. South of town, opposite the entrance to Morro Bay State Park, the Morro Bay State Park Museum of Natural History has displays of some of the life that teems along the shore, including the peregrine falcon and sea otter. An observation deck gives a perfect view of the shore birds of the region. In town, seafood restaurants serve the freshest catch from the boat-filled harbor below Morro Rock.

▶ *Continue on Hwy 1 for 4 miles (6km).*

9 Los Osos
Juan Gaspar de Portola named this area "Valley of the Bears" in 1769 because of the abundance of grizzly bears in the region. The bears are long gone, and it is now safe to follow the hiking trails that meander through Montana de Oro, one of California's loveliest state parks. Take the Los Osos Valley Road west until it turns into Pecho Road, which winds through the heart of this sanctuary.

▶ *Follow Los Osos Road east, then Foothill Boulevard east past the Madonna Inn to San Luis Obispo.*

10 San Luis Obispo
It is difficult not to like San Luis Obispo, a quiet, country town dominated by the agricultural students of California Polytechnic University. Be sure to stop at the Madonna Inn on the drive into town. Mr. Madonna, owner of a road construction business, built the first 12 rooms of the inn in 1958. This has now expanded to 109, and each room has a different theme, such as Jungle Rock or Floral Fantasy: the ultimate in kitsch. The men's room even has a waterfall cascading down for a urinal. If you survive this sensory experience, continue to the more refined atmosphere of

The 18th-century Mission San Luis Obispo de Tolosa

quiet streets lined with Victorian homes that make up the bulk of the town. San Luis Obispo Creek wanders through the central plaza close to the Mission San Luis Obispo de Tolosa, built by Father Junípero Serra in 1772, and unremarkable except for the fact that it is the birthplace of the red roof-tiles that have become synonymous with Spanish mission architecture. Three fires ravaged the mission before the fathers decided to replace the thatched roof with a less flammable material, and settled for tiles made from local clay. These were so successful that by 1784 they had been adopted by all the California missions. Near by is the County Historical Museum.

FOR HISTORY BUFFS

In 1925, at a time when the mass production of cars was changing the nation's travel habits, a hotel at 2223 Monterey Street in San Luis Obispo had its name changed to the Milestone Motel, and became the first "motorists' hotel" – or motel – in the world.

RECOMMENDED WALKS

The historic center of San Luis Obispo is best seen on foot. A walking guide to the town is available from the San Luis Obispo County Visitors Bureau, 1039 Chorro Street, Suite E.

▶ Take **Hwy 101** north inland for 10 miles (16km).

11 Santa Margarita
Vineyards and cattle ranches characterize this area, where horses graze on golden hillsides dotted with ancient California oaks. The whole landscape is typical of central California.

▶ Continue north on **Hwy 101** for 20 miles (32km) to Paso Robles.

12 Paso Robles
Wine-making in this region dates back to 1797 and there are now over 150 wineries, with more than 10,000 acres (4,050 hectares) of vineyards. Most of the wineries have tasting rooms and many offer tours. The town was named after the numerous oak trees that grow here; almond orchards are now as prominent, and during the spring their pink

and white blossoms color the surrounding countryside.

▶ Continue north on **Hwy 101** for 4 miles (6km).

13 San Miguel
Mission San Miguel must be the most easily accessible mission in the state, lying within a few yards of the Highway 101 exit ramp, and one of the more interesting missions in the chain. It was built by Father Fermin Lasuen in 1797, on the lush banks of the Salinas River. Brown-robed Franciscan monks still live here and there has been less restoration than at many of the other missions: the interior is particularly elaborate and well preserved.

▶ Continue north on **Hwy 101** for 11 miles (18km) to Bradley. Turn west on **Hwy G18** and drive for 21 miles (34km) to Jolon. Continue west on **Hwy G18** for another 5 miles (8km), entering Fort

Hunter-Liggett, a U.S. military training base.

14 San Antonio

The most remote mission in the chain, San Antonio de Padua, is incongruously located in the middle of a huge military base. Built by Father Junípero Serra in 1771, it was the third mission in the chain and has, for the most part, been reconstructed. The first attempt at renovation was destroyed in the 1906 earthquake, and the present work dates back to 1948. However, its isolation gives a feel of what the missions must have been like when they were built – in spite of the tanks and heavy artillery that now rumble by, just a little too close. In the spring, the whole area is covered in wildflowers.

▶ *Return on **Hwy G18** to Jolon and turn north onto **Hwy G14** for 18 miles (29km) to King City, then north on **Hwy 101** for 9 miles (14km).*

15 Greenfield

This agricultural town is surrounded by many of the crops common to this part of the state including alfalfa, apples and chili peppers. A brief tour of the area provides a good general introduction to California's farming industry.

▶ *Continue north on **Hwy 101** for 10 miles (16km).*

16 Soledad

The oldest settlement in the Salinas Valley was established in 1791, with the founding of a mission. By the late 19th century, it had become a dairy community, and it is now a major agricultural produce center with a distinctly Mexican feel – due, no doubt, to the high population of Mexican agricultural workers. The mission, which lies to the west of town, is one of the smallest in the chain, and has undergone extensive restoration.

▶ *Return south on **Hwy 101** to the Elm Avenue west exit. Elm Avenue becomes Arrayo Seco Road; continue until reaching Carmel Valley Road, turn right and follow all the way through Carmel Valley to **Hwy 1**.*

17 Carmel Valley

Clint Eastwood owns a ranch in this peaceful valley of green, rolling hills, studded with oak trees. Even when the coast is shrouded in fog, the sun is often shining on the valley; all along it are fruit orchards, nurseries, strawberry fields and even artichoke fields. About 6 miles (10km) past the town of Carmel Valley are the Begonia Gardens, which reach their peak during July and August.

▶ *Continue west along Carmel Valley to join **Hwy 1** by Carmel. Turn north and return to Monterey.*

Tranquil Carmel Mission, the resting place of Father Junípero Serra

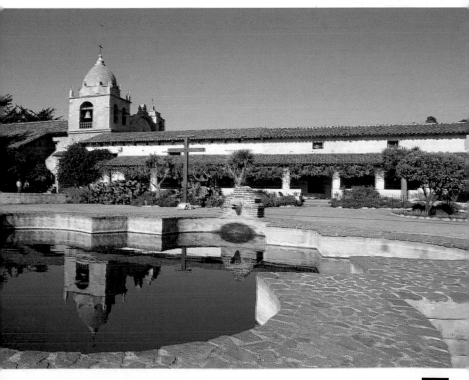

Southern
Central Coast

Some of the most sought-after property in Southern California is included in this tour, from Malibu to Santa Barbara, to the Santa Ynez Valley. The rich and famous tend to gravitate to this area, which is less than two hours' drive north of Los Angeles – and with good reason. The towns are delightful and the climate is perfect; add to this beautiful beaches and rolling hills with vineyards and horse ranches, and the appeal becomes quite obvious.

2 DAYS • 229 MILES • 370KM

ITINERARY		
SANTA MONICA	▶	**The Getty Villa** **(5m-8km)**
THE GETTY VILLA	▶	**Ojai (67m-108km)**
OJAI	▶	**Santa Barbara** **(34m-55km)**
SANTA BARBARA	▶	**Santa Ynez (31m-50km)**
SANTA YNEZ	▶	**Los Olivos (6m-10km)**
LOS OLIVOS	▶	**Solvang (6m-10km)**
SOLVANG	▶	**La Purisima Mission** **(18m-29km)**
LA PURISIMA MISSION	▶	**Lompoc (5m-8km)**
LOMPOC	▶	**Santa Barbara** **(57m-92km)**

i *Santa Monica Convention and Visitors Bureau, 1920 Main Street, Santa Monica*

▶ *Leave Santa Monica on the Pacific Coast Highway, driving along the beautiful coastline past Pacific Palisades to Topanga Canyon Boulevard. High on the right is the world's richest museum.*

❶ The Getty Villa

This extravagant replica of a Roman villa owned by Julius Caesar's father housed one of the world's most priceless collections of art until the new Getty Museum opened at the Getty Center in the Santa Monica Mountains. The Getty Villa will reopen in the near future and will house the antiquity exhibits. The remarkable collection of paintings and drawings, as well as illuminated manuscripts, 19th- and 20th-century American and European photography, furniture and porcelain can now be seen at the Getty Center.

Malibu is the favored address for many Hollywood stars, but is not particularly interesting. After the Getty Museum, the beaches and mountains are the main attraction, and although Malibu State Beach is known as one of the best surfing areas in the state, it is also good scuba-diving country.

FOR HISTORY BUFFS

Mission San Buenaventura was originally built in 1782 as part of Junípero Serra's chain. The building that occupies the original site, on a delightful plaza in Ventura's town center, is a modern restoration, but it contains many relics dating back to the late 18th century. Close by, at 100 East Main Street, the Ventura County Museum of History and Art has outstanding collections of Chumash Indian treasures and an impressive display of artifacts from the Mexican-American war.

▶ *Continue along the Pacific Coast Highway, past several golden beaches. After Mugu Point the road swings inland*

to Oxnard, where strawberry stands are a common sight during the season. Continue through Oxnard; the Pacific Coast Highway joins **Hwy 101**, which continues to Ventura, where the 1782 Mission San Buenaventura sits in the center of town. Leave Ventura on **Hwy 33** and drive north for 15 miles (24km) to Ojai.

❷ Ojai

The Ojai Valley was settled 2,000 years ago by Chumash Indians; its present-day settlers are artists, writers and New Age thinkers, who enjoy the peace and clean, clear air of this small coastal mountain town. The colonnaded main street is filled with art galleries and antiques shops, and less materialistic visitors can seek out the Krishnamurti Foundation or the Krotona Institute of Theosophy. The idyllic valley was used as the location for Shangri-La in the 1937 film *Lost Horizon*.

La Purisima Mission, near Lompoc, rebuilt to its original 1787 design

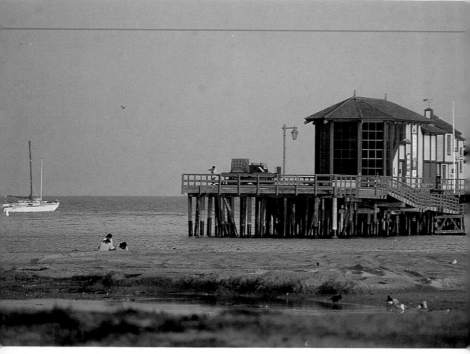

▶ *Leave Ojai on **Hwy 150** and follow it back to the coast to rejoin **Hwy 101**. Turn north and pass Carpintaria State Beach, which has inviting sand and the safest swimming on the coast, thanks to an offshore reef. Continue up to Santa Barbara.*

3 Santa Barbara

Sitting on a curving, sandy bay, with the Santa Ynez Mountains as its backdrop, Santa Barbara is one of the loveliest towns in the nation. Add to this a near perfect climate, and you have the closest an American town gets to paradise. Red-tiled roofs, white-washed buildings and palm trees give the town a strong Mediterranean atmosphere, which hints at its Spanish origins. Santa Barbara Bay was first explored by the Spanish in 1602 and by 1786 the town was a growing Spanish stronghold. The Spanish element is still seen everywhere in the town's architecture and new development is strictly controlled by

building codes that were established in 1925, to maintain the character of the town for future generations. In the same year Santa Barbara was flattened by a massive earthquake, so most of its buildings are no more than 70 years old. The mission remained standing, however, and the grandest established by the Spanish is often called the "Queen of Missions." Founded in 1786, it sits on a knoll high above the town, its design based on the work of 1st-century Roman engineers. There are restored rooms and a museum recording the mission's history and in the adjoining cemetery are the unmarked remains of 4,000 Chumash Indians.

Santa Barbara's oldest buildings are downtown. El Presidio de Santa Barbara State Historic Park, still being excavated and restored, has two of the buildings that were part of the original Spanish fort blessed by Father Junípero Serra in 1782: El Cuartel, the second-oldest surviving building in California,

Stearns Wharf, Santa Barbara, the boundary between town and sea

and La Canedo Adobe. A reconstructed chapel and padre's quarters complete the site.

The grandest building in town is the County Courthouse, built in 1929, in the exaggerated mission-style architecture adopted after the 1925 earthquake. This Spanish-Moorish castle has fine Tunisian tilework, hand-painted frescoes and exceptional murals, making it one of the great public buildings of the West. An elevator goes to the top of the El Mirador Bell Tower, which gives unparalleled views of Santa Barbara and the bay.

The waterfront is separated from town by Highway 101 but Stearns Wharf, the oldest pier on the West Coast, is an extension of Santa Barbara's main street, State Street. It was built in 1872 and has the usual mixture of souvenir shops, restaurants and seafood stands. To the west of the wharf is Santa Barbara Yacht

Harbor and, to the east, Palm Park where a trail of art is spread beneath the palm trees every Sunday for the Santa Barbara Arts and Crafts Show. Joggers, roller-bladers and cyclists fill the space for the rest of the week.

BACK TO NATURE

Go to the end of Santa Barbara's Stearns Wharf to see once-endangered brown pelicans trying to sneak fish from the fishermen. Until 20 years ago, these big marine birds were on the verge of extinction. Control of pesticides rectified the situation, and they are now as common as seagulls.

▶ *Leave town on State Street and drive north for 10 miles (16km) on* **Hwy 154** *over the Santa Ynez Mountains. Turn right on Painted Cave Road, which winds its way to the*

RECOMMENDED WALK

The Red Tile Walking Tour covers 12 blocks of downtown Santa Barbara and includes a dozen or more points of interest, such as the earliest building in town and the Spanish-Mediterranean buildings that replaced losses from the 1925 earthquake. Maps of the tour are available from The Visitors Center, at 1 Santa Barbara Street.

Chumash Painted Cave State Historic Park. A screen covers the entrance to the cave but you can catch a glimpse of brightly colored, 1,000-year-old abstract paintings used in rituals by the Chumash. Return to **Hwy 154** *and continue north across the San Marcos Pass and past Lake Cachuma.*

The exquisitely painted altar of Mission Santa Ines, in Solvang

▶ Continue on **Hwy 154** to Los Olivos.

FOR CHILDREN

The Santa Barbara Zoological Gardens at 500 Ninos Drive, off Cabrillo Beach Boulevard, can be seen in about 30 minutes, but the 700 animals, miniature train ride and petting zoo are beautifully presented and, unlike most zoos, on a scale that children can enjoy.

5 Los Olivos

Once a major stop for Butterfield Stage Lines, Los Olivos attracts visitors today with its restored 19th-century buildings, including Mattei's Tavern, which was the original stagecoach inn. To sample the wines of Santa Ynez visit the Los Olivos Tasting Room at 2905 Grand Avenue for a "one-stop" comparison.

▶ Take Alamo Pintado Road out of Los Olivos and drive south to Solvang.

4 Santa Ynez Valley

Celebrities trying to escape the city head for Santa Ynez. Michael Jackson built his Neverland Ranch here, among the Arabian horse farms and vineyards. In recent years, this valley has become a prime wine-growing region, made famous by the 2004 movie *Sideways*. Charming wineries producing excellent wines are scattered along picturesque country roads that can get

6 Solvang

This Danish Disneyland was built in 1911, complete with windmills, half-timbered houses, thatched roofs and wooden storks. Supposedly, two-thirds of the population of 3,500 are of Danish descent; the shops are

very congested during summer months. The town of Santa Ynez, on Highway 154, at the north end of the valley, is a sleepy community with a white steeple church dating back to 1897. The Valley Historical Society Museum and Parks-Jane Carriageway House have exhibits that illustrate the 19th-century settlement and history of the valley.

Above: Santa Ynez Valley, the perfect anti-dote to city life
Right: children still flock to Hans Christian Andersen, whose bust stands in the Danish community of Solvang

HANS CHRISTIAN ANDERSEN

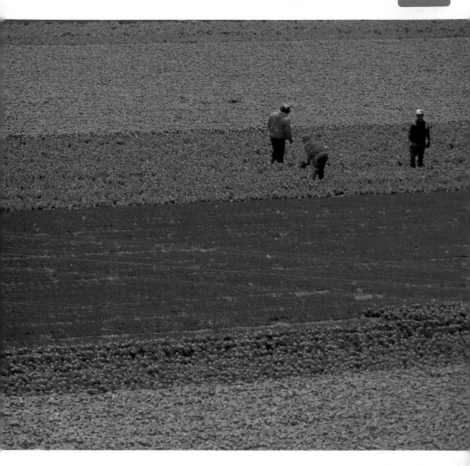

filled with Danish porcelain and brassware, and cafés offer *aebleskivers* (donut-like pastries) and Danish buttermilk pancakes. Despite a slightly phoney feel, as though it were manufactured for tourists, the town was, in fact, established by Danes, when a group of immigrant educators from Minnesota selected the area for a folk school. The Bethania Lutheran Church still holds services in Danish on the first Sunday of every month. Just to the east of the main business district is Mission Santa Ines, built in 1804 and one of the best restored of all the California missions, with a brilliantly painted altar and a colonnaded courtyard filled with flowers. A small museum in the mission building displays bibles and song books.

▶ *Leave Solvang on* **Hwy 246** *and drive through Buellton. Continue for 17 miles (27km) to Mission La Purisima Concepcion.*

7 La Purisima Mission
The original buildings at this mission, which were erected here in 1787, have long since been destroyed. Everything on the present-day site is a reconstruction, but so well executed that there is an impressively authentic atmosphere. Animals graze in the fields, crops are growing in the kitchen garden, tables are set, pans are on the stove and the store's barrels are overflowing with corn and beans. Costumed interpreters contribute to the most informative of the mission visits available in the state.

Lompoc's fields in full bloom, bringing a fiery flash of color to the surrounding countryside

▶ *Take* **Hwy 246** *to* **Hwy 1** *and turn left to Lompoc.*

8 Lompoc
More than half the world's flower seeds are grown in the fields around Lompoc, and for nearly half of every year, from June to September, they are ablaze with color, as thousands of acres of fields are in bloom. A 19-mile (30km) self-guiding tour has been designed to allow visitors to enjoy the spectacle to the full: maps of the Valley Flower Drive are available from the Chamber of Commerce.

▶ *Take* **Hwy 1** *back to Santa Barbara.*

THE FAR NORTH

Any journey north in California soon leaves the big cities and crowded freeways behind. Once past Sacramento, you enter a vast wilderness area, bigger than the state of Ohio, but with a population of little more than 250,000. This region extends from the giant redwood forests on the coast to the volcanic lava fields of remote Modoc County and up to the Oregon border. In between are mountain ranges, active volcanoes, alpine lakes, white-water rivers and dense forests. Mount Shasta, 14,162 feet (4,361m) high, has permanent glaciers; 10,457-foot (3,187m) Mount Lassen still vents steam, and the boiling mud pots at Bumpass Hell rival those at Yellowstone.

One of the great advantages of this region is that it attracts relatively few visitors, even to the national parks. Everything is on an enormous scale; back-country roads lead off into wilderness areas bigger than many counties in other parts of the state. You can drive all day and see only a few cars, which in California is quite exceptional.

This is certainly a place to get away from it all, and any number of outdoor activities are offered, from house-boating on Lake Shasta to mountain-climbing, llama-trekking or gold-panning. The only towns of any size in the region are Eureka, on the coast, and Redding, in the heart of the Shasta Cascade country. Eureka is an interesting, Victorian town; Redding has a good selection of lodging and dining establishments. Both are perfect bases from which to explore the region.

Although there are no real dangers here, the remoteness of the roads demands a reliable vehicle; otherwise, it may be a long wait for someone to drive by and get help. During the winter, sudden snow storms can close roads completely, and care should be taken not to venture into the back country when weather prospects look uncertain.

Tour 23
The so-called "Redwood Empire" extends from San Francisco all the way to the Oregon border. The mighty redwoods, the tallest trees on earth, grow along this coastal region and although they have been decimated by logging, several major forests are still in existence. California Highway 1 continues its spectacular journey up the coast past Muir Woods National Monument, 45 minutes from downtown San Francisco; Point Reyes National Seashore, Bodega, where Alfred Hitchcock filmed *The Birds*, and on to an old Russian fort on the Sonoma coast. Passing through increasingly wild scenery, the road continues to the charming artists' colony of Mendocino, skirts numerous secluded beaches and runs through redwood forests to the perfectly preserved Victorian town of Ferndale. From Eureka, the major town on the north coast, Redwood National Park is a short drive north. The return route, on the inland highway, passes through the vineyards of

Left: Mount Tamalpais, Mill Valley, with San Francisco in the distance

Mendocino County and Alexander Valley on the way back to San Francisco.

Tour 24
North of Redding, California is as wild and challenging as any area in the country. This tour heads north across Lake Shasta, created to generate electricity with the enormous Shasta Dam, the second tallest in the world. The dam can be visited on a short side trip. As the scenery becomes increasingly dramatic, the route passes Castle Crags before the white summit of Mount Shasta comes into view, looming over the highway. To the north are high, wide open spaces and the old gold town of Yreka, which still feels like a frontier settlement. From Yreka the road continues south past the remote Marble Mountains and through the forests of the Trinity Alps. The tour then returns toward Redding, stopping at the restored Chinese Joss House in Weaverville, and continues east from Redding to Lassen Volcanic National Park, rivaling Yellowstone in the variety and drama of its thermal displays. It then proceeds past

Lassen Volcanic National Park's eerie, steaming landscape

Burney Falls to the southern side of Mount Shasta and the old lumber town of McCloud, before returning to Redding, across Lake Shasta.

Tour 25
This tour samples some of the more attractive and accessible areas of California's North Country. Starting in Sacramento, it crosses the agricultural basin of the northern Central Valley and continues to Napa, on the southern fringe of the Wine Country. The old, historic town of Sonoma was the birthplace of the modern wine industry, and from here the tour continues through vineyards to the orchards of Anderson Valley and the Mendocino wineries en route to the coast. The journey reaches its prettiest section from Elk to Mendocino and continues up to Fort Bragg, returning inland past Clear Lake, the largest body of water entirely within California. After passing through the orchards of Capay Valley the tour heads back to Sacramento.

The Redwood
Empire

4 DAYS • 700 MILES • 1,128KM

Redwood forests, rugged cliffs, secluded beaches and old logging communities line this spectacular drive along California's northern coast. Highway 1 is tortuous and the going is slow, but the tour returns more speedily through the vineyards of the warm valleys.

CRESCENT CITY

Redwood National Park

0   20 miles
0   20 km

19 Orick

18 Trinidad

McKinleyville

Arcata
17 Eureka

16 Ft Humboldt State Historic Park
Ferndale
Fortuna
15
Scotia

HUMBOLDT REDWOOD STATE PARK   Weott

14 Avenue of the Giants

Richardson Grove State Park   **13** Garberville

Standish-Hickey State Rec Area   **12** Leggett

Rockport

Westport   Laytonville

Fort **11** Bragg   JACKSON STATE FOREST

Russian Gulch State Park   **10** Mendocino   **20** Willits

Van Damme State Park   **9**

8   Ukiah   **21**

Manchester

Point Arena   **22**

Gualala   Hopland

7   Lake Sonoma   Cloverdale

Salt Point State Park   **6**   Plantation   **23** Healdsburg

Fort Ross State Historic Park   **5**   **24**   Santa Rosa
Jenner
Bodega   **4**

POINT REYES NATIONAL SEASHORE   **3**   Olema   Petaluma

Novato

Stinson Beach   San Rafael

2
1
Muir Woods National Monument

SAN FRANCISCO

ITINERARY		
SAN FRANCISCO	▶	Muir Woods (13m-21km)
MUIR WOODS	▶	**Stinson Beach (5m-8km)**
STINSON BEACH	▶	**Point Reyes National Seashore** (14m-22km)
POINT REYES NATIONAL SEASHORE		
BODEGA	▶	Bodega (35m-56km)
	▶	**Fort Ross State Historic Park** (19m-30km)
FORT ROSS STATE HISTORIC PARK	▶	**Salt Point State Park** (10m-16km)
SALT POINT STATE PARK	▶	**Gualala (20m-32km)**
GUALALA	▶	**Point Arena** (18m-29km)
POINT ARENA	▶	**Van Damme State Park** (31m-50km)
VAN DAMME STATE PARK	▶	**Mendocino (3m-5km)**
MENDOCINO	▶	**Fort Bragg** (11m-17km)
FORT BRAGG	▶	**Leggett (45m-76km)**
LEGGETT	▶	**Garberville** (25m-40km)
GARBERVILLE	▶	**Avenue of the Giants** (13m-21km)
AVENUE OF THE GIANTS	▶	**Scotia** (29m-47km)
SCOTIA	▶	**Ferndale** (18m-29km)
FERNDALE	▶	**Eureka** (20m-32km)
EUREKA	▶	**Trinidad** (25m-40km)
TRINIDAD	▶	**Orick** (21m-34km)
ORICK	▶	**Willits** (184m-296km)
WILLITS	▶	**Ukiah** (24m-39km)
UKIAH	▶	**Hopland** (14m-22km)
HOPLAND	▶	**Cloverdale** (16m-26km)
CLOVERDALE	▶	**Healdsburg** (18m-29km)
HEALDSBURG	▶	**San Francisco** (69m-111km)

i Redwood Empire Association,
2 Beach Street, San Francisco

▶ From San Francisco, drive north
across the Golden Gate Bridge
on Hwy 101. Exit onto Hwy 1
at Mill Valley, continue along
Hwy 1 to Muir Beach and
follow the signs to Muir
Woods.

1 Muir Woods

Sequoia sempervirens, the ancient
coastal redwoods, can grow to
more than 360 feet (110m) and
live for 2,000 years, and they are
found only along a narrow coastal
strip of California, between
Monterey and the northern
border. The trees in Muir Woods
are the closest to San Francisco,
only a 15 minute journey from
downtown hotels. This ease of
accessibility generates more traffic than at the more northerly
redwood groves, but seeing the
trees with people is better than
not seeing them at all.

The 502-acre (203-hectare)
National Monument was named
for naturalist John Muir, and six
of the 27 miles (43km) of trails
are on a level stretch of the forest
floor, making this one of the
most accessible redwood groves.

▶ Return to Hwy 1 and continue
north for 5 miles (8km) to
Stinson Beach.

2 Stinson Beach

Stinson Beach is the name both
of a small town, with a distinctive arty feel, and of the finest
stretch of sand on the North
Coast. The 4,500-foot-long
(1,372m) beach is one of the
few in the area that are safe for
swimming, and the water is
warmed by the shoal of Bolinas
Bay. The beach is part of the
Golden Gate National
Recreation Area and during the
summer it is so popular with San
Franciscans looking for an easy
weekend escape that it can be
impossible to park. If swimming
doesn't appeal, the fishing is
very good, and there are numerous nearby hikes on Mount
Tamalpais rising above the town.

Audubon Canyon Ranch
overlooks the Bolinas Lagoon,
just north of Stinson Beach. This
1,000-acre (304-hectare) bird
sanctuary in the redwoods is
home to nesting egrets and great
blue herons from March to July
each year. There is also a small
museum dedicated to the
wildlife of the area.

▶ Continue north along Hwy 1
for 12 miles (19km) to
Olema. Turn left on Bear Valley
Road to Point Reyes Visitor
Center.

3 Point Reyes National
Seashore

Point Reyes is separated from
the mainland by the San
Andreas fault. Geologically, it
sits on the Pacific plate, and
during the 1906 earthquake the
Point Reyes Peninsula moved
20 feet (6m) northward. The
epicenter of that earthquake was
at Olema, close to the park, and
an earthquake trail and exhibit is
based in Bear Valley, near the
main visitor center. The
windswept peninsula covers
more than 66,000 acres (26,710
hectares) with some 100 miles
(160km) of trails and a 100-mile-

Sharks and whales share the waters
of Point Reyes National Seashore

long coastline. It is the foggiest and windiest spot between Mexico and Canada, so warm clothes are always advisable. This is a good location for watching whales migrate from Alaska to Mexico, and some historians claim that it was here that Sir Francis Drake first landed in the *Golden Hinde* in 1579, at what is now called Drake's Bay.

Tomales Bay, formed by the San Andreas Fault, separates the Point Reyes Peninsula from the mainland. The 13-mile-long (21km) stretch of water is a breeding ground for great white sharks and swimming is discouraged – but there are excellent fishing and bird-watching opportunities. Inverness, on the south side of the bay, has several small stores, galleries and restaurants along its single street overlooking the

Russian fur traders once occupied wooden Fort Ross, now rebuilt

water. The town of Point Reyes Station is the agricultural center of West Marin and has a thriving arts and crafts community.

▶ *Continue north for 32 miles (51km) on **Hwy 1** through Tomales to Bodega Bay.*

4 Bodega
This tiny village is a short distance from the coast where Alfred Hitchcock made his film *The Birds*. The old schoolhouse still looks as it did in his day and next door stands the picturesque village church. Bodega Bay, on the coast, was discovered by the Spanish in 1775 and developed into an important fishing harbor. Fishing still plays a significant part in the economy, though sport fishing for salmon has now overtaken the commercial business.

▶ *Continue north on **Hwy 1** for 20 miles (32km) to Fort Ross.*

5 Fort Ross State Historic Park
The wooden buildings of Fort Ross can be spotted from the tortuous bends of Highway 1. During the 19th century this was the North American outpost for Russian fur traders; the Russians arrived in 1812 and over the next 30 years decimated the sea otter population almost to the point of extinction. The fort was devastated by fire and earthquakes but has been painstakingly restored to its original appearance. A recorded audio tour directs visitors around the buildings, which include a tiny Orthodox chapel and are furnished with displays of contemporary artifacts.

SCENIC ROUTES

From Jenner, at the mouth of the Russian River, Highway 1 climbs spectacularly to follow the coast, high above steep cliffs and crashing waves, as it winds up past Fort Ross to Salt Point. All along this section of road are sweeping views of the rugged coastline.

▶ *Continue north on Hwy 1 for 10 miles (16km) to Salt Point.*

6 Salt Point State Park
Waves crash over weird sandstone formations here, and batter clumps of sea palms, creating the impression of a miniature tropical island in a hurricane. An underwater park, rich with abalone, attracts scuba divers, and there is a pygmy pine forest. A short distance inland, the Krause Rhododendron State Reserve is at its spectacular peak between April and June.

Just north of Salt Point, with an equally beautiful coastline, is an extensive private development named Sea Ranch. Many architectural awards have been won by the houses built here, to a design that ensures minimum impact upon the environment. Some houses are available for

Colorful shopfronts brighten the pretty town of Point Arena

short rentals, and there is also a lodge and restaurant. Six marked trails lead to the seashore: the Black Point Trail is the most dramatic.

▶ *Leave Sea Ranch; Gualala is immediately to the north on Hwy I.*

7 Gualala
The Gualala River was a favorite fishing haunt of Jack London, who used to cast for steelhead here. This former lumber town still retains much of its turn-of-the-century character but, apart from an attractive stretch of coastline, there is little to occupy your time here. A few art galleries include one devoted exclusively to fine photography, and there are two interesting hotels: the Gualala Hotel, built in 1903, and, just outside town, St. Orres, whose onion domes reflect the Russian influence in the area.

▶ *Continue north on Hwy I for 14 miles (22km) to Point Arena.*

8 Point Arena
Point Arena is typical of the small towns that extend up the Mendocino coast, one of the prettiest in the state. It was originally a logging community, but little happens here now, and this is principally a pleasant rest stop en route to the north. A pier and boat launching facility serve both commercial and sports fishermen. Point Arena Lighthouse was first built in 1870, but the present 115-foot-tall (35m) structure was built in 1908, after the original was badly damaged in the 1906 earthquake. It was the first steel reinforced concrete lighthouse in America. Both the lighthouse and its museum are well worth a tour.

▶ *Drive north on Hwy I for 34 miles (55km) to Little River.*

9 Van Damme State Park
Dozens of little coastal parks dot the highway, and this park is typical. Located on the scenic Little River, it offers campsites, safe but cold swimming, hiking trails and skin-diving. Close by is a forest of dwarf conifers. Hard soil prevents deep root systems and poor drainage adds to the

problem, resulting in trees only a foot (30cm) high that elsewhere reach a height of 50 feet (15m).

▶ *Continue for 3 miles (5km) on Hwy I to Mendocino.*

10 Mendocino
(See also page 156)
If there is time to visit only one town on the north coast, this should be the one. In many ways, it is not typical: a cluster of wooden Gothic houses cling together on a bluff overlooking the Pacific Ocean, resembling a New England fishing village more than a Californian town. In fact, the entire village was established by New England loggers in the mid-19th century, and is now on the National Register of Historic Places. In recent years it has been the location for many films and television shows, including the television series *Murder She Wrote* – supposedly set on Cape Cod.

Mendocino has become an important artists' colony, and the village is bursting with art galleries, including the highly respected Mendocino Art Center. Kelley House Historical Museum and Library features changing exhibits in a restored 1861 residence, and is the best place to learn about the history of Mendocino (it also acts as an unofficial tourist center). Across the road, the Ford House has displays on the history of the logging industry and a model miniature village of Mendocino as it looked in 1890.

RECOMMENDED WALKS

The only satisfactory way to see Mendocino is on foot, and the visitor center at the Kelley House has maps of a suggested walking tour through this immaculate town.

▷ *Continue on **Hwy 1** for 10 miles (16km) to Fort Bragg.*

Harbor seals take time to bask along the shore near Mendocino

❶❶ Fort Bragg

(See also page 156)
This 100-year-old seaport retains its commercial atmosphere, with lumber mills and freight yards marring the otherwise scenic setting. At the south end of town is Noyo Harbor, where there is a thriving commercial fishing fleet and charter boats are available for sport fishing. The ornate Guest House Museum was built in 1892 to house visitors to the reigning lumber company. It now houses exhibits that illustrate the area's logging, shipping and general history. Fort Bragg's highlight is the 19-acre (8-hectare) Mendocino Botanical Gardens, where magnificent blooms cover the bluffs.

▷ *Continue north on **Hwy 1** to Rockport where the road turns inland to become **Hwy 101** (Redwood Highway). After 46 miles (74km), enter Leggett.*

FOR CHILDREN

Fort Bragg is the headquarters of the Western Railroad Skunk Trains. Laid in 1885 as a logging railroad, the Skunk Line now offers scenic excursions to the town of Willits. Trains originally ran on gas, giving rise to the comment: "You can smell 'em before you can see 'em," and the line's name.

❶❷ Leggett

Leggett marks the official start of journeys through the forests of coastal redwoods. A short distance north of the town is a drive-through tree, set in a private grove: its tunnel, quite big enough for a car, was formed when the tree was damaged by fire. A little farther north is the Standish Hickey State Recreation Area, which has ample camping space available

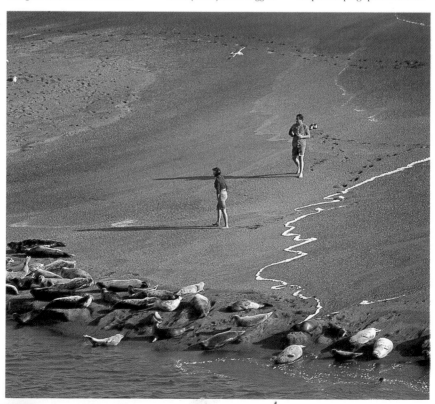

but only one mature redwood in its dense forest. A better bet is the Smithe Redwoods State Preserve, where you can hike to a waterfall or take a footpath down to the Eel River.

i Leggett Valley Chamber of Commerce Tourist Information Center, Highway 1, PO Box 218, Leggett

▶ Continue north on **Hwy 101** to Garberville.

13 Garberville
This southern gateway to Humboldt County gained notoriety for its prominence in marijuana cultivation. At one time, the economy of the town was said to revolve around this lucrative cash crop, and there is still a distinct flavor of the 1960s in the bars and cafés in town.

▶ Continue north on **Hwy 101** to Phillipsville and turn onto **Hwy 254**.

14 Avenue of the Giants
A 33-mile (53km) stretch of road running through Humboldt Redwoods State Park is home to 60 percent of the tallest trees in the world. The road winds along beneath these giants, along the banks of the Eel River, and passes a number of redwood attractions, including the Shrine Drive-Thru Tree, One Log House, Chimney Tree, Immortal Tree and Eternal Tree House.

▶ Rejoin **Hwy 101** and continue north for 3 miles (5km) to Scotia.

15 Scotia
Owned and operated by the Pacific Lumber Company since the late 1880s, Scotia is one of the few company towns left in the United States. Don't miss the self-guiding walking tour through the world's largest redwood lumber mill, for an in-depth look at the logging industry.

▶ Continue north on **Hwy 101** for 16 miles (26km) and

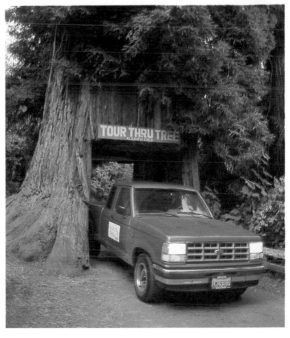

turn west at Fernbridge. Cross the Eel River to reach Ferndale after a further 4 miles (6km).

16 Ferndale
The entire town of Ferndale has been designated as a State Historic Landmark and a National Register Historic District. Visitors can step back 100 years and take a horse-drawn carriage ride down the main street, which has remained largely untouched since the 1890s. This is perhaps the best

> SPECIAL TO...
>
> One of the state's most unusual events takes place in Ferndale every May. The annual World Champion Kinetic Sculpture Race attracts all manner of bizarre human-powered vehicles that speed over land and water to gain the crown. Recent examples of the competing vehicles are displayed in Ferndale's museum on Main Street.

A truck negotiates the "trunk road" through the Drive-Thru Tree

and most complete example of California's Victorian era in existence. In spite of earthquakes and natural disasters, Ferndale has remained surprisingly intact and authentic.

▶ Return to **Hwy 101** and continue north for 18 miles (29km) to Eureka.

17 Eureka
Eureka has more Victorian buildings than any other incorporated city in California: more than 10,000, each one with more ornate detail than the next. The Carson Mansion is the best example of this "gingerbread" style of architecture, and as such is reputed to be the most photographed Victorian house in the world. It is certainly extremely striking, located in a commanding position on 2nd and M streets. Built by pioneer lumber baron William Carson between 1884 and 1886, years of depression for the lumber industry, the mansion was effectively a

625-acre (253-hectare) park set on a headland covered by forests and meadows, with beaches, sea stacks and a rim trail that is particularly beautiful at sunset.

▶ *Continue north on Hwy 101 to Orick.*

🔟 Orick

Orick is the gateway to the Redwood National Park. The main road through this tiny town is lined with souvenir shops selling bears, windmills, deer, totem poles, furniture, clocks and more – all made out of redwood.

The park itself encompasses 106,000 acres (42,898 hectares), with 8 miles (13km) of coastal roads and more than 100 miles (160km) of trails. A taste of the park can obtained by traveling a few miles north of Orick, and a shuttle departs from the information center in town to take visitors to the Tall Trees Grove, where the world's tallest known tree measures 367.8 feet (112m).

▶ *Return south on Hwy 101 for 182 miles (293km) to Willits.*

Gingerbread architecture at its best: the Carson Mansion, Eureka

job creation scheme, financed by Carson specifically in order to avoid laying off his best workmen. Today, the Carson Mansion houses a private club.

Samoa lies just across the Humboldt Bay, via Highway 255 and the Humboldt Bridge; the primary attraction here is the last operating lumbercamp-style cookhouse in the West. The Samoa Cookhouse first started serving mill workers in 1893, and today visitors can dine at the long communal tables and experience the world of the lumberjack. In the restaurant's museum and dining room are early culinary items, as well as various historical mementos from the early years of the lumber and logging industries.

▶ *Continue north on Hwy 255 to join Hwy 101 at Arcata. Turn north on Hwy 101 for 15 miles (24km) to Trinidad.*

🔟 Trinidad

Trinidad fishing village is one of the oldest settlements on the North Coast. Its site was discovered by a Portuguese navigator in 1595; the present town, which dates from 1850, sits on a bluff overlooking the ocean. Trails lead down to beautiful, rocky beaches, the pier is still a working commercial fishing dock, and a working replica of the original 1870 lighthouse warns vessels of the rocky coast. A marine lab aquarium operated by Humboldt State University provides an introduction to the sea life of this part of the coast.

Patrick's Point State Park, just to the north of Trinidad, is a

---

BACK TO NATURE

In the early 1920s, there were no more than 100 Roosevelt Elk in the Orick area, and practically none elsewhere in California. A refuge was established in 1948, at Prairie Creek State Park, and today it is estimated that the population has grown to exceed 2,000. Every November, gray whales begin their 4,000-mile migration from Alaska to Mexico, swimming along the California coast. The migration continues until early February, when they return with their calves to Alaska. The northern coast of California juts out into the Pacific farther than any other point in the continental United States, making this the best area for whale-watching. The whales usually swim closer to the coast on their way down, so November to February are the best months for sightings.

20 Willits
This small lumber town, the eastern terminus of the Skunk Train (see pages 146 and 157), has seen better days. Closure of several businesses hit the economy hard, but Willits is still a pleasant community. Near the station is the Mendocino County Museum, full of pioneer period artifacts and Indian basketry.

▶ *Continue south on Hwy 101 for 22 miles (35km) to Ukiah.*

21 Ukiah
Ukiah has been the seat of Mendocino County since 1859, when the population of the Russian River Valley was little more than 100. Near town, on Vichy Springs Road, naturally carbonated water comes bubbling out of the ground at 90°F (32°C) to fill 130-year-old outdoor tubs and an Olympic-sized swimming pool. Jack London, Teddy Roosevelt, Robert Louis Stevenson and Mark Twain all bathed here. In town, the Sun House is an excellent example of "California Craftsman" redwood architecture, and the adjoining Grace Hudson Museum houses Pomo Indian artifacts.

▶ *i Greater Ukiah Chamber of Commerce, 200 South School Street, Ukiah*

▶ *Continue south on Hwy 101 for 14 miles (22km) to Hopland.*

22 Hopland
It would be easy to drive straight past Hopland without noticing it at all, but there are good reasons to stop, such as the Solar Living Institute, where you can study the latest developments in sustainable living. On the main road is the Hopland Brewery Brewpub and Beer Garden, which opened in 1983 as the first brewpub in California since Prohibition.

Hopland is home to the winery giant Fetzer now owned by a massive conglomerate that closed the public facilities. However there are ten family-owned wineries in town, including Jeriko, owned by Danny Fetzer, and for relaxation after a hard days wine tasting, Brutocao Cellers have a championship bocce ball court.

▶ *Continue south on Hwy 101 for 16 miles (26km) to Cloverdale.*

23 Cloverdale
(See also page 156)
At one time, this was the northernmost citrus-growing area in California. Now it is the center of an emerging grape-growing industry, and just south of town is the Asti Winery. A citrus fair is held in Cloverdale every February.

▶ *Continue south on Hwy 101 for 16 miles (26km) to Healdsburg.*

24 Healdsburg
(See also pages 118 and 156)
This appealing town, built around a traditional square, is the center of one of California's premium wine-growing areas. Its setting, in the Alexander Valley, on the edge of both Dry Creek and the Russian River regions, makes it a wine-lover's dream. The downtown plaza has a small museum and the Sonoma County Wine Library – but the 50 wineries within 15 minutes of town really steal the show.

▶ *Return to San Francisco, 64 miles (103km) south on Hwy 101.*

Trinidad's replica 1870 lighthouse

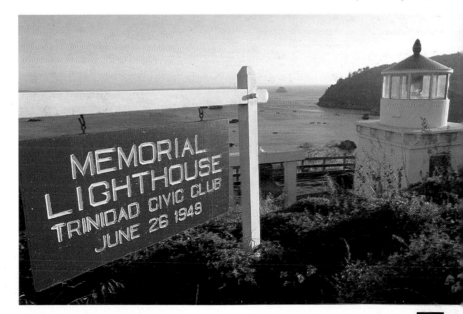

Shasta
Cascade

3 DAYS • 453 MILES • 729KM   Redding, the starting point of this tour (a five-hour drive north of San Francisco), is the gateway to the Far North, a wild region where old Gold Rush towns cling to the slopes of Mount Shasta and the remote Trinity Alps, and weird volcanic landscapes still bubble and steam – between eruptions.

ITINERARY

ⓘ *Redding Chamber of Commerce,*
777 Auditorium Drive

▶ *From Redding, drive north to*
Lake Shasta.

FOR HISTORY BUFFS

A few miles west of Redding is
the old gold-mining town of
Shasta. In the 1850s, it was the
pride of the region, producing
$100,000 of gold dust a week.
Now it is a ghost town, with
only a few buildings remaining,
including the courthouse, the
jail and a refurbished general
store. The ruins now form
Shasta State Historic Park.

❶ Lake Shasta

The highway crosses this huge
lake, whose 370-mile-long
(595km) shoreline and 30,000-
acre (12,141-hectare) expanse
make it the largest man-made
lake in the state. The dam that
created it is the second biggest
in the world – three times taller
than Niagara Falls – and can be
reached on Highway 151,
5 miles (8km) west of I-5. At the
visitor center, a film describes
the construction of the dam,
which diverts three rivers to irri-
gate Central Valley's agricultural
land. I-5 crosses the Pit River
Bridge, the world's biggest
double-decked bridge, which
carries a railroad track in addition
to the highway.

Lake Shasta is a mecca for
water sports enthusiasts and a
popular destination for houseboat holidays. For landlubbers
there is a boat trip across from
O'Brien, on the eastern side of
the lake, to the Shasta Caverns,
which feature interesting stalactite and stalagmite formations in
the limestone caves. After the
boat trip, there is a bus ride 800
feet (244m) above the lake to
the cavern's entrance.

▶ *Continue north on I-5.*

Left: boating on Lake Shasta
Above right: the Castle Crags,
created in the age of glaciers

❷ Castle Crags State Park

After 25 miles (40km), the
forested mountainsides give way
to a group of 2,000–6,000-foot-
high (609–1,829m) glacier-
polished crags towering over the
Sacramento River. The Castle
Crags were formed 225 million
years ago, when they were
forced up through a blanket of
serpentine and glacial debris;
they are the oldest rocks in the
area, considerably older than the
relatively recent volcanic
creation of Mount Shasta.

▶ *Continue north on I-5.*

❸ Dunsmuir

At the old railroad town of
Dunsmuir, 19th-century steam
locomotives and rolling stock
have been converted into motel
units at the Railroad Park
Resort.

▶ *As I-5 continues north, mighty*
Mount Shasta looms into view,
dominating the landscape.

❹ Mount Shasta

The tiny town of Mount Shasta
sits at the foot of its giant name-
sake. Only 3,000 inhabit this
outdoor pursuits center, which is
also home to a fish hatchery that,
until 1979, was the biggest in the
world. The Mount Shasta State
Fish Hatchery and Sisson
Museum was built in 1888, on a
site chosen for its proximity to
fresh water and the railroad; the
old hatchery is now a museum
with extensive displays on the
geology and human history of

the Mount Shasta region.
Behind the museum, a new
hatchery produces 5 to 10
million trout a year to stock the
streams and lakes of California.
Mount Shasta's 14,162-foot
(4,316m) peak is only the sixth
highest in the state, but it is
certainly the most impressive,
and can be seen towering over
the landscape from 100 miles
(160km) away. Five glaciers
creep down the mountains, and
at the summit are bubbling hot
springs where, according to
Indian legend, the Great Spirit
dwells. The mountain is popular
with both mountaineers and the
more spiritually inclined, who
believe in the mystic powers of
the peak. About 7,000 climbers
attempt to reach the summit
every year – but only about half
of them make it to the top.
Shasta was a favorite mountain
of John Muir, who founded the
Sierra Club, and first climbed it
in 1874.

SCENIC ROUTES

For a closer look at Mount
Shasta, take route A10, off I-5,
at Mount Shasta town.
The road winds up to 6,800
feet (2,073m) and gives a different perspective of the
mountain at every turn.

▶ *Continue north on I-5, past*
Weed, through high, wild, open
landscapes with very sparse
habitation.

5 Yreka

Yreka is a surprisingly big town for such a remote area, founded in 1857 soon after the discovery of gold in the area, and given the Indian name for Mount Shasta. Wild West lawlessness, internecine Chinese wars and a fire in 1871 were not enough to destroy the town, and many 1850s buildings have been restored. If the traffic disappeared, Miner Street, in the center of town, would look little different now from 100 years ago. Several Victorian homes have also been restored and are preserved in a nationally registered Historic District; some operate as bed-and-breakfast inns.

exhibit of restored buildings from the pioneer period in an 1800s village setting.

FOR CHILDREN

During the summer, the Blue Goose Steam Train leaves from the depot in Yreka on a tour through high cattle-ranch country, and visits the old railroad town of Montague. There are great views of Mount Shasta during the three-hour journey.

▶ Leave Yreka on **Hwy 3** west and drive through the Scott Valley for 17 miles (27km)

6 Weaverville

During the early 1850s, some 2,500 Chinese settled at this Trinity County seat to prospect for gold. Their legacy is the Weaverville Joss House State Historic Park and the 1873 Temple Amongst the Forest Beneath the Clouds, beautifully restored to its original splendor.

▶ Take **Hwy 299** east back to Redding, passing the Whiskeytown Lake Recreation Area on the way. Continue past Redding on **Hwy 44** for 50 miles (80km) and turn south onto **Hwy 89** through Lassen Volcanic National Park.

Yreka has shed its turbulent past but retains its Victorian elegance

The Siskiyou County Courthouse, at 311 Fourth Street, has displays of gold in various forms from Yreka's glittering past, and the nearby County Museum, at 910 S. Main Street, contains exhibits from the region dating from prehistoric times to the present day. Outside, there is an impressive

to Fort Jones, with views ahead of the Marble Mountains, that connect with the Trinity Alps. From Fort Jones, continue for 12 miles (19km) to the old mining supply town of Etna. Another 13 miles (21km) along **Hwy 3** is Callahan, a one-block town; continuing south, the road passes through the forests and mountains of the Trinity Alps and joins **Hwy 299** at Weaverville.

7 Lassen Volcanic National Park

Known to Native Americans as "Fire Mountain," "Broken Mountain" and "Mountain-Ripped-Apart," Lassen Peak is the southernmost volcano of the Pacific northwest's vast Cascade Range. It sits within a huge caldera formed by the collapse of its mother mountain, 30,000 years ago. Lassen is much more famous, however, for its recent behavior: surprise volcanic eruptions, culminating in a dramatic blast of steam and smoke that tossed five-ton boulders into the sky in 1915. These theatrics created such a thrill throughout the U.S. that the peak and its breathtaking setting were protected as a national park in 1916.

Lassen has easy access during the few short months when the main road traversing the park is not blocked by snow. Many of the park's most notable features are either visible or accessible from the road. Three of the world's four types of volcanoes are here, in addition to boiling lakes, mudpots and sulphurous steam plumes. The best place to appreciate Lassen's fiery presence, not to mention the wild flowers along the way, is at Bumpass Hell, where the careless Mr. Bumpass lost one of his legs to a boiling mudpot!

▶ *Leave Lassen Park by returning to* **Hwy 44** *and continuing north on* **Hwy 89**.

8 McArthur-Burney Falls
Teddy Roosevelt called these 129-foot (39m) falls, west of Highway 89, "the eighth wonder

Right: McCloud and Mount Shasta
Below: Bumpass Hell

of the world" – but don't hold your breath! Though they are one of the most scenic waterfalls in the state, they are no Niagara Falls. A trail from the parking lot leads to the foot of the falls and during the morning beautiful rainbows form in the mist.

▶ *Continue north on* **Hwy 89** *around the southern flank of Mount Shasta to McCloud.*

9 McCloud
This queen of the lumber mill days was a company town where the workers were paid in script, which they spent at the company store, and their houses were built from the lumber that they had milled. McCloud has

changed very little since it was founded in 1827, and gas lamps still light the streets at night.

▶ *Continue west on* **Hwy 89** *for 10 miles (16km) and turn onto* **I-5** *back to Redding.*

BACK TO NATURE

The McCloud River Preserve is a 6-mile (10km) stretch of wild trout stream protected by the Nature Conservancy, just south of McCloud. Take Squaw Valley Road to Lake McCloud and follow the Ah-Di-Na Camp signs along a dirt road to its end.

Capital to
Coast

Leave California's capital, passing through the northern Central Valley, and head for the Wine Country. The Sonoma and Alexander valleys lead to the Anderson Valley's fruit orchards. The tour then leads up the rugged Mendocino coast to Fort Bragg and returns to Sacramento via Clear Lake, the largest body of water entirely within California.

3 DAYS • 434 MILES • 696KM

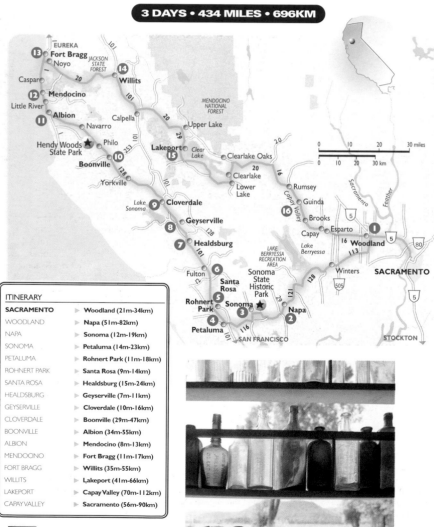

i Sacramento Convention and
Visitors Bureau, 1109 2D Daily,
Sacramento

► *Leaving Sacramento, take I-5
north for 15 miles (24km).*

❶ Woodland

What was once a typical little
farming community has grown to
become the seat of Yolo County.
Just off the main street is a
reminder of the past, in the
form of the old Opera House,
originally built in 1885 and
burned in 1892. It was rebuilt in
its present form in 1896, and
there are regular tours and
special performances. Nearby
is a fine example of an early
20th-century courthouse.

► *Take Hwy 113 south and exit
on Hwy E6 west to Winters.
Continue west on Hwy 128
past the southern tip of Lake
Berryessa and turn left onto
Hwy 121. Continue into
Napa.*

❷ Napa

(See also page 116)
The town from which the world-
famous wine valley derives its
name is a world away from the
vineyards and expensive country
clubs a few miles north of town.
Like so many northern
Californian towns, this was a
Gold Rush center during the
1850s. The old historic downtown area on the bank of the
Napa River has good examples
of 18th- and early 19th-century
architecture. Maps of suggested
walking tours are available from
the tourist office.

Napa is also the base of the
controversial Napa Wine Train,
restored in the late 1980s to offer
three-hour, 36-mile (58km)
round trips to St. Helena, in the
heart of Napa Valley, while lunch
or dinner is served in restored
Pullman dining cars. Many vintners opposed the intrusion of the
train into the previously peaceful
vineyards, but commerce once
again won over environment.
Although the train makes stops
at selected wineries in the valley,
it apparently does nothing to

ease the notorious traffic congestion on Highway 37.

i Napa Valley Conference and
Visitors Bureau, 1310 Napa Town
Center

► *Leave Napa on Hwy 12 and
continue west past the "neo-
chateau" of Domaine Carneros
on the left. Continue for
5 miles (8km) past the winery
and turn right onto Napa
Road to continue into Sonoma.*

❸ Sonoma

(See also page 119)
It was in Sonoma Plaza in 1846
that the Bear Flag was raised to
declare California a republic;
less than one month later it was
replaced by the Stars and
Stripes. The history of the
Republic is preserved with the
help of period displays shown
in the Depot Museum, which
is housed in the original town
depot.

The City Hall in Sonoma

On the north side of the
attractive town square is Sonoma
State Historic Park, a group of
old adobe buildings including
the Toscano Hotel and Sonoma
Barracks, both of which are open
for tours. Also included in the
park is the home of General
Vallejo, the founder of Sonoma,
where tours are offered throughout the week. Just off the plaza
is the Mission San Francisco
Solano, the last in the chain of
missions that stretch up from
Baja California in Mexico, which
houses a collection of water-
colors of *The Missions of
California* by Chris Jorgensen.

► *Leave Sonoma driving south
on Hwy 12. Turn right onto
Hwy 121; at the stop light at
the junction with Hwy 116,
turn right. Follow Hwy 116
through Lakeville into
Petaluma.*

4 Petaluma

Riverside Petaluma retains a small-town America atmosphere: its streets needed little help to give the necessary 1950s look when the town was used as a location for *American Graffiti* and *Peggy Sue Got Married*. Petaluma grew up on poultry farming and dairy farming but it has increasingly become a bedroom community for San Francisco. On the eastern edge of town is the Petaluma Adobe State Historic Park, where the restored 1836 two-story adobe building was at the center of General Vallejo's vast land holdings.

▷ *Continue north on* Hwy 101.

5 Rohnert Park

Suburban Rohnert Park is another bedroom community, with the Sonoma Wine Information Center located just off the freeway, where interactive displays and literature cover most of the wineries in the county.

▷ *Continue north on* Hwy 101 *to Santa Rosa.*

6 Santa Rosa

(See also pages 118–19)
Fast-growing Santa Rosa boasts among its attractions a restored 1920s shopping area in Railroad Square and the intriguing Church of the One Tree, at Sonoma Avenue, a steepled church which, as its name suggests, was made from a single tree – a redwood chopped down in the 19th century. The Luther Burbank Home and Gardens deserves a visit.

▷ *Continue north on* Hwy 101 *for 17 miles (27km).*

7 Healdsburg

(See also pages 118 and 149)
Strategically positioned between three wine-growing areas, Healdsburg is a good base for visiting wineries. It also has an excellent display of Pomo Indian artifacts at the old Carnegie Library.

▷ *Continue north on* Hwy 101 *for 9 miles (14km).*

8 Geyserville

(See also page 118)
This small town sits in the heart of the Alexander Valley, one of California's most important wine regions, and Chateau Souverain's hop kiln design winery can clearly be seen from the west side of Highway 101.

▷ *Continue north on* Hwy 101.

9 Cloverdale

(See also page 149)
This grape-growing center is a pleasant town with several restaurants and plentiful accommodations. It holds a citrus fair every February.

SCENIC ROUTES

The section of road from Cloverdale to Boonville, along Highway 128, winds through high, rolling hills typical of northern California. Clinging to the hillside, the route gives beautiful vistas at every turn. Winter rains turn the hills bright green for a few months during the spring, but they soon revert to their normal golden color in the heat of California's summer.

▷ *From Cloverdale take* Hwy 128 *for 27 miles (43km) through beautiful pastoral scenery to Boonville.*

10 Boonville

This secluded farming community is best known for the local language it invented in the 1880s: "Boontling" has a vocabulary of about 1,000 words, and the local paper still publishes a column in the language every week. Boonville is at the head of an important wine-growing region, and the Anderson Valley Brewing Company, a local microbrewery, produces some of the best beer in the state. The Anderson Valley Historical Museum is housed in the little

1891 Conn Creek School House, and displays lumber industry relics and Indian artifacts.

▷ *Continue on* Hwy 128 *through the Anderson Valley, where apple orchards climb up the valley until Philo, when vineyards take over. Drive another 30 miles (48km) to the coast.*

BACK TO NATURE

Just north of Philo, in the Anderson Valley, Hendy Woods State Park contains a grove of giant coastal redwoods towering more than 300 feet (91m) above the valley floor. Several walking trails meander through the forest and there are also camp sites available.

---

11 Albion

Albion is a tranquil fishing village, part of a century-old series of "dog hole" ports, where steamers navigated between craggy inlets to pick up loads of lumber.

▷ *Continue north on* Hwy 1 *for 8 miles (13km) to Mendocino.*

12 Mendocino

(See also pages 145–6)
This handsome village was built by New England loggers in the 19th century, and now has a large and active community of artists. A model of historic Mendocino and a display on its history are shown at Ford House.

▷ *Continue north on* Hwy 1 *for 11 miles (18km) to Fort Bragg.*

13 Fort Bragg

(See also page 146)
Fort Bragg is a working lumber town and harbor, with an impressive show of flowers in the 19-acre (8-hectare) Mendocino Botanical Gardens, set on bluffs overlooking the sea.

▷ *Return down* Hwy 1 *to Noyo and take* Hwy 20 *east for 34*

miles (55km) to Willits. The
road passes through Jackson
State Forest which has more
than 52,000 acres (21,000
hectares) of redwoods,
Douglas fir, hemlock and
bishop pine trees.

14 Willits
(See also pages 146 and 149)
Willits is the terminus of the
Skunk Train and home of the
Mendocino County Museum,
where items illustrate the area's
Indian and pioneer history.

▶ Drive south on **Hwy 101** for
17 miles (27km) to Calpella
and turn east onto **Hwy 20** for
19 miles (30km) to Upper
Lake. Turn south onto **Hwy 29**.

15 Lakeport
The "lake" in question is Clear
Lake, the largest natural body of
water entirely within California,
which, though off the beaten
track, provides boating, water
skiing, sailing and fishing.
Lakeport, the county seat, is the
first town on Highway 29, in an
area of pear and walnut orchards

and a growing wine industry.
The Historic County
Courthouse is a regional history
museum with re-creations of
rooms from the turn of the
century and exhibits of Pomo
Indian culture. South of
Lakeport, Highway 281 hugs
the western shore of the lake
and continues to Lower Lake,
where the Anderson Marsh State
Historic Park interprets 10,000
years of Native American
history, culture and archaeology.
Its headquarters are in an 1870s
restored ranch house surrounded
by 500 acres (202 hectares) of
freshwater tule marsh that
provides a winter home for bald
eagles and other rare birds.

▶ Drive north on **Hwy 53** for 8
miles (13km) to **Hwy 20** and
east on **Hwy 20** for 18 miles
(29km). Take **Hwy 16** south
for 33 miles (53km) to Capay.

16 Capay Valley
Pastures and almond orchards
make this part of the drive
particularly scenic in the spring,
when the hillsides are emerald

Sunset over Clear Lake

green and the almond trees
are covered in pink blossom.
Highway 16 runs south through
the farming communities of
Rumsey, Guinda, Brooks, and
Capay, and has a number of idyllic picnic sites. The road follows
Cache Creek as it flows the
length of the valley, providing
fishing and swimming in the
spring and summer. Along this
route look for turn-of-the-20th-
century homesteads with sturdy
wooden houses, windmills and
long-obsolete tank houses. On
the approach to Brooks, the 1868
schoolhouse stands by an even
older oak tree and in town you
can play "High Stakes Bingo"
at the Cache Creek Indian
Rancheria. The southern gateway to Capay Valley is Esparto,
where an almond festival is held
every February.

▶ Continue on **Hwy 16** through
rich farmlands for 15 miles
(24km) to Woodland and then
on **I-5** for 15 miles (24km)
back to Sacramento.

ACCOMMODATIONS

Where possible, reserve in advance if you plan to stay in a city hotel or inn. Nevertheless, in many parts of the state, you may find rooms in roadside motels simply by looking out for a likely place and stopping. The inexpensive Motel 6 and EZ-8 chains are good bets for reasonable accommodations. All motels have ample parking, and the majority of the national chain motels are clean and offer good basic amenities, including televisions, telephones and, increasingly, internet access Normally there is no restaurant or room service, but there will almost always be an inexpensive restaurant close by. Hotels vary greatly in price and services, and some may not have parking spaces.

At major inner-city hotels, overnight parking can be as expensive as a cheap motel room. In general, the more expensive the hotel, the higher the cost of incidentals, which include in-room minibars, internet access and telephone charges. Always check prices at the front desk to avoid a nasty shock at check out.

An increasingly popular accommodations option is the bed-and-breakfast inn, often a restored 19th-century house serving huge breakfasts (cooked or Continental) in communal dining rooms. Again, prices vary and some inns may not offer private bathrooms, but unlike Europe, bed-and-breakfast inns do not offer cheap alternative accommodations. They are usually antique-filled mansions, designed for romantic getaways. The rooms rarely have telephones or television, neither of which would be a priority for the intended occupants. Smoking and pets are generally not allowed and children may be difficult to accommodate: check any age limits beforehand.

Camping is popular and widely available in the state and national parks, many of which are fully booked well in advance. Reservations can be made up to two months ahead through MISTIX (tel: 800/444-7275).

Campgrounds vary from the basic to comfortable areas with washing, eating and shopping facilities. Anyone planning to camp in the wild outdoors, beyond the campgrounds, needs a wilderness permit (available from park rangers' offices) and adequate supplies, including emergency rations of food and drink; a first-aid kit including bandages and diarrhea tablets; maps; a whistle; insect repellent; a waterproof groundsheet and sleeping bag; and sun protection. The ranger should be given details of your whereabouts and your planned route and schedule, and all campers should be sensitive to the environment and have an awareness of snakes and/or bears and fire hazards.

Youth hostels provide an alternative budget option, and many are in the most popular walking and hiking regions. Reserve in advance during the peak season. Members pay slightly less than non-members. Most hostels have kitchen facilities and a night curfew, and all forbid smoking, drinking and drug-taking.

For information on youth hostels in California contact the following offices:
Central CA Council, PO Box 3755, Merced, CA 95344 (tel: 209/725-0407);
Golden Gate Council, 425 Divisadero Street, San Francisco, CA 94117 (tel: 415/863-1444);
Los Angeles Council, 1436 2nd Street, Santa Monica, CA 90401 (tel: 310/393-9913);
San Diego Council, 521 Market Street, San Diego, CA 92101 (tel: 619/525-1531).

CALIFORNIA CALENDAR OF EVENTS

January

• Tournament of the Roses, Pasadena. A spectacular parade down Colorado Boulevard, with lavish floats, music and extraordinary equestrian entries, followed by the Rose Bowl Game. Call 626/449-4100 for details or just stay home and watch it on TV. January 1.

February

• AT&T Pebble Beach National Pro-Am, Pebble Beach. A PGA-sponsored tour where pros are teamed with celebrities to compete on three world-famous golf courses. Call 831/644-0333. Lasts a week; dates vary.

• Chinese New Year Festival and Parade. The largest Chinese New Year Festival in the United States is San Francisco's, which includes a Golden Dragon parade with lion-dancing, marching bands, street fair, flower sale, and festival food. Call 415/986-1370.

L.A.'s celebration is colorful too, with dragon dancers parading through the streets of Chinatown. Chinese opera and other events are scheduled. Contact the Chinese Chamber of Commerce at 213/617-0396. Late January to early February.

• Mustard Festival, Napa Valley. Celebrating the blossom of yellow-petaled mustard flowers, which coat the valley during February and March, the event was originally conceived to drum up interest in visiting during this once-slow season. Events range from a kick-off gourmet gala at the CIA Greystone to a wine auction, golf benefit, recipe and photography competitions, and plenty of food and wine celebrations. For information and a schedule of events, call 707/259-9020.

March

• Return of the Swallows, San Juan Capistrano. Each St. Joseph's Day (March 19), visitors flock here for the arrival of the mission's swallows that will nest and remain until October. The celebration includes a parade, dances, and special programs. Call 949/234-1300 for details. March 19–21.

• Santa Barbara International Film Festival. For 10 days each March, Santa Barbara does its best impression of Cannes. There's a flurry of foreign and independent movie premieres, personal appearances by actors and directors, and symposia on hot cinematic topics. Call 805/963-0023 for details.

• Redwood Coast Dixieland Jazz Festival, Eureka. Three days of jazz featuring some of the best Dixeland bands. Call 707/445-3378. Last weekend in March.

April

• San Francisco International Film Festival. One of America's oldest film festivals, featuring more than 100 films from over 30 countries. Tickets are relatively inexpensive, and screenings are very accessible to the general public during two weeks early in the month. Call 415/561-5022.

• Toyota Grand Prix, Long Beach. An exciting weekend of Indy-class auto racing and entertainment in and around downtown Long Beach, drawing world-class drivers from the United States and Europe. Contact the Grand Prix Association at 888/82SPEED. Mid-April.

• Renaissance Pleasure Faire, San Bernardino. One of America's largest Renaissance festivals, set in Glen Ellen Regional Park. Performers dress in 16th-century costume and revel in this festive re-creation of a medieval English village. For ticket information,

call 800/52-FAIRE. Weekends late April to Memorial Day.

• Ramona Pageant, Hemet. A unique outdoor pageant that portrays the lives of the Southern California Mission Indians. The play was adapted from Helen Hunt Jackson's 1884 novel *Ramona*. Call 800/645-4465 for details. Late April to early May.

May

• Cinco de Mayo. A week-long celebration throughout Los Angeles of one of Mexico's most jubilant holidays. The fiesta's Carnival-like atmosphere is created by large crowds, live music, dance and food. The main festivals are in El Pueblo de Los Angeles State Historic Park, downtown; other events around the city. Call 213/628-1274 for information.

There's also a Cinco de Mayo celebration in San Diego, with folklore, music, dance, food and historical reenactments. Held in Old Town. Call 619/220-5422 for information.

• Venice Art Walk, Venice Beach. An annual weekend event that gives visitors a chance to take docent-guided tours, visit artist's studios, or take a Sunday self-guiding art walk through private studios and homes of more than 50 emerging and well-known artists. Call 310/392-9255. Mid-May.

• Calaveras Country Fair and Jumping Frog Jubilee, Angel's Camp. The event is inspired by Mark Twain's story *The Celebrated Jumping Frog of Calaveras County*. Entrants from all over the world arrive with their frog participants. Also children's parade, livestock competition, rodeo, carnival and fireworks. Call 209/736-2561. Third weekend in May.

• Bay to Breakers Foot Race, Golden Gate Park, San Francisco. One of the city's most popular annual events,

it's really more fun than run. Thousands of entrants show up dressed in their Halloween-style costumes for the approximately 7½-mile (12km) run across the park. Call 415/777-7770. Third Sunday of May.

• Carnival, San Francisco. The Mission District's largest annual event is a two-day festival that culminates with a parade on Mission Street over Memorial Day weekend. More than a half-million spectators line the route, and the samba musicians and dancers continue to play on 14th Street, near Harrison, at the end of the march. Call the Mission Economic and Cultural Association at 415/920-0125. Memorial Day weekend.

June

• Playboy Jazz Festival, Los Angeles. Bill Cosby is the traditional Master of Ceremonies, presiding over top artists at the Hollywood Bowl. Call 800/279-4444. Mid-June.

• Wine Auction, Napa Valley. Napa's most renowned event brings close to 2,000 deep-pocketed wine aficionados to the Napa Valley wine country and includes a weekend of culinary events, barrel tastings, a live auction and a vintners' ball. Tickets to the event are $1,500 per couple and sell out every year. Fax 707/963-3488.

• Lesbian and Gay Freedom Day Parade. Celebrated all over the state, but San Francisco's party draws up to a half-million participants. The parade's start and finish has been moved around in recent years to accommodate road construction but traditionally it begins and ends at Civic Center Plaza. Call 415/864-3733. Usually the third or last weekend of June.

• Ojai Music Festival. This three-day event has been drawing world-class classical and jazz personalities to the open-air Libbey Bowl since 1947. Seats (and local lodgings) fill up quickly. Call 805/646-2094 for more information.

• Hot-Air Balloon Classic, Windsor. Hundreds of brilliant balloons float silently across the sky above, while gawkers enjoy a food-and-crafts fair. Call 707/837-1884. Usually last weekend in June.

July
• Independence Day. It's celebrated all over the country, but it's terrific in Pasadena, which offers Southern California's most spectacular display of fireworks following an evening of live entertainment at the Rose Bowl. Call 626/577-3100 for further information.

• Festival of Arts and Pageant of the Masters, Laguna Beach. A fantastic performance-art production in which live actors re-create famous Old Masters paintings. Ticket prices range from $15 to $40. Call 800/487-FEST or 949/494-1145. July through August.

• Gilroy Garlic Festival. A gourmet food fair with more than 85 booths serving garlicky food from almost every ethnic background, plus close to 100 arts, crafts, and entertainment booths. Call 408/842-1625. Last full weekend in July.

• Shakespeare at the Beach, Lake Tahoe. Experience the Bard at Sand Harbor on the shore beneath the stars. Call 800/747-4697. Three weeks in late June and August.

• International Surf Festival, Los Angeles. Hermosa Beach, Manhattan Beach, Redondo Beach, and Torrance collaborate in the oldest international surfing festival in California. Competitions include surfing, boogie boarding and sandcastle building. Call 310/376-6911 for details. End of July.

August
• Old Spanish Days Fiesta, Santa Barbara. The city's

biggest annual event, this five-day festival features a grand parade with horse-drawn carriages, two Spanish marketplaces, a carnival, a rodeo, and dancers. Call 805/962-8101. Early August.

• California State Fair, Sacramento. At the California Exposition grounds, a gala celebration, with livestock, food, exhibits, entertainment on 10 stages, thoroughbred racing and a 1-mile (1.5km) monorail for panoramic views of it all. Call 916/263-3000. Late August to early September.

September
• Sausalito Art Festival. A juried exhibit of more than 180 artists, accompanied by music from Bay Area jazz, rock and blues performers and international cuisine with wines from some 50 Napa and Sonoma producers. Call 415/332-3555 for information. Labor Day weekend.

• Monterey Jazz Festival. Top names in traditional and modern jazz. One of the oldest annual jazz festivals in the world. Call 831/373-3366. Mid-September.

• San Francisco Blues Festival, on the grounds of Fort Mason. The largest outdoor blues music event on the West Coast. Local and national musicians perform during two marathon days. Call 415/826-6837. Usually in mid-September.

• Los Angeles County Fair. Horse racing, arts, agricultural displays, celebrity entertainment and carnival rides at the largest county fair in the world, held at the Los Angeles County Fair and Exposition Center, in Pomona. Call 909/623-3111 for information. Late September.

• Danish Days, Solvang. Since 1936, this three-day event has been celebrating Old World customs and pageantry with a

parade, gymnastics by local schoolchildren, and demonstrations of traditional Danish arts and crafts. Call 800/GO-SOLVANG for information.

October
• Oktoberfest, Big Bear Lake. Enjoy a heady beer at the best Oktoberfest in Southern California. Activities range from log-sawing competitions to yodeling contests. Call 909/585-3000. The action takes place at the Convention Center on weekends starting in late September and continuing through the end of October.

• Half Moon Bay Pumpkin and Art Festival, Half Moon Bay. Features hundreds of artisans' booths, pumpkin carvings, music and a contest for the largest pumpkin. Colorful to the extreme. Call 650/726-9652. Dates vary.

• Western Regional Final Championship Rodeo, Lakeside. Top cowboys from 11 western states compete in events, including calf roping, barrel racing, bull riding, team roping and steer wrestling. Held at the Lakeside Rodeo Grounds, Calif. 67 and Mapleview Avenue, Lakeside. Call 619/561-4331 for information. Mid-October.

• Halloween, San Francisco. The "City by the Bay" celebrates with a fantastical parade which is organized at Market and Castro, and a mixed gay-straight crowd revels in costumes of extraordinary imagination. October 31.

November
• Hollywood Christmas Parade. This spectacular star-studded parade marches through the heart of Hollywood. For information, call 310/631-0691. Sunday after Thanksgiving.

December
• Christmas Boat Parade of Lights. Following long-standing tradition, sailors love to

decorate their craft with colorful lights for the holidays. Several Southern California harbors hold nighttime parades to showcase these creations, which range from tiny dinghies draped with a single strand of lights to yachts with entire Nativity scenes twinkling on deck. Call the following for information: Marina del Rey (310/821-0555); Long Beach (562/435-4093); Mission Bay (619/276-8200); Ventura Harbor (805/642-6746); Huntington Harbor (714/840-7542).

• New Year's Eve Torchlight Parade, Big Bear Lake. Watch dozens of nighttime skiers follow a serpentine path down Snow Summit's ski slopes bearing glowing torches—it's one of the state's loveliest traditions. Afterward, the party continues indoors with live bands and plenty to eat and drink. For information on this 21-and-over event, call 909/866-5766.

GETTING AROUND
Motoring
Accidents
Set up warning signs. Call police, Highway Patrol and ambulance if required. Take names and addresses of all involved, names and numbers of insurance policies and make and license plate of other vehicle(s). Take names and addresses of all witnesses. Under no circumstances admit to or sign any statement of responsibility.

Breakdowns
The American Automobile Association (AAA) is a member of a worldwide association of motoring organizations (AIT) and, as such, makes certain services available to visitors from member organizations. Call AAA's nationwide road service number: 1-800-400-4222 (24-hour) and you will be given information for obtaining emergency assistance.

If you break down on a highway, lift up the hood (bonnet); remain in your vehicle until the Highway Patrol arrives. Do not open doors or windows to anyone else. If you spot another driver who seems to need help, contact the police (dial 911).

Some precautions can be taken before setting off on a drive, to avoid unnecessary trouble. Have the car's oil level checked every time you fill the tank; check tire pressure regularly. Tires should be fully inflated, without any worn or uneven patches, before you set out on your journey. Have the coolant level checked, and make sure there are no leaks in the radiator. Ideally the brakes and brake fluid should also be checked, and you should have plenty of antifreeze, especially if traveling into skiing areas, in which case snow chains for tires are advisable (obligatory in some places).

Make sure all lights work and that there is washing liquid supplied for cleaning the windshield.

Car Rentals
California is one of the cheapest states to rent a car. All the major car rental companies are represented, but better rates can usually be obtained from local companies that are listed in the Yellow Pages. These are generally not based in airports, but they will provide a free shuttle service to their facility. None of the major companies will rent to anyone under the age of 25. It may be possible to find a local company that will do so, but be prepared to pay a loaded insurance premium.

Make sure you understand the conditions that apply to each firm's policy. Some may charge an extra fee for renting a car in one place and leaving it in another; some may include a full gas tank in the overall price, others may not.

It is advisable to find out whether your own insurance would cover damage to a rented car, and what the details are of Collision Damage Waiver (CDW).

Car rental companies with offices in California include: Alamo (tel: 800/327-9633); Avis (tel: 800/331-1212); Budget (tel: 800/527-0700); Dollar (tel: 800/800-4000); Hertz (tel: 800/654-3131); National Car Rental (tel: 800/328-4567); Thrifty Car Rental (800/367-2277).

Documents
Drivers need a valid license. Car registration numbers and proof of insurance must be carried.

Route Directions
The following abbreviations for U.S. roads have been used throughout this book:
Hwy – Highway
I – Interstate
Most Interstate roads are freeways (motorways) and although they are theoretically the fastest roads, around major urban areas, particularly at rush hour, they can quickly become parkings lots.

Rules and Regulations
On many rural freeways the limit is up to 70mph (110kph). Road signs always clearly indicate specific limits and they are strictly enforced.

Drivers and passengers must wear seat belts, and children under four years old or lighter than 40 pounds (18kg) must sit in approved safety seats.

Rail Travel
Rail travel in California is limited. On some routes, passengers must transfer to a bus to complete their journey, which somehow defeats the objective. Several local narrow-gauge trains operate in the state, such as the Skunk Train in Mendocino and Roaring Campo Railroad in Santa Cruz, but these are novelty rides rather than serious alternative transportation.

Amtrak operates rail services in California, with a particularly scenic line running along the coast – the Coast Starlight –

from Seattle to Los Angeles or on to San Diego via Oakland, Salinas, San Luis Obispo, Santa Barbara and the Malibu coast. Reserve ahead. Visitors from outside the U.S. can buy the USA Railpass, allowing 15 or 30 days' unlimited travel on Amtrak lines. Amtrak offices in San Francisco and Los Angeles sell passes within the U.S. to holders of foreign passports.

Travelers with disabilities should specify their needs when reserving seats with Amtrak. Some stations are not well equipped with facilities; discounts may be available.

Air Travel

(See also Travel to the U.S. from Overseas, below.) Several airlines operate regular flights within California, including:
American Eagle (800/433-7300); Southwest (800/435-9792); United (800/241-6522); and USAir Express (800/428-4322).

Bus Travel

Traveling by bus is inexpensive but time-consuming, and bus stations are often located in unsavory parts of town. Greyhound operates bus lines between all the major cities in California, but some routes (such as those between Los Angeles and San Francisco, for example) are as expensive as air fares. Travelers from outside the U.S. can buy Ameripass tickets, giving bus travel for seven, 15 or 30 days and available from Greyhound offices.

The Green Tortoise bus line operates between Los Angeles and San Francisco, and is geared toward younger travelers (tel: San Francisco 415/956-7500 or 800/867-8647).

Alternative Travel

San Francisco probably provides the best public transportation system in California, its best-known option being the bay ferries: the Red and White boats, that link San Francisco, Angel Island,

Tiburon and Vallejo (tel: 415/447-0591), and the Golden Gate Ferry Service, between San Francisco and Sausalito (tel: 415/923-2000).

Underground trains operated by the Bay Area Rapid Transit company (BART) run between 33 stations in the San Francisco Bay area.

Golden Gate Transit buses serve the North Bay, across the Golden Gate Bridge, an area that is not served by BART (tel: 415/455-2000).

San Diego's Tijuana Trolley makes regular journeys to the Mexican border and between San Diego neighborhoods.

Safety

Certain areas of certain towns and cities are not safe for tourists. Talk to staff at the travel agency, tourist information center or car rental company and ascertain which neighborhoods should be avoided. If possible, get a map showing the safe areas clearly, and be sure of the directions to your destination.

If you are involved in a motoring accident in an area that may be dangerous, stay in the car and keep doors and windows locked until police arrive on the scene. If you are bumped from behind, or if something is wrong with the car, head straight for a service station rather than stopping in an unknown area.

Never leave expensive equipment such as cameras or cell (mobile) phones visible in the car.

Try to park in well-lit or monitored parking lots, and to fill the tank in daylight. See also **Motoring: Accidents**, page 161.

HOLIDAYS

1 January – New Year's Day;
Third Monday in January – Martin Luther King Jr. Day;
Third Monday in February – Presidents' Day;
Last Monday in May – Memorial Day;
4 July – Independence Day;

First Monday in September – Labor Day;
Second Monday in October – Columbus Day;
11 November – Veterans Day/ Armistice Day;
Last Thursday in November – Thanksgiving Day;
25 December – Christmas Day. The Tuesday following the first Monday in November is Election Day.

LIQUOR LAWS

Liquor and grocery stores, as well as some drugstores, can legally sell packaged alcoholic beverages between 6am and 2am. Most restaurants, nightclubs, and bars are licensed to serve alcoholic beverages during the same hours.

The legal age for the purchase and consumption of alcoholic beverages is 21; note that proof of age is strictly enforced.

TAXES

Sales tax is levied on goods and services by state and local governments and is not included in the price tags you'll see on merchandise. These taxes are not refundable.

TRAVEL TO THE U.S. FROM OVERSEAS

Several airlines fly regularly from Europe to the U.S., either direct to California or to states with connecting flights. Non-U.S. airlines with flights to California include:
British Airways (tel: London (0345) 222 111);
Virgin Atlantic (tel: London (01293) 747 747);
Aer Lingus (tel: Dublin (01) 844 4747; Shannon (061) 415 556);
Qantas (tel: Sydney (008) 177 767);
Air New Zealand (tel: Auckland (0800) 737-000; Christchurch (643) 379-5200);
Air Canada (tel: (800) 268-7240).

VISITOR INFORMATION

For information on the state as a whole, contact California

Tourism, 801 K Street, Suite 1600, Sacramento, CA 95814 (tel: 800/862-2543), and ask for their free information pack. Almost every city and town in the state has a dedicated tourist bureau or chamber of commerce that will be happy to send you information.

To find out more about California's national parks, contact the Western Region Information Center, National Park Service, Fort Mason, Building 201, San Francisco, CA 94123 (tel: 415/556-0560).

For state park information, contact the Department of Parks and Recreation, P.O. Box 942896, Sacramento, CA 92496-0001 (tel: 916/653-6995).

Campsites can be reserved up to eight weeks in advance by calling Park-Net (tel: 800/444-7275). Daily 8am–5pm.

For information on fishing and hunting licenses, contact the California Department of Fish and Game, License and Revenue Branch, 3211 South Street, Sacramento, CA 95816 (tel: 916/227-2244).

Telephones
For local directory assistance ("Information"), dial 411; for long-distance information in the United States and Canada, dial 1, then the appropriate area code and 555-1212.

For collect (reversed-charge) calls and person-to-person calls, dial 0 (zero, not the letter O) followed by the area code and the number you want; an operator or recording will then come on the line, and you should specify that you are calling collect or person-to-person, or both. If your operator-assisted call is international, dial 0 and wait for the operator.

Business Hours
Offices: usually weekdays 9–5. Banks: weekdays 9–3 or later; sometimes Saturday mornings. Stores, especially those in shopping complexes, tend to stay open late: until about 9 weekdays and until 6 on weekends.

Taxes
In the United States there is no value added tax (VAT) or other direct tax at a national level. Every state and city is allowed to levy its own local sales tax on all purchases, including hotel and restaurant checks and airline tickets.

Taxes are included in the price of certain services, such as public transportation, cab fares, phone calls, and gasoline (petrol).

The amount of sales tax varies from 4 to 10 percent, depending on the state and city, so when you are making major purchases, such as photographic equipment, clothing, or hi-fi components, it can be a significant part of the cost.

Many cities charge a separate "bed" or room tax on accommodations, above and beyond any sales tax.

Time
The United States is divided into four time zones (six, if Alaska and Hawaii are included).

From east to west, these are eastern standard time (EST), central standard time (CST), mountain standard time (MST), and Pacific standard time (PST).

There are also Alaska standard time (AST) and Hawaii standard time (HST).

California is on PST; eight hours behind Greenwich Mean Time (GMT).

Tipping
Service in America is some of the best in the world, and is rarely included in the price of anything. It's part of the American way of life to tip, on the principle that you must expect to pay for any service you get.

In restaurants it is usual to add 15–20 percent to the check. It is a common practice for an 18 percent service charge to be added automatically if the party is six or more people. Normally this is clearly stated on the menu.

WHEN TO GO
California's climate is so varied that it is impossible to generalize about the state as a whole.

San Francisco's temperate marine climate means relatively mild weather year-round. In summer, temperatures rarely top 70°F (21°C), and the city's famous fog rolls in most evenings. In winter, it seldom falls below freezing. Because of San Francisco's fog, summer rarely sees more than a few hot days in a row. Head a few miles inland though, and it's likely to be clear and hot.

The Central Coast shares San Francisco's climate, though it gets warmer as you get farther south. Seasonal changes are less pronounced south of San Luis Obispo, where temperatures remain relatively stable year-round. The northern coast is rainier and foggier; winters tend to be mild but wet.

Summers are refreshingly cool around Lake Tahoe and in the Shasta Cascades – perfect for hiking, camping and other outdoor activities and a popular escape for residents of California's hot deserts and valleys. Skiers flock to this area for terrific snowfall from late November through early April.

Southern California is usually much warmer than the Bay Area, and it gets significantly more sun. This is *the* place to hit the beach. Even in winter, daytime temperatures regularly reach into the 60s (15–20°C) and warmer. Summers can be stifling inland, but Southern California's coastal communities are always comfortable.

You can sunbathe throughout the year, but only die-hard enthusiasts and wet-suited surfers venture into the ocean in winter. The water is warmest in summer and fall, but even then, it is too chilly for many.

The Southern California desert is sizzling hot in summer; temperatures regularly top 100°F (38°C). Winter is the best time to visit the desert resorts (remember, it gets surprisingly cold at night in the desert).

ACCOMMODATIONS AND RESTAURANTS

Following is a selection of hotels and bed-and-breakfasts (☼) which can be found along the routes of each tour, as well as suggestions for restaurants (🕮) to take a break.

Accommodations prices
Accommodations are divided into five price brackets, based on the cost of a double room:

$	under $75
$$	$75–150
$$$	$150–225
$$$$	$225–300
$$$$$	more than $300

Restaurant prices
Restaurants are divided into three price categories based on the cost of a three-course meal for one, excluding drink:

$	under $20
$$	$20–50
$$$	more than $50

TOUR I
LOS ANGELES
☼ **Hotel Bel Air $$$$**
701 Stone Canyon Road, Bel Air, CA 90077. Tel: 310/472-1211; fax: 310/476-5890.
91 rooms.

☼ **Hotel Palomar Los Angeles $$$**
10740 Wilshire Boulevard, Los Angeles, CA 90028.
Tel: 310/475-8711.
268 rooms.

☼ **Magic Castle Hotel $**
7025 Franklin Avenue, Hollywood, CA 90028.
Tel: 323/851-0800.
49 rooms.

☼ **The Standard $$**
8300 Sunset Boulevard, West Hollywood, CA 90069.
Tel: 323/650-9090.
139 rooms.

🕮 **La Botte Ristorante $$**
620 Santa Monica Boulevard, Los Angeles, CA 90401.
Tel: 310/576-3072.
Italian cuisine.

🕮 **The Ivy $$$**
113 N. Robertson Boulevard, West Hollywood, CA 90048.
Tel: 310/274-8303.
California cuisine.

🕮 **Patina $$$**
141 S. Grand Avenue, Los Angeles CA 90012.
Tel: 213/972-3331.
French/California cuisine.

🕮 **Spago $$$**
176 N. Canyon Drive, Beverly Hills, CA 90210.
Tel: 310/385-0880.
California cuisine.

🕮 **Yamashiro $$$**
1999 N. Sycamore Avenue, Holywood, CA 90068.
Tel: 323/466-5125.
Japanese cuisine.

PASADENA
☼ **Pasadena Hilton $$$**
150 S. Los Robles Avenue, Pasadena, CA 91101. Tel: 626/577-1000; fax: 626/584-3148.
296 rooms.

LONG BEACH
☼ **Hotel Queen Mary $$**
1126 Queen's Highway, Long Beach, CA 90802. Tel: 562/435-3511; fax: 562/437-4531.
365 rooms.

SANTA MONICA
☼ **Hotel California $**
1670 Ocean Avenue, Santa Monica, CA 90401.
Tel: 310/393-2363.
26 rooms.

🕮 **Border Grill $$**
1445 Fourth Street, Santa Monica, CA 90401.
Tel: 310/451-1655.
Mexican haute cuisine.

TOUR 2
VENICE
☼ **Ritz Carlton Marina del Rey $$$$$**
4375 Admiralty Way, Marina del Rey, CA 90212.

Tel: 310/823-1700.
304 rooms.

☼ **Lincoln Inn $$**
2447 Lincoln Boulevard, Venice Beach, CA 90291.
Tel: 310/822-0686; fax: 310/822-3136.
27 rooms.

🕮 **Sidewalk Café $**
1401 Ocean Front Walk, Venice, CA 90291.
Tel: 310/399-5547.
Hamburgers etc.

TOUR 3
REDLANDS
🕮 **Joe Greensleeves $$**
220 North Orange Street, Redlands CA 92374.
Tel: 909/792-6969.
California cuisine. Closed major holidays.

LAKE ARROWHEAD
☼ **Arrowhead Tree Top Lodge $–$$**
27992 Rainbow Drive, Lake Arrowhead, CA 92352.
Tel: 800/358-8733.
24 rooms.

RIVERSIDE
☼ **The Mission Inn $$$**
3649 Mission Inn Avenue, Riverside, CA 92501.
Tel: 800/843-7755; fax: 909/784-5525.
239 rooms.

🕮 **Los Amigos Drive In $**
3162 Main Street, Riverside, CA 92501. Tel: 909/877-1490.
Mexican fast food.

TOUR 4
NEWPORT BEACH
☼ **Balboa Bay Club and Resort $$$$**
1221 West Coast Highway, Newport Beach, CA 92663.
Tel: 888/445-7153.
138 rooms.

Opposite: Golden Gate Bridge, San Francisco

Fleming's Steak House $$
455 Newport Center Drive,
Newport Beach, CA 92660.
Tel: 949/720-9633.
Steaks and lobster.

Roy's of Newport Beach $$$
453 Newport Center Drive,
Newport Beach, CA 92660.
Tel: 949/640-7697.
Asian fusion.

LAGUNA BEACH
◇ **Inn at Laguna Beach $$$**
211 N. Coast Highway, Laguna
Beach, CA 92651. Tel: 949/497-
9722; fax: 949/497-9972.
70 rooms.

TOUR 5
SAN DIEGO
◇ **Balboa Park Inn $$**
3402 Park Boulevard, San
Diego, CA 92103. Tel: 619/
298-0823.
26 rooms.

◇ **Hotel del Coronado $$$$**
1500 Orange Avenue, San
Diego, CA 92118. Tel: 619/435-
6611; fax: 619/522-8338.
688 rooms.

Anthony's Fish Grotto $$
11666 Avena Place, San Diego,
CA 92128. Tel: 619/291-7254.
Seafood. Closed major holidays.

El Agave Tequileria $$
2304 San Diego Avenue, Old
Town, San Diego, CA 92110.
Tel: 619/220-0692.
Mexican cuisine.

Star of the Sea $$$
1360 N. Harbor Drive, San
Diego, CA 92101.
Tel: 619/232-7408.
Seafood.

LA JOLLA
◇ **La Valencia $$$**
1132 Prospect Street, La Jolla,
CA 92037. Tel: 858/454-0771;
fax: 858/456-3921.
118 rooms.

Nine-Ten $$$
910 Prospect Street, La Jolla,
CA 92037. Tel: 858/964-5400.
California cuisine.

Roppongi $$
875 Prospect Street, La Jolla,
CA 92037. Tel: 858/551-5232.
Asian cuisine.

TOUR 6
CARLSBAD
◇ **Inns of America $$**
751 Raintree Drive, Carlsbad,
CA 92009. Tel: 760/931-1185;
fax: 760/931-0970.
126 rooms.

Tuscany $$
6981 El Camino Real, Carlsbad
CA 92009. Tel: 760/929-8111.
Northern Italian cuisine.

ENCINITAS
Savory $$
267 N. El Camino Real,
Encinitas, CA 92024.
Tel: 760/634-5556.
"Casual" fare with an international twist.

TOUR 7
PALM SPRINGS
◇ **Casa Cody Country Inn $$**
175 S. Cahuilla Road, Palm
Springs, CA 92262. Tel: 760/
320-9346; fax: 760/325-8610.
27 rooms.

◇ **Parker Palm Springs $$$$$**
4200 E. Palm Canyon Drive,
Palm Springs, CA 92264.
Tel: 760/770-5000.
144 rooms.

Palmie $$
44-491 Town Center Way, Suite
G, Palm Desert, CA 92260.
Tel: 760/341-3200.
French cuisine.

RANCHO MIRAGE
Wally's Desert Turtle $$$
71-775 Highway 111,
Rancho Mirage, CA 92274.
Tel: 760/568-9321.
Continental cuisine. Closed mid-Jun to Sep.

TOUR 8
TWENTYNINE PALMS
◇ **29 Palms Inn $$**
73950 Inn Avenue, Twentynine
Palms, CA 92277. Tel: 760/367-
3505; fax: 760/367-4425.
19 rooms.

BARSTOW
Idle Spurs Steak House $$
690 Old Highway 58, Barstow,
CA 92311. Tel: 760/256-8888.
*Prime rib & steaks. Closed
Thanksgiving & Christmas.*

TOUR 9
DEATH VALLEY
◇ **Furnace Creek Inn $$$**
Furnace Creek, CA 92328.
Tel: 760/786-2345;
fax: 760/786-2514.
224 rooms.

BISHOP
◇ **Days Inn $$**
725 N. Main Street, Bishop,
CA 93514. Tel: 760/872-1095.
89 rooms.

Whiskey Creek $
524 North Main Street, CA
93514. Tel: 760/873-7174.
*American cuisine. Closed
Christmas.*

TOUR 10
JAMESTOWN
◇ **Jamestown Hotel $**
18153 Main Street, Jamestown,
CA 95327. Tel: 209/984-3902.
8 rooms.

◇ **National Hotel $**
77 Main Street, Jamestown,
CA 95327. Tel: 209/984-3446.
9 rooms.

SONORA
◇ **Gunn House Hotel $**
286 S. Washington Street,
Sonora, CA 95370.
Tel: 209/532-3421.
20 rooms.

COLUMBIA
◇ **City Hotel $**
Main Street, Columbia State
Park, CA 95310. Tel: 209/532-
1470.
10 rooms.

◇ **Fallon Hotel $**
Washington Street, Columbia
State Park, CA 95310.
Tel: 209/532-1479.
14 rooms.

MURPHYS
◇ **Dunbar House 1880 $$**
271 Jones Street, Murphys,

CA 95247. Tel: 209/728-2897.
5 rooms.

🍽 **Firewood $**
420 Main Street, Murphy's. CA
95247. Tel: 209/728-3248.
American fare.

AUBURN
🍽 **Headquarter House $$**
14500 Musso Road, Auburn,
CA 95603. Tel: 530/878-1906.
*Continental cuisine. Closed
Christmas.*

TOUR 11
YOSEMITE
◇ **Tenaya Lodge $$$**
1122 Highway 41, Fish Camp,
CA 93623. Tel: 559/683-6555;
fax: 559/683 8684.
244 rooms.

◇ **Yosemite Lodge $$**
Yosemite Valley, CA 93389.
Tel: 559/252-4848.
245 rooms.

🍽 **Ahwahnee Dining Room
$$$**
Yosemite Valley, CA 95379
Tel: 209/372-1489.
International cuisine.

🍽 **Wawona Hotel Dining
Room $$**
Wawona Road, Yosemite, CA
95379. Tel: 209/375-1425.
California cuisine.

LEE VINING
◇ **Tioga Lodge $$**
54411 Highway 395, Lee
Vining, CA 93541. Tel: 760/
647-6423; fax: 760/647-6074.
14 rooms.

TOUR 12
SOUTH LAKE TAHOE
◇ **Camp Richardson
Resort $**
Jameson Beach Road, South
Lake Tahoe, CA 96158.
Tel: 530/541-1801.
78 rooms.

◇ **Inn By The Lake $$**
3300 Lake Tahoe Boulevard,
South Lake Tahoe, CA 96150.
Tel: 530/542-0330; fax: 530/
541-6596.
100 rooms.

🍽 **Sprouts Natural Foods
Café $**
3123 Harrison Street, South
Lake Tahoe, CA 96150.
Tel: 530/541-6969.
Health food.

TAHOE VISTA
🍽 **Le Petit Pier $$$**
7238 North Lake Boulevard,
Tahoe Vista, CA 96148.
Tel: 530/546-4464.
French cuisine. Closed Tue.

TRUCKEE
◇ **Truckee Hotel $$**
10007 Bridge Street, Truckee,
CA 96161. Tel: 530/587-4444;
fax: 530/587-1599.
37 rooms.

TOUR 13
FRESNO
◇ **San Joaquin $$**
1309 Shaw Avenue, Fresno,
CA 93711. Tel: 559/225-1309.
68 rooms.

🍽 **The Ripe Tomato $$$**
5064 N. Palm Avenue, Fresno,
CA 93704. Tel: 559/225-1850
French cuisine.

🍽 **Veni, Vidi, Vici $$**
1116 N. Fulton Street, Fresno,
CA 93728. Tel: 559/266-5510.
California cuisine.

SEQUOIA NATIONAL
PARK
◇ **Wuksachi Lodge $$$**
64740 Wuksachi Way, Sequoia
N P, CA 93262. Tel: 810/
559-5000.
102 rooms.

TOUR 14
SAUSALITO
◇ **Casa Madrone $$$**
801 Bridgeway Sausalito,
CA 94965. Tel: 415/332-0502.
63 rooms.

◇ **Inn Above Tide $$$**
30 El Portal, Sausalito,
CA 94965. Tel: 415/332-9535.
29 rooms.

🍽 **Poggio $**
777 Bridgeway, Sausalito,
CA 94965. Tel: 415/332-7771.
Italian cuisine.

FAIRFIELD
🍽 **Adalberto's $**
936 N. Texas Street, Fairfield,
CA 94533. Tel: 707/428-3604.
Mexican cuisine.

BENICIA
◇ **Captain Walsh House $$**
235 East L Street, Benicia,
CA 94510. Tel: 707/747-5653;
fax: 707/746-1639.
3 rooms.

TOUR 15
SACRAMENTO
◇ **Delta King Riverboat $$**
1000 Front Street, Sacramento,
CA 95814. Tel: 916/444-5464.
44 cabins.

◇ **Hartley House $$**
700 22nd Street, Sacramento,
CA 95816. Tel: 916/444-8085;
fax: 916/447-1820.
5 rooms.

◇ **Sterling House $$**
1300 H Street, Sacramento,
CA 95814. Tel: 916/448-1300.
17 rooms.

🍽 **Biba $$$**
2801 Capitol Avenue,
Sacramento, CA 95816.
Tel: 916/455-2422.
*Italian cuisine. Closed Sun and
major holidays.*

🍽 **Paragary's Bar and
Oven $$**
1401 28th Street, Sacramento
CA 95816. Tel: 916/457-5737.
Mediterranean cuisine.

🍽 **The Waterboy $$**
20th Street and Capitol
Avenue, Sacramento,
CA 95814. Tel: 916/498-9891.
French/Italian cuisine.

TOUR 16
SAN FRANCISCO
◇ **Campton Place Hotel
$$$$**
340 Stockton Street, San
Francisco, CA 94108.
Tel: 415/781-5555.
110 rooms.

◇ **Golden Gate Hotel $**
775 Bush Street, San Francisco,
CA 94108. Tel: 415/392-3702;
fax: 415/392-6202.
25 rooms.

◇ **Hotel Vintage Court $$**
650 Bush Street, San Francisco,
CA 94108. Tel: 415/392-4666.
107 rooms.

⑪ **Boulevard $$$**
1 Mission Street, San Francisco,
CA 94105. Tel: 415/543-6084.
California cuisine.

⑪ **Farallon $$**
450 Post Street, San Francisco,
CA 94102. Tel: 415/956-6969.
Seafood. Closed major holidays.

⑪ **Grand Café $$**
501 Geary Street, San
Francisco, CA 94102.
Tel: 415/292-0101.
French cuisine.

⑪ **Swan Oyster Depot $**
1517 Polk Street,
San Francisco, CA 94109.
Tel: 415/673-1101.
Seafood.

TOUR 17
SAN FRANCISCO
◇ **Hotel Boheme $$**
444 Columbus Avenue,
San Francisco, CA 94133.
Tel: 415/433-9111.
15 rooms.

◇ **The Triton Hotel $$$**
342 Grant Avenue, San
Francisco, CA 94108. Tel: 415/
394-0500; fax: 415/394-0555.
140 rooms.

⑪ **Boulevard $$$**
I Mission Street, San Francisco,
CA 94108. Tel: 415/543-6084.
California/French cuisine.

⑪ **Empress of China $$**
838 Grant Avenue, San
Francisco, CA 94108.
Tel: 415/434-1345.
*Chinese cuisine. Closed Sun and
major holidays.*

TOUR 18
SAN FRANCISCO
◇ **Tuscan Inn $$$**
425 North Point, San Francisco,
CA 94133. Tel: 415/561-1100.
221 rooms.

⑪ **Jeanty at Jacks $$$**
615 Sacramento Street,
San Francisco, CA 94111.
Tel: 415/693-0941.
French cuisine.

⑪ **L'Osteria del Forno $**
519 Columbus Avenue,
San Francisco, CA 94133.
Tel: 415/982-1124.
Italian cuisine.

TOUR 19
YOUNTVILLE
◇ **Napa Valley Lodge $$$**
2230 Madison Street,
Yountville, CA 94559.
Tel: 707/944-2468.
55 rooms.

⑪ **Bistro Jeanty $$**
6510 Washington Street,
Yountville, CA 94599.
Tel: 707/944-0103.
French cuisine.

⑪ **The French Laundry $$$$**
6640 Washington Street,
Yountville, CA 94599.
Tel: 707/944-2380.
French/California cuisine.

ST. HELENA
◇ **El Bonita Motel $$–$$$**
195 Main Street, St. Helena,
CA 94574. Tel: 707/963-3216;
fax: 707/963-8838.
41 rooms.

◇ **Meadowood Resort $$$$**
900 Meadowood Lane,
St. Helena, CA 94574.
Tel: 707/963-3646.
85 rooms.

⑪ **Terra $$$**
1345 Railroad Avenue,
St. Helena, CA 94574.
Tel: 707/963-8931.
California cuisine.

CALISTOGA
◇ **Mount View Hotel $$$**
1457 Lincoln Avenue,
Calistoga, CA 94515. Tel: 707/

942-6877; fax: 707/942-6904.
32 rooms.

TOUR 20
HALF MOON BAY
◇ **Beach House Inn $$**
4100 N. Cabrillo Highway,
Half Moon Bay, CA 94109.
Tel: 650/712-0220.
54 rooms.

⑪ **Pasta Moon $$**
315 Main Street, Half Moon
Bay, CA 94019. Tel: 650/
726-5125.
Italian cuisine.

SANTA CRUZ
◇ **Casa Blanca Inn $$**
101 Main Street, Santa Cruz,
CA 95060. Tel: 831/423-1570.
39 rooms.

◇ **Mission Inn $$**
2250 Mission Street, Santa
Cruz, CA 95060. Tel: 831/425-
5455; fax: 831/469-4870.
53 rooms.

⑪ **Omei $**
2316 Mission Street, Santa
Cruz, CA 95060.
Tel: 831/425-8458.
Chinese cuisine.

MONTEREY
◇ **Cypress Tree Inn $**
2227 N. Fremont Street,
Monterey, CA 93940.
Tel: 831/372-7586.
55 rooms.

◇ **Lodge at Pebble
Beach $$$$$**
17-Mile Drive, Pebble Beach,
Monterey, CA 92953. Tel: 831/
624-3811; fax: 831/644-7960.
161 rooms.

⑪ **Sardine Factory $$$**
701 Wave Street, Monterey,
CA 93940. Tel: 831/373-3775.
*Italian cuisine. Closed week of
Dec 25.*

TOUR 21
BIG SUR
◇ **Ventana Inn $$$$**
Highway 1, Ventana, CA 93920.
Tel: 831/667-2331; fax: 831/
667-2512.
60 rooms.

SAN LUIS OBISPO
◇ **La Questa Motor Inn $$**
2074 Monterey Street,
San Luis Obispo, CA 93401.
Tel: 805/543-2777; fax: 805/
544-0696.
72 rooms.

Ⓣ **Big Sky Café $**
1121 Broad Street, San Luis
Obispo, CA 93401.
Tel: 805/545-5401.
California cuisine. Open daily.

TOUR 22
SANTA MONICA
◇ **Channel Road Inn $$$**
219 W. Channel Road, Santa
Monica, CA 90402. Tel: 310/
459-1920; fax: 310/454-9920.
14 rooms.

OJAI
◇ **Blue Iguana Inn $$$**
11794 N. Ventura Avenue,
Ojai, CA 93923. Tel: 805/
646-5277.
23 rooms.

SANTA BARBARA
◇ **Inn of the Spanish
Garden $$$**
91 Garden Street, Santa
Barbara, CA 93101.
Tel: 805/564-4700.
23 rooms.

◇ **Hotel Oceana $$$**
202 W. Cabrillo Boulevard,
Santa Barbara, CA 93101.
Tel: 805/965-4577;
fax: 805/965-9937.
122 rooms.

Ⓣ **Bouchon $$**
9 W. Victoria Street, Santa
Barbara CA 93101.
Tel: 805/730-1160.
French cuisine.

Ⓣ **Wine Cask $$$**
813 Anacapa Street, Santa
Barbara, CA 93101.
Tel: 805/966-9463.
California cuisine.

LOS OLIVOS
Ⓣ **Los Olivos Café $$**
2879 Grand Avenue,
Los Olivos, CA 93441.
Tel: 805/688-7265.
California cuisine.

SOLVANG
◇ **Royal Scandinavian Inn $$**
400 Alisal Road, Solvang,
CA 93464. Tel: 805/688-8000.
133 rooms.

TOUR 23
BODEGA
◇ **Inn at the Tides $$**
800 Coast Highway 1, Bodega
Bay, CA 94923. Tel: 707/
875-2751.
86 rooms.

Ⓣ **Tides Wharf Restaurant
$$**
835 Highway 1, Bodega Bay,
CA 94923. Tel: 707/875-3652.
Seafood.

GUALALA
◇ **Whale Watch Inn $$$$**
35100 Highway 1, Gualala,
CA 95445. Tel: 707/884-3667;
fax: 707/884-4815.
18 rooms.

MENDOCINO
◇ **Brewery Gulch Inn $$$**
9401 Coast Highway 1,
Mendocino, CA 95460.
Tel: 800/578-4454.
10 rooms.

Ⓣ **Café Beaujolais $$**
961 Ukiah Street, Mendocino,
CA 95460.
Tel: 707/937-5614.
French cuisine. Closed Dec 25.

TRINIDAD
◇ **Bishop Pine Lodge $–$$**
1481 Patricks Point Drive,
Trinidad, CA 95570. Tel: 707/
677-3314; fax: 707/677-3444.
13 rooms.

TOUR 24
REDDING
◇ **La Quinta Inn $$**
2180 Hilltop Drive, Redding,
CA 96003. Tel: 530/221-8200.
133 rooms.

Ⓣ **Buz's Crab Stand $**
2159 E. Street, Redding, CA
96001. Tel: 530/243-2120.
Seafood.

MOUNT SHASTA
Ⓣ **Piemont $**
1200 South Mount Shasta

Boulevard, Mount Shasta,
CA 96067. Tel: 530/926-2402.
*Italian/American cuisine. Closed
Mon, Thanksgiving & Christmas.*

MCCLOUD
◇ **McCloud Hotel $$**
408 Main Street, McCloud,
CA 96057. Tel: 530/964-2822;
fax: 530/964-2844.
16 rooms.

TOUR 25
SONOMA
◇ **Gaige House Inn $$$**
13540 Arnold Drive, Glen
Ellen, CA 95442. Tel: 707/
935-0237.
23 rooms.

◇ **Sonoma Mission Inn $$$**
Boyes Boulevard and Highway
12, Sonoma, CA 95476.
Tel: 707/938-9000.
226 rooms.

Ⓣ **The Girl and the Fig $$**
110 West Spain Street, Sonoma,
CA 95476. Tel: 707/938-2064.
Rustic Provençal-inspired cuisine.

Ⓣ **Swiss Hotel $$**
18 W. Spain Street, Sonoma,
CA 95476. Tel: 707/938-2884.
Italian cuisine.

SANTA ROSA
◇ **Los Robles Lodge $–$$**
1985 Cleveland Street, Santa
Rosa, CA 95401. Tel: 707/545-
6330; fax: 707/575-5826.
104 rooms.

HEALDSBURG
Ⓣ **Cyrus $$$$**
29 North Street, Healdsburg,
CA 95448. Tel: 707/433-3311.
*California cuisine. Closed
Thanksgiving & Christmas.*

BOONVILLE
◇ **Boonville Hotel $$**
14050 Highway 128, Boonville,
CA 95415. Tel: 707 895 2210;
fax: 707 895 2243.
8 rooms, studio and bungalow.

The famous Hollywood sign
originally said Hollywoodland

Practical Information

Practical Information
The addresses, telephone numbers and opening times of the attractions mentioned in the tours, including the telephone numbers of the local Tourist Information Offices are listed below tour by tour.

Many attractions are closed for major holidays, including Thanksgiving, Christmas, and the New Year, so check before visiting.

TOUR 1

[i] Hollywood Visitors Information Center, 6801 Hollywood Boulevard, CA 90028.
Tel: 323/467-5412.

1 Hollywood Boulevard
Mann's Chinese Theatre
6925 Hollywood Boulevard.
Tel: 323/464-8111, 818/784-6266.
Call for show times.

2 Griffith Park
Park Ranger Visitor Center, 4730 Crystal Springs Drive.
Tel: 323/913-4688.

Griffith Observatory and Planetarium
2800 East Observatory Road.
Tel: 213/473-0800.
Hours vary, call for information.

Gene Autry Western Heritage Museum
4700 Western Heritage Way.
Tel: 323/667-2000.
Open Tue–Sun 10–5.

Travel Town Museum
5200 Zoo Drive.
Tel: 323/662-5874.
Open Mon–Fri 10–4, weekends 10–5.

3 Forest Lawn
1712 South Glendale Avenue.
Tel: 323/254-3131.
Open daily 9–5.

4 Pasadena
Norton Simon Museum of Art
411 West Colorado Boulevard.
Tel: 626/449-6840.
Open Thu–Sun noon–6.

Huntington Library
1151 Oxford Road, San Marino.
Tel: 626/405-2100.
Open Tue–Fri 1–4.30, Sat–Sun 10.30–4.30; Jun, Jul, daily 10.30–4.30.

Descanso Gardens
1418 Descanso Drive, La Canada.
Tel: 818/949-4290.
Open daily 9–4.30.

5 El Pueblo de Los Angeles State Historic Park
Avila Adobe, E-10 Olvera Street.
Tel: 213/628-1274.
Open Mon–Sat 10–5.

6 Music Center
135 North Grand Avenue.
Tel: 213/972-7211.
Call for performance times.

7 Museum of Contemporary Art
250 South Grand Avenue.
Tel: 213/626-6222.
Open Tue, Wed, Fri, Sun 11–5, Thu 11–8.

9 Exposition Boulevard
Museum of Natural History and Museum of Science and Industry
Los Angeles Coliseum, 700 State Drive.
Tel: 213/763-3466.
Call for opening times.

10 Long Beach
Queen Mary
1126 Queens Highway.
Tel: 562/435-3511.
Call for tour information.

14 The Getty Center
1200 Getty Center Drive.
Tel: 310/440-7300.
Open Tue, Wed, Sat, Sun 11–6, Thu, Fri 11–9.

15 Beverly Hills
Los Angeles County Museum of Art
5905 Wilshire Boulevard.
Tel: 323/857-6000.

Open Tue–Fri 10–5, Sat–Sun 10–6.

George C. Page Museum
5801 Wilshire Boulevard.
Tel: 323/934-7243.
Open Tue–Sun 10–5.

TOUR 2

[i] Hollywood Visitors Information Center, 6801 Hollywood Boulevard, CA 90028.
Tel: 323/467-5412.

TOUR 3

[i] LA INC, LA CVB, 685 South Figueroa Street, Los Angeles, CA 90017.
Tel: 213/689-8822

1 Redlands
Kimberly Crest House
1325 Prospect Drive.
Tel: 909/792 2111.
Open Thu–Sun 1–4.

5 Riverside
The Mission Inn
3649 Mission Inn Avenue.
Tel: 800/344 4225.
Call for tour times.

California Citrus State Historic Park
1879 Jackson Street.
Tel: 909/780 6222.
Open daily 8–5.

California Museum of Photography
3824 Main Street.
Tel: 951/827-4787.
Open Tue–Sun 11–5.

6 Chino
Planes of Fame Air Museum
7000 Merrill Avenue.
Tel: 909/597-3722.
Open daily 9–5.

TOUR 4

[i] Hollywood Visitors Information Center, 6801 Hollywood Boulevard, CA 90028.
Tel: 323/467-5412.

[i] Visitors Bureau, Suite 208, 301 Main Street, Huntington Beach, CA 92647.
Tel: 714/969-3492.

[i] Visitors Bureau, 252 Broadway, Laguna Beach, CA 92651.
Tel: 949/497-9229.

1 Bolsa Chica Ecological Reserve
17851 Pacific Coast Highway.
Tel: 714/846-3460.
Open daily, daylight hours.

2 Huntington Beach
International Surfing Museum
411 Olive Street.
Tel: 714/960-3483.
Open Wed–Sun noon–5.

4 Balboa
Fun Zone
600 East Bay.
Tel: 949/673-0480.
Call for opening hours.

TOUR 5

[i] San Diego Visitor Information Center, 2688 E. Mission Bay Drive, San Diego, CA 92109.
Tel: 619/276-8200.

1 Balboa Park
San Diego Zoo
2000 Zoo Drive.
Tel: 619/234-3153.
Open daily 9–5.

Museum of Man
1350 El Prado.
Tel: 619/239-2001.
Open daily 10–4.30.

San Diego Aerospace Museum
2001 Pan American Plaza.
Tel: 619/234-8291.
Open daily 10–4.30.

San Diego Automotive Museum
2080 Pan American Plaza.
Tel: 619/231-2886.
Open daily 10–4.30.

2 Mission San Diego de Alcala
10818 San Diego Mission Road.
Tel: 619/283-7319.
Open daily 9–5.

3 Old Town San Diego State Historic Park
4002 Wallace Street.
Tel: 619/220-5422.
Open daily 10–5.

Practical Information

[4] University of California at San Diego (UCSD)
Birch Aquarium at Scripps
2300 Expedition Way.
Tel: 858/534-FISH.
Open daily 9–5.

[5] La Jolla
La Jolla Museum of Contemporary Art
700 Prospect Street.
Tel: 858/454-3541.
Open Tue–Sat 10–5, Wed until 8, Sun noon–5. Free entry on 1st Tue of month.

[7] SeaWorld
1720 Shores Road.
Tel: 619/226-3901.
Open Jun–Aug, daily 9am–10pm; Sep–May, daily 10–5.

[9] Maritime Museum
1306 North Harbor Drive.
Tel: 619/234-9153.
Open daily 9–8.

TOUR 6

[i] San Diego Visitor Information Center, 2688 E. Mission Bay Drive, San Diego, CA 92109.
Tel: 619/276-8200.

[1] El Cajon
Heritage of the Americas Museum
2952 Jamacha Road.
Tel: 619/670-5194.
Open Tue–Fri 10–4, Sat noon–4.

[3] Julian
Eagle and High Peak Mine
P.O. Box 624.
Tel: 760/765-0036.
Call for tour times.

[4] Santa Ysabel
Mission Santa Ysabel
23013 Highway 79.
Tel: 760/765-0810.
Open daily 9–5.

[5] Mount Palomar
Palomar Observatory
35899 Canfield Road.
Tel: 760/742-2119.
Open daily 9–4.

[6] Pala
Mission San Antonio de Pala
Mission Road.

Tel: 760/742-3317.
Open Tue–Sun 10–4.

[7] Mission San Luis Rey de Francia
4050 Mission Avenue.
Tel: 760/757-3651.
Open daily 9–5.

[9] Escondido
San Diego Wild Animal Park
15500 San Pasqual Valley Road.
Tel: 760/480-0100.
Open daily 9–5.

TOUR 7

[i] Palm Springs Desert Resorts Convention and Visitors Bureau, 70–100 Highway 111, Rancho Mirage, CA 92270. Tel: 760/770-9000, 800/41-RELAX.

[2] Desert Hot Springs
Cabot's Pueblo Museum
67616 East Desert View Avenue.
Tel: 760/329-7610.
Call for times.

[3] Palm Springs
McCullum Adobe
221 South Palm Canyon Drive.
Tel: 760/323-8297.
Open Thu–Sat 10–4, Wed, Sun noon–3.

Palm Springs Desert Museum
101 Museum Drive.
Tel: 760/325-0189.
Open Tue–Sat 10–5, Sun noon–5.

Moorten Botanical Garden
1701 South Palm Canyon Drive.
Tel: 760/327-6555.
Open Mon, Tue, Thu–Sat 9–4.30, Sun 10–4.

[5] Palm Desert
Living Desert Wild Animal Park
47900 Portola Avenue.
Tel: 760/346-5694.
Open daily 9–5. Closed Aug.

TOUR 8

[i] Hollywood Visitors Information Center, 6801 Hollywood Boulevard, CA 90028.
Tel: 323/467-5412.

[i] California Welcome Center, 2796 Tanger Way, Suite 106. Barstow, CA 92311.
Tel: 760/253-4813.

[3] Chiriaco Summit
General Patten Memorial Museum
2 Chiriaco Road.
Tel: 760/227-3483.
Open daily 9.30–4.30.

[8] Calico Ghost Town
I-15 at Ghost Town Road, Yermo.
Tel: 760/254-2122.
Open daily 9–5.

Calico Early Man Archaeological Site
P.O. Box 535, Yermo.
Open Wed–Sun 9.30–1.

[9] Barstow
Mojave River Valley Museum
270 East Virginia Way.
Tel: 760/256-5452.
Open daily 11–4.

TOUR 9

[i] Hollywood Visitors Information Center, 6801 Hollywood Boulevard, CA 90028.
Tel: 323/467-5412.

[1] San Fernando
Universal Studios
100 Universal City Plaza.
Tel: 818/622-3801.
Open Oct–May, daily 9–7; Jun–Sep 8am–10pm.

NBC Studios
3000 West Alameda Avenue, Burbank.
Tel: 818/840-3537.
Call for hours.

[8] Ridgecrest
Maturango Museum
North China Lake Boulevard & Las Flores Avenue.
Tel: 760/375-6900.
Open daily 10–5.

[13] Independence
Eastern California Museum
155 North Grant Street.
Tel: 760/878-0364.
Open Wed–Sun 10–4.

Manzanar National Historic Site
P.O. Box 426.
Tel: 760/878-2932.
Open daily dawn–dusk.

[16] Bishop
Paiute Shoshone Indian Cultural Center
2300 West Line Street.
Tel: 760/873-4478.
Open daily 10–3.

TOUR 10

[i] San Francisco Visitor Information, 900 Market Street, lower level of Hallidie Plaza near Powell and Market streets, San Francisco, CA 94102.
Tel: 415/974-6900.

[i] California Welcome Center, 13411 Lincoln Way, Auburn, CA 95603.
Tel: 530/887-2111.

[2] Jamestown
Railway 1897 State Historic Park
5th and Reservoir streets.
Tel: 209/984-3953.
Open daily 9.30–4.30.

[3] Sonora
Tuolumne County Museum
158 West Bradford Avenue.
Tel: 209/532-1317.
Open daily 10–4.

[4] Columbia
Columbia State Historic Park
Highway 49 at Parrot's Ferry Road.
Tel: 209/588-9128.
Open daily 8–6.

[5] Moaning Cavern
5350 Moaning Cave Road.
Tel: 209/736-2708.
Open daily 9–6 (summer); 10–5 (winter).

Mercer Caverns
1665 Sheepranch Road.
Tel: 209/728-2101.
Open Sun–Thu 10–4.30, Fri–Sat 10–6.

i Tourist Information Office
12 Number on tour

6 Murphys
Old Timers Museum
P.O. Box 94.
Tel: 209/728-1160.
Call for hours.

7 Angels Camp
Angels Camp Museum
753 South Main Street.
Tel: 209/736-2963.
Open daily 10–3.

8 San Andreas
Calaveras County
Museum
30 North Main Street.
Tel: 209/754-1058.
Open Mon–Fri 9–4.

11 Jackson
Amador County Museum
225 Church Street.
Tel: 209/223-6386.
Open Wed–Sun 10–4.

14 Placerville
Gold Bug Mine
Tel: 530/642-5207.
*Open May–Dec, daily 10–4;
Jan–May, weekends only.*

**15 Marshall Gold
Discovery State
Historic Park**
310 Back Street.
Tel: 530/622-3470.
Open daily 10–5.

16 Auburn
Gold Country Museum
1273 High Street.
Tel: 530/889-6500.
*Open Tue–Fri 10–3.30,
Sat–Sun 11–4.*

TOUR 11

i San Francisco Visitor
Information, 900 Market
Street, lower level of
Hallidie Plaza and Powell
and Market streets, San
Francisco, CA 94102.
Tel: 415/974-6900.

i California Welcome
Center, 710 W. 16th Street,
Suite A, Merced,
CA 95340.
Tel: 209/384-2791.

2 Mariposa
Mariposa Museum
5119 Jessie Street.
Tel: 209/966-2924.
Open daily 10–4.30.

California State Mining
and Mineral Museum
5005 Fairgrounds Drive.

Tel: 209/742-7625.
Open Wed–Sun 10–4.

8 Bodie
Bodie State Historic Park
P.O. Box 515, Bridgeport.
Tel: 760/647-6445.
*Open 8–7 (summer); 8–4
(rest of year)*

TOUR 12

i Sacramento Visitor
Information Center, 16081
Street, CA 95814.
Tel: 916/808-7777.

i Nevada City Chamber
of Commerce, 132 Main
Street, Nevada City,
CA 95959.
Tel: 530/265-2692.

2 South Lake Tahoe
Lake Tahoe Historical
Society Museum
3058 Lake Tahoe
Boulevard.
Tel: 530/541-5458.
Call for hours.

3 Tallac Historic Site
South Lake Tahoe.
Tel: 530/541-5227.
Open Jun–Sep, daily 10–4.

4 Emerald Bay
Vikingsholm
Emerald Bay.
Tel: 530/525-7277.
Open Jun- Sep. Call for times.

**5 Sugar Pine Point
State Park**
Ehrmann Mansion
P.O. Box 266.
Tel: 530/525-7982.
Open Jun–Aug, daily 11–4.

6 Truckee
The Emigrant Trail
Museum
12593 Donner Pass Road.
Tel: 530/582-7892.
Open daily 9–4.

8 Grass Valley
Empire Mine State
Historic Park
10556 East Empire Street.
Tel: 530/273-8522.
Open daily 9–5.

TOUR 13

i Fresno Convention
and Visitors Bureau, 848 M
Street, Fresno, CA 93721.
Tel: 800/788-0836.

1 Fresno
Kearney Mansion
7160 West Kearney
Boulevard.
Tel: 559/441-0862.
Open Fri–Sun 1–4.

Forestiere Underground
Gardens
5021 West Shaw Avenue.
Tel: 559/271-0734.
Call for hours.

Fresno Metropolitan
Museum of Art
1515 Van Ness Avenue.
Tel: 559/441-1444.
Open Tue–Sun 11–5.

4 Crystal Cave
HCR 89, Box 10, Three
Rivers.
Tel: 559/565-3759.
*Open mid-May to mid-Jun,
Fri–Mon 11–4; mid-Jun to
Labor Day, daily 11–4.*

6 Visalia
Tulare Historical
Museum
444 West Tulare Avenue.
Tel: 559/686-2074.
*Open Mon and Wed– Fri
10-4, Sat–Sun 12.30–6.30.
Closed Tue. Shorter hours
and also closed Wed in
winter.*

TOUR 14

i San Francisco Visitor
Information Center,
Benjamin Swig Pavilion,
Hallidie Plaza, Market and
Powell streets, San
Francisco, CA 94101.
Tel: 415/974 6900.

1 Sausalito
San Francisco Bay Model
2100 Bridgeway.
Tel: 415/332-3871.
Open Tue–Sat 9–4.

**2 Western Railway
Museum**
5848 State Highway 12,
Suisun City.
Tel: 707/374-2978.
Open Sat–Sun 11–5.

7 Benicia
Benicia State Capitol
Building
115 West G Street.
Tel: 707/745-3385.
Open daily 10–5.

Camel Barn Museum
2024 Camel Road.
Tel: 707/745-5435.
Open Wed–Sun 1–4.

8 Martinez
John Muir National
Historic Site
4202 Alhambra Avenue.
Tel: 925/228-8860.
Open daily 10–5.

TOUR 15

i Sacramento Visitor
Information Center, 16081
Street, Sacramento,
CA 95814.
Tel: 916/808-7777.

1 Sutter's Fort
2701 L Street.
Tel: 916/445-4422.
Open daily 10–5.

2 Governor's Mansion
1526 H Street.
Tel: 916/323-3047.
Open daily 10–5.

3 State Capitol
10th Street & Capitol Mall.
Tel: 916/324-0333.
Open daily 9–5.

**4 Crocker Art
Museum**
216 O Street.
Tel: 916/264-5423.
Open Tue–Sun 10–5.

**5 Old Sacramento
State Historic Park**
1102 Second Street.
Tel: 916/445-6645.
Open business hours.

California State Railroad
Museum
1119 2nd Street.
Tel: 916/445-6645.
Open daily 10–5.

TOUR 16

i San Francisco Visitor
Information Center,
Benjamin Swig Pavilion,
Hallidie Plaza, Market and
Powell streets, CA 94101.
Tel: 415/974-6900.

2 Fisherman's Wharf
Aquarium of the Bay
Pier 39, Beach Street.
Tel: 415/623-5300.
Open daily 10–8.30.

i Tourist Information Office
12 Number on tour

Maritime National Historic Park
2905 Hyde Street.
Tel: 415/447-5000.
Open daily 9.30–5.30 (4.30 during winter).

4 Fort Mason
Mexican Museum
Building D.
Tel: 415/202-9700.
Open Wed–Fri noon–5, Sat–Sun 11–5.

Museo Italo Americano
Building C.
Tel: 415/673-2200.
Open Wed–Sun noon–5.

Craft and Folk Art Museum
51 Yerba Buena Lane.
Tel: 415/227-4888.
Open Tue–Fri, Sun 11–5, Sat 10–5.

S.S. *Jeremiah O'Brian*
Pier #3.
Tel: 415/544-0100.
Open daily 9–4.

6 The Presidio
Presidio Army Museum
Montgomery Street.
Tel: 415/561-4323.
Call for hours.

7 Fort Point
Long Avenue, off Lincoln Boulevard.
Tel: 415/556-1693.
Open daily 10–5.

8 California Palace of the Legion of Honor
34th Avenue and Clement Street.
Tel: 415/750-3600.
Open Tue–Sun 9.30–5.

10 San Francisco Zoological Gardens
Sloat Avenue at Pacific Ocean.
Tel: 415/753-7080.
Open daily 10–5.

11 Golden Gate Park
M.H. de Young Memorial Museum
Tel: 415/750-3600.
Open Tue–Sun 9.30–5.30 (until 8.45 on Fri).

Japanese Tea Garden
Tel: 415/8752-4227.
Open daily 9–6.

California Academy of Sciences
Tel: 415/750-7145.
Open daily 10–5.

17 Asian Art Museum
Tel: 415/581-3500.
Call for information.

TOUR 17

i San Francisco Visitor Information Center,
Benjamin Swig Pavilion,
Hallidie Plaza, Market and Powell streets, CA 94101.
Tel: 415/974-6900.

5 Cable Car Barn
1201 Mason Street.
Tel: 415/474-1887.
Open daily 10–6.

7 Financial District
Wells Fargo History Room
420 Montgomery Street.
Tel: 415/396-2619.
Open Mon–Fri 9–5.

8 Pacific Heritage Museum
608 Commercial Street.
Tel: 415/399-1124.
Open Tue–Sat 10–4.

TOUR 18

i San Francisco Visitor Information Center,
Benjamin Swig Pavilion,
Hallidie Plaza, Market and Powell streets, CA 94101.
Tel: 415/974-6900.

6 Coit Tower
1 Telegraph Hill.
Tel: 415/362-0808.
Open daily 10–6.

TOUR 19

i San Francisco Visitor Information Center,
Benjamin Swig Pavilion,
Hallidie Plaza, Market and Powell streets, CA 94101.
Tel: 415/974-6900.

i California Welcome Center, 9 Fourth Street, Santa Rosa, CA 95401.
Tel: 800/404-7673.

1 Vallejo
Six Flags Discovery Kingdom
Marine World Parkway.

Tel: 707/643-6722.
Open mid-Mar to Memorial Day, Fri–Sun 10–8; Memorial Day–Oct, daily 10–10.

2 Napa
COPIA
500 First Street.
Tel: 707/259-1600.
Call for information.

3 Yountville
Domaine Chandon
1 California Drive.
Tel: 707/944-2280.
Open May–Oct, daily 10–5; Nov–Apr, Wed–Sun 10–4.

Trefethen Vineyards
1160 Oak Knoll Avenue.
Tel: 707/255-7700.
Open daily 10–4.

Robert Mondavi Winery
7001 St Helena Highway.
Tel: 888/766-6328.
Open daily 10–4.

St. Supéry Winery
8440 St. Helena Highway.
Tel: 707/963-4507.
Open daily 10–4.

5 St Helena
Silverado Museum
1490 Library Lane.
Tel: 707/963-3757.
Open Tue–Sun noon–4.

Beringer Vineyards
2000 Main Street.
Tel: 707/963-7115.
Open daily 10–4.

Charles Krug Winery
2800 St. Helena Highway.
Tel: 707/963-5057.
Open daily 10–4

6 Calistoga
Old Faithful of California
1299 Tubbs Lane.
Tel: 707/942-6463.
Open daily 9–6.

7 Geyserville
Rossi & Bianco
400 Souvrain Road.
Tel: 707/433-8282.
Open daily 10–5.

8 Healdsburg
Sonoma County Wine Library
139 Piper Street.
Tel: 707/433-3772.
Open Mon, Wed 9.30–9, Tue, Thu–Sat 9.30–6.

Healdsburg Museum
221 Matheson Street.
Tel: 707/431-3325.
Open Tue–Sun 11–4.

10 Glen Ellen
Jack London State Historic Park
2400 London Ranch Road.
Tel: 707/938-5216.
Open daily dawn to dusk.

Benziger Winery
1883 London Ranch Road.
Tel: 707/935-3000.
Open daily 10–4.

Buena Vista Winery
18000 Old Winery Road.
Tel: 707/938-1266.
Open daily 10–4; guided tours at 2.

TOUR 20

i San Francisco Visitor Information Center
Benjamin Swig Pavilion,
Hallidie Plaza, Market and Powell streets, CA 94101.
Tel: 415/974-6900.

2 Santa Cruz
Surfing Museum
West Cliff Drive.
Tel: 831/420-6289.
Open Thu–Mon noon–4 (winter), Wed Mon noon–5 (summer).

3 Monterey
Monterey Bay Aquarium
886 Cannery Row.
Tel: 800/756-3737, 800/225-2277.
Open daily 10–6.

TOUR 21

i Monterey Peninsula Visitor and Convention Bureau, P.O. Box 1770, Monterey CA 93942.
Tel: 877/MONTEREY.

2 Carmel-by-the-Sea
Tor House
26304 Ocean View Road.
Tel: 831/624-1813.
Open Fri–Sat 10–3.

3 Point Lobos State Reserve
Highway 1, 3 miles (5km) south of Carmel.
Tel: 831/624-4909.
Open daily 9–7 (summer); 9–5 (winter).

5 Hearst Castle
750 Hearst Castle Road,
San Simeon.
Tel: 805/927-2020.
*Open daily – tours start at
8.20.*

8 Morro Bay
Morro Bay Natural
History Museum
Morro Bay State Park
Road.
Tel: 805/772-2694.
Open daily 10–5.

10 San Luis Obispo
Mission San Luis Obispo
de Tolosa
751 Palm Street.
Tel: 805/781-0220.
*Open daily 9–4 (winter);
9–5 (summer).*

13 San Miguel
Mission San Miguel
775 Mission Street.
Tel: 805/467-3256.
Open daily 9.30–4.30.

14 San Antonio
Mission San Antonio de
Padua
1 Mission Creek Road,
Jolon.
Tel: 831/385-4478.
Open Mon–Sat 9.30–4.30.

TOUR 22

⟨i⟩ Santa Monica
Convention and Visitors
Bureau, 1920 Main Street
Santa Monica, CA 90405.
Tel: 310/319 6263.

1 The Getty Villa
17985 Pacific Coast
Highway, Malibu.
Tel: 310/440-7300.
Open Thu–Mon 10–5.

3 Santa Barbara
Mission Santa Barbara
Laguna and Olivos streets.
Tel: 805/682-4713.
Open daily 9–5.

El Presidio de Santa
Barbara State Historic
Park
Tel: 805/965-0093.
Open daily 9–5.

County Courthouse
1100 Anacapa Street.
Tel: 805/568-2220.
*Open for tours Mon–Sat at
2, Wed and Fri 10.30.*

6 Solvang
Mission Santa Innes
1760 Mission Drive.
Tel: 805/688-4815.
*Open Mon–Sat 9–7, Sun
1.30–4.30 (summer);
Mon–Sat 9–4.30, Sun
1.30–4.30 (winter).*

7 La Purisima Mission
Tel: 805/733-3713.
Open daily 9–4.30.

TOUR 23

⟨i⟩ Redwood Empire
Association, 2 Beach
Street, San Francisco,
CA 94133.
Tel: 800/619-2125.

⟨i⟩ Leggett Valley
Chamber of Commerce,
Highway 1, PO Box 218,
Leggett, CA 95455.
Tel: 707/925-6470.

⟨i⟩ Greater Ukiah
Chamber of Commerce,
200 South School Street,
Ukiah, CA 95482.
Tel: 707/462-4705.

2 Stinson Beach
Audubon Canyon Ranch
4900 Highway 1.
Tel: 415/868-9244.
*Open weekends and
holidays 10–4.*

**5 Fort Ross State
Historic Park**
19005 Coast Highway 1.
Tel: 707/847-3286.
Open daily 10–4.30.

10 Mendocino
Kelly House Museum
45007 Albion Street.
Tel: 707/937-5791.
*Open Fri–Mon 1–4 (winter);
daily 1–4 (summer).*

Mendocino Art Center
45200 Little Lake Road.
Tel: 707/937-5818.
Open daily 10–5.

11 Fort Bragg
Mendocino Coast
Botanical Gardens
18220 North Highway 1.
Tel: 707/964-4352.
*Open Mar–Oct, 9–5;
Nov–Feb, 9–4.*

15 Scotia
Pacific Lumber Company
1125 Main Street.
Tel: 707/764-2222.
Open Mon–Thu 8–2.

20 Willits
Mendocino County
Museum
400 East Commercial
Street. Tel: 707/459-2736.
Open Wed–Sun 10–4.30.

21 Ukiah
Grace Hudson Museum
431 South Main Street.
Tel: 707/467-2836.
*Open Wed–Sat 10–4, Sun
noon–4.*

22 Hopland
Fetzer Valley Oaks Food
and Wine Center
13601 Eastside Road.
Tel: 707/744-1250.
Open daily 9–5.

TOUR 24

⟨i⟩ Redding Chamber
of Commerce, 777
Auditorium Drive,
Redding, CA 96001.
Tel: 530/225-4433.

4 Mount Shasta
Sisson Museum
1 North Old Stagecoach
Road.
Tel: 530/926-5508
Open daily 1–4.

5 Yreka
Siskiyou County
Courthouse
311 Fourth Street.
Tel: 530/842-8340.
Open Mon–Fri 8–5.

Siskiyou County
Museum
910 South Main Street.
Tel: 530/842-3836.
Open Tue–Sat 9–5.

6 Weaverville
Joss House State Historic
Park
Main and Oregon streets.
Tel: 530/623-5284.
*Open Jun–Sep, 10–5;
Oct–Dec, Wed–Sun 10–5;
Jan–Apr, Sat 10–5; May,
Wed–Sun 10–5.*

TOUR 25

⟨i⟩ Sacramento
Convention and Visitors
Bureau, 1608 I Street,
Sacramento CA 95814.
Tel: 916/808-7777.

⟨i⟩ Napa Valley
Conference and Visitors
Bureau, 1310 Napa Valley
Town Center, CA 94559.
tel: 707/226-7459.

3 Sonoma
Sonoma State Historic
Park
20 East Spain Street.
Tel: 707/938-1519.
Open daily 10–5.

Mission San Francisco
Solano de Sonoma
First and Spain streets.
Tel: 707/938-9560.
Open daily 10–5.

4 Petaluma
Petaluma Adobe State
Historic Park
3325 Adobe Road.
Tel: 707/762-4871.
Open daily 10–5.

10 Boonville
Anderson Valley Historical
Society Museum
Between Boonville and
Philo on Highway 128.
Tel: 707/895-3207.
Call for hours.

10 Lakeport
Lake County Museum
Old County Courthouse,
255 North Main Street.
Tel: 707/263-4555.
Open Wed–Sun 9–4.

INDEX

Index

Index & Acknowledgments

The Automobile Association

wishes to thank the following libraries and photographers for their assistance in the preparation of this book.
MARY EVANS PICTURE LIBRARY 74c; SPECTRUM COLOUR LIBRARY 19, 20; UNIVERSAL STUDIOS, HOLLYWOOD 21

The remaining photographs are held in the Association's own photo library and were taken by Robert Holmes with the exception of page 12 taken by Max Jourdan; pages 40, 41a, 100, 101, 102, 103, 105, 106/7, 107, 108, 112, 164 which were taken by Ken Paterson; pages 170/1 taken by Clive Sawyer; and pages 5, 7, 8, 9, 11, 13, 15, 16 taken by Phil Wood.

Thanks also to Daniel Millington for his contribution to this book.

Contributors

Copy editor: Nia Williams   **Indexer:** Marie Lorimer
Thanks to **Robert Holmes** for his updating work.

Atlas

OREGON　　　IDAHO

Yreka
Orick
Weed
182-183　**184**

Eureka
Weaverville
Redding

NEVADA

Leggett

Fort
Bragg　**185**　**186-187**
Ukiah　Nevada
City
Auburn

Santa Rosa　Sacramento
Napa
Sonora
San Francisco **188-189**　**190-191**
Modesto

Santa Cruz
Monterey　Fresno　Independence
Big Sur　**192-193**　**194-195**　**196**

San
Simeon　San Luis
Obispo　Ridgecrest

197　**198-199**　**200-201**

Santa Barbara　Ventura　Los
Angeles　San Bernardino
Santa Monica
Venice　Palm
Springs
Long
Beach　**202-203**　**204**

A
R
I
Z
O
N
A

San Diego

MEX

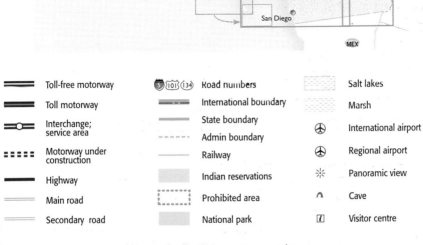

═══ Toll-free motorway	Road numbers	Salt lakes
═══ Toll motorway	International boundary	Marsh
═○═ Interchange; service area	State boundary	International airport
▪▪▪▪▪ Motorway under construction	Admin boundary	Regional airport
━━ Highway	Railway	Panoramic view
═══ Main road	Indian reservations	Cave
═══ Secondary road	Prohibited area	Visitor centre
	National park	

0　10　20　30　40 km
0　10　20 miles

D

Toiyabe National Forest F

Gillis Range

Gabbs Valley Range

361

Walker Lake

Thorne
HAWTHORNE AMMUNITION DEPOT
Babbitt
Hawthorne
359
95
Luning
7564ft
Table Mtn

Garfield Hills

Mina
Sodaville
9187ft
Pilot Peak

Ione Wash

Cedar Mountain

Dry Lake

San Antonio Mts

9530ft
well Mtn
oiyabe
ational
orest

Excelsior Mountains

Marietta

Tonopah Junction
95

360

Candalaria Hills

Candalaria

Monte Cristo Range

Columbus Salt Marsh

Coaldale

Blair Junction

6
95

9108ft
Lone Mtn

Tonopah

Inyo National Forest

Mount Montgomery
6

264

773

95

265

20

13140ft
Boundary Peak

Benton Hot Springs
Benton

11123ft
Glass Mtn

13559ft
Mt Dubois

Silver Peak Range

Silver Peak

8376ft
Montezuma Peak
Goldfield

Montezuma Range

3

ke
owley

as Place

Dyer
264

14246ft
White Mtn Peak

Inyo National Forest

9450ft
Piper Peak

Palmetto Mts

395

Chalfant
6

11278ft
Blanco Mtn

266

Oasis

Lida

9046ft
Magruder Mtn

266

774

4

Gold Point

3748ft
Morgan
Rovana
Scheelite

Laws
Bishop

168
7703ft
Chocolate Mtn

Deep Springs

NEVADA
CALIFORNIA

13986ft
Mt Humphreys

Keough Hot Springs

9083ft
Black Mtn

Deep Lake Springs

Eureka Valley

8456ft
Last Chance Mtn

Oriental Wash

11188ft
Round Mtn

168

13830ft
Mt Darwin
Glacier Lodge

Big Pine

168

Last Chance Range

Death Valley Wash

Scottys Castle

5

14242ft
North Palisade

Fish Springs

Inyo National Forest

12219ft
Mt Woodworth

14058ft
Split Mtn

11123ft
Waucoba Mtn

Saline Range

10608ft
Burnt Mtn

194

13495ft
Mt Pinchot

OWENS

Owens River

195

8953ft
m Mtn

Kings Canyon National Park
D

395

E

Willow Creek Camp

F

191

Atlas Index

Atlas Index